Author Bio

SCOTT JONES HAS WRITTEN HUMOR COLUMNS (*Life in the Laugh Lane, Humor Me, Jest A Minute, Innocent Bystander, The Marble Column*) for newspapers and magazines in the USA and Thailand (*Bangkok Post, Chiang Mai Post, Chiang Mai Mail, and Cynosure* newspapers, *Encounter, Tom Yum, and Programming* magazines). Scott has authored two novels and two humor books, recorded four albums of original music, and performed his unique style of music, comedy, and stand-up photography in Asia, Canada, and all 50 states in America. ("I traveled a lot. With a show like mine, you had to keep moving.")

He currently lives in Thailand with his wife and Chance the Husky, whose name has evolved into Chancellor, the Exalted Ruler of Their General Vicinity.

~ ~ ~

Author Reviews Along the Way

"You are a stand-up comedian in print."
—*Somewhere in England*

"I'm reading your book, but am having trouble with it.
I keep dropping it when I start laughing so much."
—*Bangkok, Thailand*

"I laughed so hard I passed an ice cube through my nose."
—*San Francisco, California*

"You had me up late two nights in a row laughing out loud!
The second half of the book was my favorite, an emotional
roller coaster. I was in tears by the end of the book."
—*Portland, Oregon*

"I write on behalf of my client, Paul Sullivan, who now
languishes in the Intensive Care Unit of the hospital.
His doctors tell me that he suffers from strained ribs, a
strangulated hernia, and a persistent attack of hiccups.
He will need rest, physiotherapy, and an arcane surgical
procedure known as a gigglectomy. The alleged cause of
my client's incapacity is your book *Life in the Laugh Lane*."
—*Chiang Mai, Thailand*

"I'm really glad you came to our school cuz we were
sposed to have a spelling test that afternoon."
—*John Huth, 4th Grader, Wisconsin*

~ ~ ~

Other Books by Scott Jones

LIFE in the LAUGH LANE:
facts, fiction and photos from America to Asia

FLESH and BLOOD and DNA
in her right mind and the wrong body

FIVE LIVES, ONE DREAM
five lives intertwined though they've never met

EDIT YOURSELF
tips and techniques to tweak your writing

~ ~ ~

Thanks

MY DEEPEST GRATITUDE TO ALL the official and unofficial editors who helped mold this book into its present state and remove the mold from some of my ancient writing which needed disinfecting.

To my father Ken Jones, one of the funniest guys I've ever met, for imbedding humor and festivity into my soul.

To Darlene Jones for loving Ken Jones, having monumental patience with his idiosyncracies, and staying with him until dropping me into the world and getting divorced.

To Amy D'Apice, the most prolific artist I've ever known, who has probably created three more paintings on canvas while I'm writing this sentence. Her artwork is on my wall; now it's on this book cover and wandering around the world. [www.artconspiracy.net] She's also responsible for creating the phrase, "the US of Angst," that I stole.

To Jim King for expert advice on any topic I requested and on several I didn't.

To all the regular and irregular editors at our Writers Without Borders meetings in Chiang Mai, who always told it like it is, honestly, even though it wasn't like it was for the person sitting next to them.

And in a completely different dimension—my hands, shoulders, lower back, cramping legs, and stiff fingers thank Chancellor the Husky for demanding I get the hell out of my chair and take us for a walk at least twice a day.

~ ~ ~

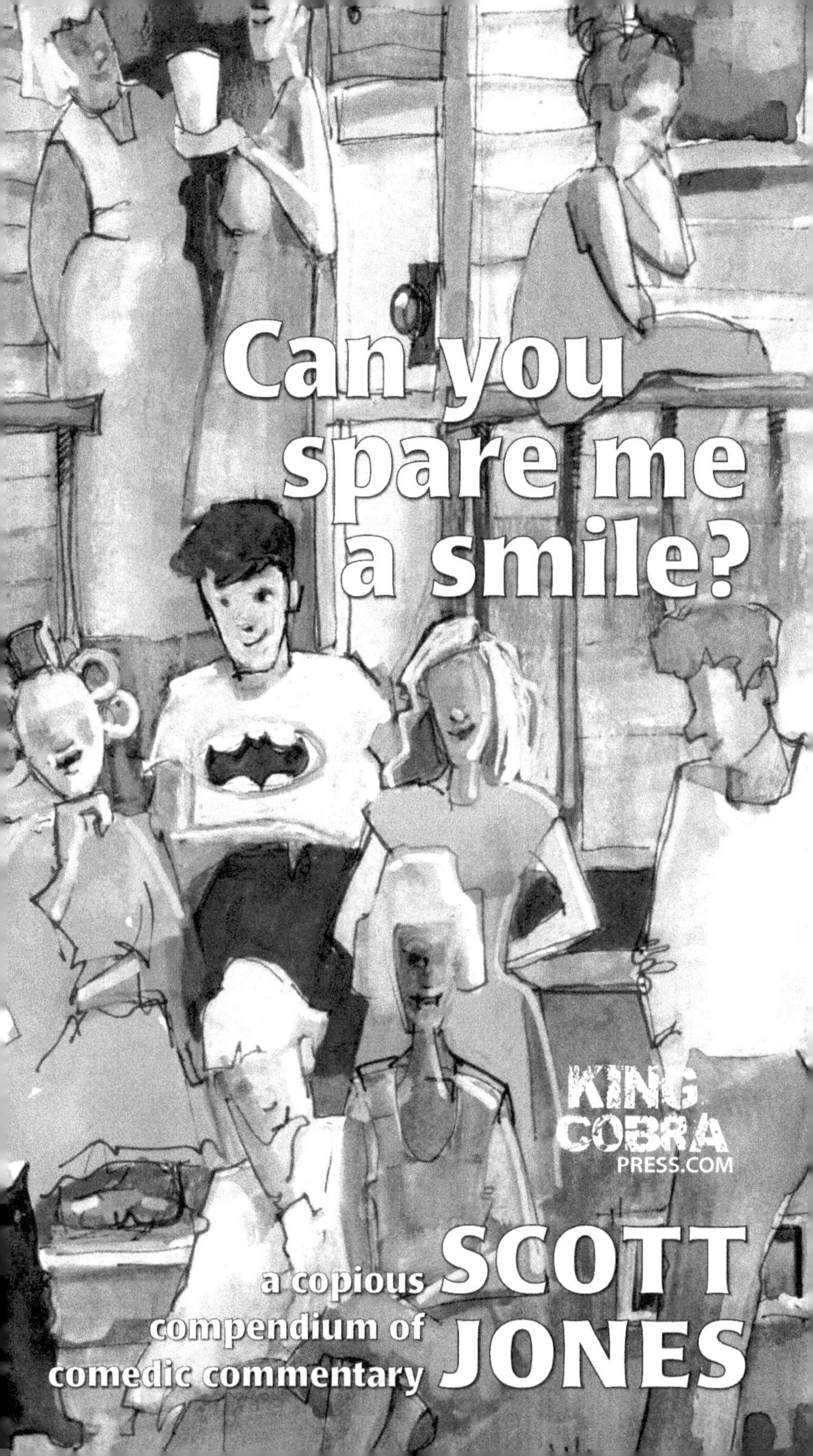
Can you spare me a smile?
KING COBRA PRESS.COM
a copious compendium of comedic commentary
SCOTT JONES

Copyright and Credits

~ ~ ~

Dedicated to the Ones I Love

Joomi the Soulmate
and, of course, Chance the Husky
but not necessarily in that order
it depends on the moment

and to the scraggly, long-haired, long-lost stranger
responsible for the title of the poem, song, and this book
who approached me on the streets of San Francisco
the dude I assumed would ask me for cash
and instead to my surprise he said,
"Can you spare me a smile?"
and walked away with
one of his own

can you spare me a smile
all this sadness just isn't your style
now get rid of that frown
your smile's on upside down

if you were walkin' along
and just saw yourself all around
wouldn't you smile at your reflection
showin' so much more affection?
you'd have a smile within your self
you'd have a smile without your self
you'd know that all those people
are your most sensitive self
in another human being

~ ~ ~

Table of Tales

WARNING!
HUMOR AHEAD

[1] This fun book is not intended to malign any human being (alive, dead, or undecided), group, company, city, country, planet (besides Earth and Uranus), galaxy or universe, except for the slandering, defaming, speaking harmful untruths about, and ruining the reputation of its author, often referred to herein as "The Village Idiot."

[2] With vast multitudes of PC (People Complaining) in the US of Angst who are freshly woke (though my outdated, somnambulant grammar checker wants me to change it to "awake"), the author finds it difficult to determine which terms and activities are currently PC (Politically Correct) and not just PC (Personally Confusing).

[3] Please read at your own risk if you are a Flat Earther, a Screaming Karen, one of Agent Orange's minions, a *Give Us This Day Our Daily Conspiracy* newspaper subscriber, refer to yourself as an acronym, or haven't worn a mask because the pandemic is a hoax, and you'd rather protect your porch with an AR-15 semi-automatic rifle.

[4] Do NOT read this if you are fanatic about any of the following categories which are the butt of jokes in this book: giant centipedes, rats, chickens, bears, Brits, snails and slugs, caterpillars, togas, clowns, doctors, vegans, carnivores, destructive construction workers, musicians and folks with Welsh or Norwegian ancestors like the author, plus Sumo wrestlers, Southern policemen, and Harley riders who wear size XXXXXXXXXXL t-shirts.

PROCEED WITH CAUTION

Making Fun

I HAVE ONLY BEEN ARRESTED ONCE… for joking at an airport. In its infancy in 1973, the airline security in Wisconsin consisted of one blue-haired lady sitting behind a folding table. "What's in your backpack?"

"Two books and a scarf," I said. "Be careful, the scarf might explode." Official charge: bomb threat, felony, $1,000 bail, reduced to disorderly conduct, $25 fine. No signs were posted that read, "No joking in the airport, you dipstick."

While I spoke with delighted students after finishing a graduation concert at a Colorado high school, an angry man stomped up to the stage, wagged his finger at me, and shouted, "Filthy obscene language! I'll see to it you **NEVER** perform in Arvada again!" And then he stormed away.

I asked the counsellor who'd hired me if he knew the man. "Yeah," he said, "That's the principal of the school."

"Why is he so bent outta shape? It was a clean show."

"You mentioned that many things 'suck.' He doesn't like that word and thinks it constitutes swearing."

Alas, no signs warned me that the principal sucked.

When I was eight, my mother overheard me yell the fun S-word a friend had taught me. She washed out my mouth with soap. If I'd said the F-word, she'd probably have used a flame-thrower. She didn't even want me to play an F-chord on the piano. Later in life while performing, if I knew Mom was in the audience, I'd never speak the F-word. I was afraid she'd charge the stage with a spray bottle of Lysol and a mop for my mouth, and clean up my act on the spot.

Meet my father, a master of making fun—in this photo age fifty-something, going on five, working part-time as a marionette. In celebration of trouncing me at gin rummy and winning several cents, he's proclaiming victory with a resounding "TA-DA" while using his arms as two exclamation points. I blame his sperm for my birth as a rapscallion with tongue in cheek or a foot in my mouth.

This first chapter you're reading is the final chapter I wrote, after a British editor had penciled "PC?" in the margin to question the political correctness of some of my observations. Near a paragraph extolling (or making fun of) the eccentricities of Scandinavians, he'd written, "If there's a statue of you in your hometown, they might tear it down."

Is it possible, I thought, that these days the North Dakota locals, who have escaped to neighboring Minnesota, are *not* pounding down cold ones while sitting around a bonfire, humming the Hamm's beer theme song—"from the land of sky blue waters"—and sharing Norwegian or Swedish jokes, depending on which clan is in the majority at the campsite?

The jokes are the same. "Did ya hear that Norwegians were throwin' sticks o' dynamite 'cross the border inta Sweden?" *The Swedes lit 'em and threw 'em back!* (Now switch the countries and tell it at the next campsite.) I mentioned this to my editor, but to appreciate it, he'd have to experience the companionship of Ole and Sven.

For decades I performed on stages; these days I perform on pages. It's safer at home, but I can't feel, see, or hear the reaction of these tiny audiences of one reader stretched across the globe. Normally I don't intend to offend anyone, well, maybe Agent Orange. And I apologize in advance regarding "INDIA: a hip story" which may well annoy 18% of the world's population in one chapter. Comedy is a perilous profession, and today, humor is not a laughing matter.

If you choose, feel free to have a ceremonial book-burning of *Can you spare me a smile?* and then upload the video on the web. Or if you come across a unique sign that commemorates the misprints, misspellings, and misjudgments that make us all human, please send me a photo.

Dear Customer Please look at the washing of you that take much. And took the cloth away by time. Because customers do not know the next time though. Kindly note And implementation
                                      Thanks

I'm sure you "do not know the next time though," but when you finally do, I'll "kindly note and implementation" the fun. Thanks.

~ ~ ~

Thailand Is Not Fargo

Born and raised in North Dakota, I loved reading stories in *National Geographic* magazine about living in exotic lands where my parents would never send me out to shovel snow. During the first fifty years of my adolescence, I imagined Thailand as a tropical paradise somewhere *over there* with tawny petite natives wearing ripe vegetables and flowers, swaying serenely under palm trees, and singing hit songs from the musical *South Pacific.*

Wake up, Scotty! You're in Fargo hanging out with frost-bitten Scandinavians, stiff in their galoshes frozen to the sidewalk, merrily singing "You oughta go ta Nor' Dakota, see the cattle and the wheat and the folks that can't be beat..." moments before expiring from hypothermia, still grinning. Search the web for "You oughta go ta" and listen with sympathy for poor little me, forced to learn marginal grammar and misspelled words so early in life.

Technically speaking, Thailand is A-OK, meaning all okay or stupendous or supernacular or eximious... and Fargo is TFC, meaning too fucking cold. In the "dead" of a "winter" at 8 a.m. in January, Thailand is likely to be a hundred degrees warmer than Fargo at thirty below zero.

Minus 196 in Minnesota? That means it's colder up north in Fargo.
(I did not alter this photo. Cross my heart and hope to survive.)

If you look up the word "flat" in a dictionary, the skyline near Fargo might be featured, though it's featureless. The origin of an unofficial state slogan is apparent in these four photographs: "Ah, North Dakota. So flat you can watch your dog run away for three weeks."

Looking east from one of the countless flat spots near Fargo

Looking west from the same flat spot near Fargo

Looking south from the same flat spot near Fargo

Looking north to the hill built next to the interstate highway which is also North Dakota's only ski area. Beginner slope to the right. Expert slope to the left and running down onto the highway.

My current home away from home lounges in a green valley surrounded by lush mountains. In the countryside near a tiny village in Chiang Mai province, my yard and street are as flat as Fargo, but I can see verdant peaks on three horizons.

Similarly, my home state in the middle of America right next to Canada, is also surrounded by mountains—if you consider the Rockies 1,500 km to the west, the Appalachians 2,000 km to the east, and the Ozarks 1,500 km to the south. And Arctic icebergs 4,000 miles to the north, which are the size and consistency of heaps of plowed snow in Fargo parking lots. However, to actually view these distant mountains, you must travel thousands of kilometers, surf the web, or dream on, baby.

Ah, North Dakota. Social distancing since the beginning of North Dakota. (FYI: the photo above would look the same in color.)

I never thought I'd be living in a travel poster, nor that behind the scenes of that alluring poster, a vast number of small, medium, and large creatures lurked.

As I write these words, my foot is burning from the bites of an ant army defending their colony from my immobile foot. Estimated ant population in my immediate vicinity? Infinite, give or take a billion. Each fierce warrior is one iota larger than invisible. This brave antic, pun intended, would be like me taking a bite out of Mt. Everest in an attempt to save the world. However, foothills cannot rise up—like my foot—and then stomp repeatedly, flattening entire battalions into a film of elemental ant particles. (Sorry, I digress, though still focused on the topic at hand, rather, at foot.)

My first daily task is to sweep the porch free of poop, liberally deposited by 150-plus bats living in the attic. Bat poop is tiny, but it's still poop, and I don't want it between my toes. (For my first task in Fargo, I'd be outside in snowshoes shoveling drifts in the dark while trying to stay alive by wearing most of the clothes I owned.)

I haven't figured out how to conquer Bat World humanely without 150 decomposing corpses flavoring the household air, so I try to enjoy the free nature show every dusk as the winged hordes begin their feeding frenzy, swooping out of the eaves like fighters from an aircraft carrier in war movies I watched as a kid in Fargo.

Okay, so they might carry rabies, suck our blood, and turn into Dracula at any moment, but one bat eats about 3,000 mosquitoes per night times 150 bats = 450,000 times 30 days = 13,500,000 mosquitoes per month. This system is more efficient than neon mosquito zappers, without the ugly blue light, annoying crackling, or stench of barbecuing bug parts.

I used to be practically unaware of mosquitoes because their bites didn't affect me in the USA. In Thailand I should be alarmed and very aware. Mosquitoes are Number One on the dangerous animals list and kill over 725,000 people each year. And in second place (drum roll) killing 500,000 per year (drum roll crescendos)—people! Unlike humans equipped with an array of ways to destroy their fellow humans, personally or from afar, mosquitoes are merely messengers carrying malaria, Dengue fever, Japanese Encephalitis, and other fatal diseases ending in "itis" that melt your organs from the inside out. In this perilous situation, you are authorized to kill the messenger.

The soft skin of my wife Joomi, on the other hand, on both arms, and all over her body, is a certified mosquito magnet. The single mosquito within twenty-five kilometers of Joomi will promptly find her. And bite her. And she'll swell up instantly and remarkably while scratching off her flesh down to bone marrow.

"Joomi! What are those bumps covering your face?"

"Mosquito bites."

"Which one is your nose?"

Although valid medical properties concerning her blood type and warmer-than-normal body temperature account for her unbidden role as Tender Morsel For The Entire Insect World, I never quite believed that every biting bug would make a beeline for Joomi—until this incident.

While we relaxed on a restaurant patio overlooking a splendid sunset in the Pai valley north of Chiang Mai, five dogs who'd adopted us slept around the table. I glanced down in abject horror to witness—and I'm not making this up—about fifty wood ticks in a semicircle on the floor, creeping straight for Joomi. They'd forsaken their familiar Rancid Hairy Canine Habitat for the Fresh Exotic Sweet Meat In The Neighborhood. We scurried out the door and never returned. The ticks are still tracking Joomi, oh so slowly, but she should be safe for a few years.

Humans are a tiny minority in the world. As a 10-year-old nerd in Fargo, I was enthralled by insects and hoped to become an official entomologist, a bug scientist. I also played the clarinet. Luckily I transcended these two childhood follies because the double-edged, unsavory sword of entomologist/clarinetist is an iron-clad method of birth control—no female on Earth has ever been attracted to

Beetle Boy Honking on a Stick.

One dream became real in Thailand. Insects are indeed glorious here, although that fact will forever prevent my stepdaughter from visiting me. Sure, multicolored butterflies ("pii sua" in Thai or "ghost clothing") flit through the flowers in my yard, but centipedes, millipedes, and gazillionipedes lurk in the nooks and crannies. (Yes, I know these multi-legged creatures are technically not insects. They're arthropods, like scorpions, lobsters, and crayfish, but most folks lump them into the Icki Disgustus species, which includes insects, spiders, some lawyers, and all politicians.)

Barefoot and groggy in the morning, I stepped onto the porch to strange pain, looked down, and expected flames to be shooting out of my toe. I saw nothing. No wasps, no bees, no red-hot needles. Movement to the right. A beige scorpion the color of the tile and the length of one toenail scuttled into the corner. I grabbed the Dust Pan of Death and pummeled it into individual scorpion molecules, then suffered as a one-legged man for several hours.

If you come to Thailand, don't forget to check inside your shoes. I found one in my motorcycle helmet (a scorpion, not a shoe) seconds before putting it on my head. At 100 kilometers per hour, I can envision my involuntary reaction to a scorpion slinking down the visor, two centimeters from my nose. My bladder, stomach, and intestines would uncork and empty, creating a slick road slime under my tires as I slam on the brakes, catapulting the bike into a swamp, where I'd be sucked dry by leeches, strangled by a python, and finally devoured by a crocodile.

My least favorite creature? The Giant Centipede aka Chinese Red Head, Jungle, Orange-legged, or Vietnamese Centipede (Latin scientific name, Scolopendra subspinipes, which sounds like two deadly diseases). Up to twelve venomous inches of ugliness and flailing legs, this beast is horror movie material. Wikipedia says, "Active and aggressive, a giant centipede preys on almost every living animal it encounters that is not longer than itself."

So if you're over a foot tall and happen upon one, it won't eat you, but your principal immediate dangers will be 1) frenzied scurrying in the opposite direction, 2) tripping over your own flailing feet, 3) firmly planting your face into the sidewalk, and/or 4) shitting in your pants.

Their poisonous sting can kill small children, or reduce adults to small children whimpering for days with fever, chills, nausea, swelling, and excruciating pain. From personal experience, I've learned that tromping on one with a sandal is less effective than pounding an advancing tank with a pillow.

"Yeah, whatever," the monster mumbles after a wee flinch. "Is that your best shot?"

I've chopped them in half with a shovel and the squig-

If you're bitten by one of these creatures, contact your next of kin before the centipede contacts his. Or hers. Okay, fine. Its.

gling continues. "Yeah, whatever. Now there are two of us."

A grim centipede victim testimonial: "I woke at midnight with a stabbing pain in my big toe. A huge centipede was hanging off my foot. The more I shook my foot, the more it held on. I finally pried it off. The burning sensation traveled up my calf, causing muscle spasms, and then up my thigh, stopping right before the important bits."

[My technical analysis of the attack—centipede grabs prey with its lower pair of prehensorial legs, then curves head quickly behind to implant venomous claws deeply and firmly into the victim's flesh like a rabid cannibal chowing down on a foot long while holding the bun with two hands.]

The previous testimonial comes from the venerable *ThaiVisa.com* which contains a plethora of information about Thailand, and its "current" immigration laws, even though new visa laws have likely been added since I started this chapter, continue to mutate as I write this paragraph, and will be outdated by tomorrow.

Danger now dwells in the virtual nooks and crannies of *ThaiVisa.com* since a subspecies of the professional complainers and whingers (British for serious whiners) who plague the web have invaded Thailand. Tyrannosaurus Expattaya—crusty curmudgeons from around the globe —will bite your head off and mangle your ego. They are difficult to spot in the wild because their true identities are cloaked behind cryptic avatars or user names like "Retired Redneck" and "Trouser Snake." If you post a seemingly noncontroversial statement in their forums like "My wife and I had a lovely afternoon in Lopburi" (or in Bangkok or Hong Kong or Bulgaria or anywhere else in the world), prepare to have your personality bulldozed, your values torpedoed, and the length of your manhood lampooned.

This treacherous creature prowls for prey at night. A Pattaya newspaper reported that a lady of the evening (Desparados Prostitutimus) approached a tourist on the beach and offered to sell the man her bodily wares. He declined her offer, so she stabbed him. I doubt if this marketing technique is effective for expanding one's customer base. What was she thinking? One less sales prospect reduces her night's workload?

Around the globe in Fargo, courteous Scandinavians would never consider this violent tactic, though a six-foot Avon lady—with flocked blond hair, frozen fake eyelashes, inch-thick foundation on her face crystallizing around the edges, who is towing a massive rolling sample case colored the same hot pink as her cheeks, her fur-lined parka, and the Cadillac parked in your driveway presented by the corporate office honoring her as Grand Exalted Titanium Salesperson of 1989—might appear on your doorstep.

Miss Avon rings the bell and shouts in her singsong Swedish accent, "Avon calling!"

Mr. Ole Politeson opens the door and invites her into his vestibule lined with goose down overcoats, arctic survival boots, and insulated mittens the size of boxing gloves. "So how can I help ya then?"

"Cold 'nuff for ya?" she purrs.

"Ya sure, you betcha," he sighs, supremely comfortable with the exact conversation he's had with everyone in the neighborhood for the past month. "Thermometer hasn't broken zero since January, ya know."

"How 'bout some peachy makeup for the little missus? Lather on enough 'n' it'll keep her face warm and toasty."

"Ya, well, you know… she left me for the meter man."

"Lands sakes alive! Musta been a nitwit to give up a stud muffin like you. Tell ya what, I got some snazzy men's cologne to help ya seduce the ladies…"

"Nah, thanks anyway. Not in the market yet."

"Remember…" Miss Avon pokes him in the ribs. "Only 326 shopping days left till Christmas!"

"Ya, well then, got some time to think about it, but now I gotta meet my friend Sven." He reaches for the doorknob.

"But dear sir, my mama's got terminal cancer," she pleads, her voice a notch below shrill, "and I gotta pay all of her 'spensive hospital bills…"

"Well, golly, God bless her, and you too." Ole turns to open the door. "Sorry, but I gotta go—"

"Alrighty then! Here's your free sample!" she screams, slams shut her display case, lunges at Ole, and imbeds a nail file into his neck. "You have a nice day now!"

(FYI: This story is feasible except for the lunging and stabbing part. The dialogue is authentic.)

I never dreamed I'd have a pet Rhino or Atlas. Depending on which source you consult, the number of insect species on our planet is between a million and thirty million, with over 10,000 new species discovered every year. Experts estimate the number of individual insects on Earth is ten quintillion—10 followed by 18 zeros—300 pounds of bugs for every human.

Scads of these species are stunning and intriguing. In Fargo I'd pore over the back pages of comic books advertising the world's largest moth and beetle: the Atlas and the Rhino. Oh, how I lusted after them, brittle and embalmed behind glass, dead relics of some exotic locale. Here in Thailand I meet gigantic live Atlas moths with twelve-inch wingspans and regularly hangout with rhinoceros beetles. As I surfed the web, a horny rhino visited for two hours and attempted to mate with my power cord while hoping he and I could Skype with his relatives in New Guinea.

Sellers set up shop with their rhinos lashed to sugar cane stalks, and kids take them home as pets—the beetles, not the sellers. At village festivals, folks pit their champion against the neighbor's, one beetle on each end of a rotating stick. They tumble toward each other like log rolling lumberjacks in the river competing in the north woods of America. No biting or fighting, just "last one on the stick wins."

In Fargo we played "King of the Hill"—"hill" meaning a mound of plowed snow in a parking lot—but it's "King of the Stick" in Thailand. No beetles or spectators get hurt unless they drink too much rice whiskey and go blind—the spectators, not the beetles. I only recall three activities in Fargo that caused blindness: 1) running with a sharp stick; 2) staring at the sun too long, tempting because we didn't see it much in the winter; or 3) excessive masturbation.

After rescuing two rhinos from one seller, I became a kid again, choosing the "buy now and save, then release" method. After extensive research on the web, I built a terrarium with sand, decaying humus, dead leaves, rotten mini-log for shade, and a stockpile of sugar cane. Inebriated from fermented cane juice, both rhinos burrowed into the sand and disappeared for three days. My terrarium looked like a desolate morass, smelled like shit, and attracted flies, which prompted my wife's terse command: "Get this away from the house! It's disgusting." I dug out the bugs, set them outside the gate, and never saw them again.

Most days at home are a face-off between our pets and the pests. Anywhere you live in Asia, rats are never far away. I used to think they were squeaky little things in city sewers. Well, they'll definitely keep you awake in the country when the foot-long rat and its family cavorts in the ceiling above the bedroom, bumping and thumping like drunken monkeys. Enter Keesha, an orphan cat abandoned at a temple, adopted by us, and ready to slay for her supper. After a few nights of rambunctious carnage in the walls and ceiling crawl spaces, the cat eliminated the rats, though we haven't had the heart to fling her into the attic with the 150 bats aka winged rats.

Very happy cat, very unhappy bat

The two dogs we inherited from the ten that my mother-in-law-next-door saved from the streets, are splendid watchdogs who sense enemies hundreds of miles away in every direction and bark incessantly to warn us of impending danger. This incites the eight dogs next door into an uproar, creating a domino "howlcast," which sets off canine communities throughout Thailand and beyond, causing spontaneous yapping in Malaysia.

Somehow I didn't kill our two dogs while training them *not* to kill Keesha the Cat, though I'm still plotting to dispose of the other eight canines next door by flinging my live scorpions and centipedes over the fence. Oddly enough, one of our dogs, who would like to eat the cat, but doesn't care for the rats, has taken down several of the bats. She's old, gentle and fat, but I'm still trying to figure out how to get her into the attic.

Though our extended family of dogs yelp, bay, and produce wailing noises that sound like an axe-murderer is loose in the yard, it's a cheap security system. The canine cacophony forces nighttime prowlers to reconsider their missions, including those malevolent intruders cruising the grass: king cobras. The only one I've seen so far was short and skinny and fencing with Keesha in broad daylight. I broke up the battle, unsure whose life I'd saved: the cat's or the cobra's. (This would *never* happen in Fargo.)

And I doubt you'd find this North Dakota scene in Thailand—a "Beware of the Dog" sign posted on the gate with no fence to prevent the AWOL dog from attacking you. He's been running away for three weeks.

~ ~ ~

Wailing on Wales

IF ENGLAND HARASSED MY WELSH ANCESTORS as much as Brits make fun of me, I understand why my relatives left Great Britain. Unfortunately, my grandparents ended up in a town and state that all of America ridicules—Fargo, North Dakota—the letters of which can be rearranged to spell "a good, hot, rank fart." This escape eventually led to my birth in the United States of America—which offers added insight into its inimitable culture by rearranging its letters: 1) "Fat, roasted, meat cuisine;" 2) "Fantastic idea? Sure, to me!" or 3) "An armistice? To us, defeat!"

Being half-Welsh was an unavoidable fate. My mother's maiden name was also Jones, meaning "offspring of John," which begs the question, "Like English, does the word John also mean "toilet" in the Welsh language?" Darlene Jones married Ken Jones, and my friends will never believe they weren't blood-related, probably brother and sister.

As the age-old saying goes, created by the explorers who named it, "North Dakota isn't the end of the world, but you can see it from there." I wish Mom had popped me across the river in the eccentric state of Minnesota, which produced Vice President Walter Mondale (name rearranged: "a real meltdown") who lost miserably in his presidential bid because of bad hair, enormous ears, too many gums when he smiled, and dark bags under his eyes the size of sofa cushions. For their governor, Minnesota once chose former professional wrestler Jesse "The Body" Ventura and changed their state slogan to "Our governor can beat up your governor." During the aftershock of 9/11 and former President Bush's War On Terrorists And Random People Who Aren't Bright White, progressive Minnesota elected the first Muslim congressman in America, quite remarkable for a bunch of tall, blonde, Scandinavian Lutherans.

North Dakota has produced one semi-famous singer

Peggy Lee (or Leggy Pee), one semi-famous baseball player Roger Maris (rearranged, Sir Ogre Arm), and several prize-winning cows—Bessie, Bossy, and Beulah, though these might be the names of their large Scandinavian owners. It's hard to tell them apart, because, like their cows, the owners appear to have five stomachs. What's the difference between a champion cow in North Dakota and her owner? Two choices: 1) about three kilos; or 2) lipstick.

Sign on Thailand truck: Do Thais go to Wales and litter?

In Thailand, though my British friends know I've permanently left the USA, they persist with their japing about my inglorious American heritage. Standing with four Brits, I plead in an attempt to salvage my reputation, "But I'm half-Welsh!" Like a well rehearsed, synchronized maneuver in a movie scene, each "friend" silently grimaces and takes a giant step away from me as if I'd passed a good, hot, rank one. Is Wales that bad, worse than America?

For years I only knew two things about Wales:

1) it's the birthplace of Tom Jones, the gold-chained, famous-to-aging-housewives, big-voiced crooner;

and 2) it promotes the city with the longest name in the world which, unlike my home town, must be difficult to chant at sporting events: "Go get 'em Lanfairpwllgwyngyll-gogerychwyrndrobwllllantysiliogogogoch! (Fargo is much simpler: "Go, Fargo, far, go far, go far, go!") With so many consonants and even four "l's" in a row, the Welsh language must've mutated in pubs after several hundred pints of beer and stuporous sessions of slurred singing.

The web told me that the negative British opinion of Wales began in 1847 with the English-speaking commissioner's official report on their educational system, then largely conducted in Welsh. It concluded that "the natives were dirty, ignorant, lazy, drunk, superstitious, lying, and cheating because they were nonconformists and spoke Welsh," which was similar to England's view of the rest the world, except for the "spoke Welsh" part.

I also learned these grim facts: a) "Jones" means "an addiction to a drug, principally heroin," and b) "Welsh" means "to cheat or swindle by failing to pay a debt," perhaps resulting in c) "wales" which are "large welts raised on the skin by the lash of a whip." And in 1841, 14% of the population in Wales was named Jones, which may verify the incestuous insinuations about my ancestors who possibly evolved from sis and bro into mumsy and pops.

I finally visited Wales, but only remember castles, more castles, and food that tasted like ground-up castles, possibly the worst meals I'd ever experienced, even more distasteful than native English cuisine. In London, dining was an anticipated event with savory selections from around the world, although I avoided local entrées.

Zealous British Waitress: "I'll bet you'd love the chef's special spotted dick!"

Suspicious American Me: "No, thanks. I went to see a

doctor about one last week."

Subdued Waitress: "Well then, have you ever tried haggis with bashit neeps?"

Me: "No, but I think stepped in some once."

Flagging Waitress: "Hmm. Our choice faggots are truly out of sight."

Me: "Let's keep 'em that way. Please bring me a dish from any other country in the world."

While planning meals in Wales, I'd ask myself, "Should I try to find something with actual flavor today, or just go with another bowl of fun-size Snickers?" The ale, however, was addicting, and I consumed significant quantities while trying to forget I'd have to eat again. I remember nothing about the capitol city of Cardiff except it was called Cardiff, which is probably the Welsh word for castle.

The conclusion and/or response to my British mates? Who cares! Make fun of me. I do!

Final facts: The city name Llanfairpwellgwyngyllgog… etcetera… means "St. Mary's Church in the hollow of white hazel near a rapid whirlpool and the Church of St. Tysilio near the red cave," but the world's longest city name is in Thailand: Krungthepmahanakornamornratanakosinmahin-tarayutthayamahadilokphopnopparatrajathaniburiromu-domrajaniwesmahasatharnamornphimarnavatarnsathit-sakkattiyavisanukamprasit, meaning "Bangkok… whatever."

Fargo doesn't really *mean* anything, except its name-sake, William G. Fargo, a financial backer of the railroad and partner in the Wells-Fargo Express Company. In some circles the acronym FARGO means "Fast Advection in Rotating Gaseous Objects" ["advection" means "the hori-zontal flow of air, water, etc."] which seems to tie back into the previously mentioned letter rearrangement of "a good, hot, rank fart." Fargo is located right across the river from Moorhead, and everyone knows what that means.

~ ~ ~

The Clown Problem

WE HIRED A THAI CLOWN to perform for the kids at the Chiang Mai ToyRide. "Her" name was "Joker Man," and though she, or he, seemed feminine, we never really knew for sure, since her, or his, baggy clothes disguised the plumbing of her/his gender, or the two petite trolls concealed under the costume. A world-class balloon twister, Joker Man—or Woman—could create most anything out of rubber and air, including a motorcycle, our solar system, and life-size water buffalo.

This reminded me of the '80s when the clown population exploded in America. You might have thought WCA stands for Warhorse Challenge Association, Wollongong College Australia, or World Cheese Awards. You are correct, but WCA also stands for the World Clown Association which was founded in 1983. In

Depending on when you read this book, he (or she) is the current or was the past president of the World Clown Association as displayed on their website.

short order, clowns were not only in the circus. You'd find them at conventions, expos, parties, family reunions… anywhere.

Dine at a fancy restaurant and a bunch of clowns might somersault in, balance dishes on their heads, and juggle the dinner rolls. Pandemonium would break loose when dessert was delivered—twelve dozen whipped cream pies. Did they tip the waitress? Of course… over.

Then it happened—a couple of clowns moved in next door. There went the whole neighborhood. They installed a trapeze in the oak tree and watered their lawn with a miniature fire engine. Soon the entire block was littered with rubber baseball bats and bowling pins, their front yard cluttered with elephant poop, and their backyard filled with a cannon. You never knew when that thing might go off and a human cannonball would drop in.

One morning a Volkswagen Bug pulled into the driveway, the doors flew open, and 36 people got out.

What about their kids? Picture little Emmet sitting at his third-grade desk, already bald, with a red plastic nose and wearing his father's make-up. His shoes are three-feet long. He's dressed in a hand-me-down polka dot suit with four huge buttons down the front. His friends have dogs and cats, but poor Emmet goes home to a rubber chicken.

It's difficult to calculate how many clowns still live in America, since millions of them have yet to reveal their true nature. 75% of all licensed drivers are clowns. Congress is completely made up of clowns and coaxed along an unstable high wire by Agent Orange, the Unpresidential Buffoon. Some of your best friends might even be clowns, but you certainly wouldn't want your sister to marry one.

The road to respectability has been rocky, and clown rights hard to achieve. Who can forget the Selzer Bottle Riots in the '60s? Millions of water-gun-toting, make-up-wielding jokers descended on Washington to paint the town red, white, and blue, green, yellow, and purple. There wasn't a statue standing without pie filling on its face and crust on its shoulders. The name "clown" had became unacceptable and they demanded to be called "Painted Americans." The law now requires colleges to fulfill their clown quotas. Students can major in Clownology by taking courses such as Fun 101, Advanced Faces, and the Fundamentals of Falling Down.

But how many still remain in the closet? I met an apparently normal woman and asked her out. Her name was Bozette. We had a great time on our date, so when I took her home, I didn't dwell on the fact that she lived in a massive tent. Nor did I notice her butler's entire tuxedo was tattooed on his body. What am I supposed to say about her roommates—the fattest lady and the thinnest man I had ever seen? I tried to kiss Bozette, but when she removed her glasses, her nose came off with them. I panicked and tried to sneak out the back flap of the tent, but the strongest man in the world stopped me.

Ever try to make love to a clown? They just can't get serious. When I took off my clothes, she couldn't stop laughing. Bozette dragged me into her bedroom—no teddy bears and no mattress—she had a real bear on a tricycle and a gigantic whoopee cushion. After one close encounter of the clown kind, she was smitten, I was smut, and we tied the knot.

Spotlights danced across the big top of the Clownitarian Church as lions roared. Men with whips herded friends, relatives, and an extended baboon family onto the packed bleachers, and then rolled a long red trampoline down the aisle. The Father of the Clown delivered Bozette in a wheel-barrow, surrounded by Clownsmaids and the Best Clown, while clownographers with squirting cameras took pictures of bouquets of squirting flowers. After a slapstick three-ring ceremony, calliope music filled the tent, and the audience burst into a rousing chorus of "Send Out the Clowns." We bounced down the aisle, jumped onto her unicycle, and rode off into the sunset.

~ ~ ~

The Jokes on Us Musicians

BOYCOTT THE INTERNET! Due to degrading, politically incorrect material I received from someone who found it somewhere on the Web, I'm asking the known world to boycott the internet immediately.

Although these accusations might be valid, especially regarding clarinet players—me, in the past—this raft of insults is damaging to musicians everywhere. I assume they came from bank managers or disgruntled fathers, since musicians are generally loved throughout the world, until they walk into a bank, or try to date your daughter.

My father was a talented musician and encouraged me heartily, but maybe I should've listened to my mother.

"Mom, I want to grow up and be a musician!"

"Love, you can't do both."

"But I'll study music in college!"

"Another term for music major is night manager at a 7-11."

The parents couldn't keep me away from the piano, even when they moved it into the basement. Dad didn't want me playing with myself all day, so he suggested I learn the clarinet and join the 7th grade concert band. I was overweight, had braces on my teeth filled with red gel so they wouldn't lacerate my lips, and wore thick glasses that made me look like an insect. The clarinet sealed my doom as the quintessential geek. The insensitive internet says:

"Why do people have an instant aversion to clarinetists?" (It saves time in the long run.)

"Why are a clarinetist and a blind javelin thrower alike?" (They both instill fear and panic, causing everyone to move out of range.)

"How do you get a clarinet player out of a tree?" (Cut the rope.)

"Why do clarinetists put their instrument cases on the dashboard?" (So they can park in handicapped zones.)

The difference between a standard and a bass clarinet?

You can hit a baseball farther with a bass clarinet.

"What do clarinet players use for birth control?" (Their personalities.)

I soon discovered a universal truth. During the entire history of the world, not *one* gorgeous teenage girl has ever swooned and snuggled up to a geek as he squawked romantic hits on the clarinet. Sooo… I switched to the guitar. Although aspiring folksingers might attract a few women, they do not impress the parents. The nasty internet says:

"What's the difference between a folksinger and a pizza?" (A pizza can feed a family of four.)

"What do you do if you run over a folksinger?" (Back up.)

"What do you call a folksinger who broke up with his girl?" (Homeless.)

Trombone players fare about as well on the web as folksingers and guitar players.

"How do you decrease wind drag on a trombonist's car?" (Take the Domino's pizza sign off his roof.)

"What's the difference between a dead chicken and a dead trombonist in the road?" (It's possible the chicken was on its way to a paying gig.)

"How many trombonists does it take to pave a driveway?" (Seventeen, if you lay them side-by-side.)

I focused on the piano again, since I couldn't set a beer on my guitar while performing. Thanks to keyboard technology magic, I could play all the sounds of an orchestra, without having to *be* a trombonist or carry a clarinet.

The internet is less abusive to keyboard players, but it's brutal on drummers and bass players:

"Wha'd'ya call a beautiful woman on a drummer's arm?" (A tattoo.)

"What did the drummer get on his IQ test?" (Saliva.)

"How can you tell if the stage is level?" (The drummer's drool comes out of both sides of his mouth.)

"What do you do if you see a bloody bass player running through your backyard?" (Laugh and shoot again.)

"What's the perfect weight of a bass player?" (One kilo, including the urn.)

"What do you do if a bass player is drowning?" (Throw him his amp.)

Since 99% of the people in Thailand seem to play the guitar, sing ancient John Denver songs, and most likely have the same problems I did, I imagine this advice—from *me,* not the internet—applies for musicians here as well.

If you see a bank manager and a disgruntled father lying in the street, who do you run over first? (The bank manager—business before pleasure.)

~ ~ ~

Bubbas, Yoga, and Togas

WALKING INTO THE ALL-AMERICAN, small-town baseball park in North Carolina, surrounded by Bubbas, Billy Bobs, Big Boys and Babes vividly reminds me that I'm smack dab in the middle of the Bible Belt, the Sun Belt, and the Gun Belt.

Sign outside the Everything Y'all Need Store in NC:
"Ah got mah new gun used! Let's eat, drink, and kill stuff!"

I attend one game every three years, like clockwork, while visiting relatives in North Carolina. I'm a vocal fan of my cousin, a semi-local teenage baseball star, although wearing ten silver bracelets, bright blue glasses, bamboo sandals, and a tie-dye shirt from Thailand, I annually ruin his reputation: I'm obviously gay, so he's gay, or queer, homosexual, metrosexual, pansexual, bisexual, LGBTQ-SOB, all of the above, plus a vegetarian and an Emissary of Satan.

North Carolina has a bevy of big baseball fans—*damn* big, okay, let's say *enormous*—200 to 400 pounds and counting. It takes serious determination to become the shape of a baseball the size of a Volkswagen. Does someone pay them to eat, as Tater Tots Tasters, or as the workers who bite the holes out of doughnuts? It's difficult to tell the gender of these folks, because the telltale chest area looks like two saddlebags hanging off an elephant. Ask a blob in NC which sex they might be, and y'all might could be dead right quick. [FYI: The phrase "might could" is not a typo; it's authentic Southern syntax.]

Back to the ball game. In between the strikes, fouls, RBIs, FBIs, MVPs, MP3s and other terms I don't understand, my mind wanders back to my touring days when I performed at a college near the town where this baseball stadium sits. (To protect the reputation of the college, and—if I ever return—my life, I will only refer to the town of Salisbury by a rearrangement of the letters in its name: *A Burly Sis*, who I believe might be perched right down the bench from me.)

I broke one of my performance rules in this town: do not accept any gigs on New Year's Eve, Halloween, or at toga parties—grim evenings when the *audience members* are the show. They don't care who or what's on stage. Their only priority in life is to get terminally hammered, then fall on their knees to drive the white porcelain bus—and they want everyone to watch it happen.

By seven p.m. the burly-sis toga party was in full-boisterous-swing. An inebriated frat boy came dressed in a white KKK sheet with two eye slits and a round mouth hole below them. He'd fill his face with mashed potatoes, and when someone asked why he wore a pointy hooded toga, he'd spew a white blob onto the innocent victim and yell, "Ah'm a whitehead!"

Around nine p.m. in the middle of my show, the drunken minions demanded that I spin their homemade "Wheel of Fortune" on stage, which would determine the price of a draft beer for the next ten minutes. I spun the wheel. It landed on five cents. Every audience member staggered to the bar, then lurched back to their tables with *twenty beers* for a dollar. I became invisible… or double… or triple.

"Hey, y'all. Ther'all was only one guy on stage a minute ago, but now ther'alls three of 'em. Er… four. Five?"

As the saying goes in the entertainment biz—"I killed 'em." My entire audience died of alcohol poisoning. The activities director was so embarrassed he gave me an extra $100 *not* to tell anyone about it.

Although born in the US of A, I always feel like the quintessential "stranger in a strange land" upon returning. This year I got even stranger.

Halfway through the baseball game, I leave the stadium because of a throbbing headache which I can cure with an immediate yoga session, my own personal seventh inning stretch. In a park-like grassy area I begin my warm-up routine: roll the head in circles, shake it side to side, pump my shoulders up and down, reach for the sky as high as possible, hang forward and relax. Twenty minutes later in the Triangle Pose—eyes closed, leaning to the side, one arm straight up, other hand on my ankle—I feel a presence. A sinister presence. I open my eyes to see two policemen standing alert but squinting, about a yard in front of me, hands on their holsters.

"Whach'all doin' here, boy?"

Blithering out of my serene daze and again reaching for the sky in the Tree Pose, I babble about headaches and not needing to use drugs because of yoga, though they probably only hear "drugs" and "yogurt." Once I open my mouth, they'all know I'all ain't from 'round these parts.

"Where y'all from?" the other asks. Luckily they're both minorities, similar to the weird foreigner confessing in front of them—a uniformed woman and a black officer—

instead of two skinhead patrolmen from the Aryan Nation.

They tentatively accept I'm not a lunatic at large, although that's how I must've been described in the three complaints they'd received from the neighborhood residents:

"Y'all better get here quick. We'all gots an escaped retard havin' one o' them 'leptic fits right in our backyard."

The tiny SWAT team of two escorts me to the parking lot—one behind me, one in front—as I religiously vow to drive straight to Thailand.

After the game, I watch Bubba and the Blobs of A Burly Sis follow their bellies to their pickup trucks. It's possible they are the same folks I'd performed for a decade earlier at that local college, still pounding down the bottles of brew. I imagine they've been practicing the teachings of Buddha for years: "Don't just do something, sit there."

~ ~ ~

Write from the Start

WHEN I FIRST HEARD ABOUT the group Writers Without Borders, I thought "Doctors Without Borders" and assumed they must be a bunch of gnarly journalists championing causes, flinging revolutionary leaflets from helicopters, and administering grammar vaccinations in underdeveloped countries.

"Your daughter is fine now, Mrs. Bangabongodrum. We cured the adjectivitis, performed a present perfect tensectomy, and relieved her subordinate claustrophobia. Give her these Vitamin ABCs daily, which should reduce her stress on the wrong syllables."

"Thanks so much, but she can't grasp the apostrophe rules for the word 'its'. It's driving her insane!"

"Hmm. An apostroholic, eh? Well, don't worry. Billions of baby emailers with raging textosterones are driving us into a Period Period, when we'll only use periods, period."

I was mistaken, and once I'd experienced this amiable group, I became addicted.

Writers Without Borders is a casual group of English language writers of articles, stories, poetry, books, blogs, columns, theater and screenplays, fiction, nonfiction, or anything in between, who meet once a week in Chiang Mai,

Thailand to share and discuss works in progress.

This august association of artists (meaning "old farts") filled a deep void in my life... *Yes! Free feedback! Credible critiques! These are savvy editors who will prevent the Terrible Typos and other ailments that plague reclusive writers!*

This advertising campaign prematurely displayed in a Japanese department store sums up the necessity for pre-publication editing.

Their marketing manikins and womanikins determined that "fuckin'" means "fantastic," which is correct, but only one of its multitudinous definitions. I suspect they learned some of its other meanings from the management, as in, "Fuck all of you fucking idiots! If you don't commit fuckin' hara-kiri immediately, I will personally fuck you up!"

At my inaugural Writers Without Borders meeting, I read a column due the next day at the newspaper, one regarding a traumatic but comical experience at immigration, and my unbridled emotions galloped across the page. They advised me to turn down the volume and substitute a few gentler words so the Thai government wouldn't deport me, along with the editor of the newspaper. Every suggestion was right on, and I made the changes later that evening.

Since the group attracts such diverse writers, the comments would come from many directions. If I'd shared this chapter at a meeting, I might have heard…

Lee: "One time I wrote a theater piece about puns. It was a play on words."

Charles: "I'm reading a book about anti-gravity. I can't put it down."

Frances: "A woman said she recognized me from the vegetarian restaurant, but I'd never met herbivore."

Stuart: "Do you think your double entendres help this piece? No pun in ten did."

More likely I'd get this feedback…

Lee: "Consider this quote from Mark Twain: 'Substitute 'damn' every time you're inclined to write 'very'; your editor will delete it and the writing will be just as it should be.'"

Charles: "I feel this should be a serious article with facts and benefits written in simple, straight-forward language."

Frances: "Good heavens! I apologize to you all. Whatever came over me to invite Mr. Jones to our little group?"

Stuart: "Scott buddy, why don't you take a break from writing for a few weeks… and then give it up altogether?"

~

Let's back up a few decades. As a child, I was very young, began writing early on, and received my first literary award in third grade. Mom fastened my poem "Dragons" to the fridge with a kitchen magnet. In high school I penned a humor column for the school newspaper and assumed the role of Roving Reporter, so I had a socially acceptable excuse for speaking to girls beyond my geek clique.

The school burned down, forcing us Central High students to attend North High in shifts. The Central shift started at noon, which allowed our folk-singing group— The Able Cainraisers—to get up late, drink coffee, lounge around, rehearse, and stay up late performing locally and around the Midwest. That sweet introduction to the entertainment biz captured my career dreams, and apart from the distraction of beginning college as a business major and graduating as an unemployable political scientist, working as a lifeguard, carpenter, painter, bus driver, cabbie, bartender, encyclopedia salesman for one day, and a few months hitching through Europe and living in Israel, destiny led me back to the stage.

The freelance freedom to do whatever I pleased was a pleasure, but the feedback could be brutal. At the Glory Hole Bar in Central City, Colorado, a month after graduating from college, I had a two-hour, happy hour gig after an eight-hour day of construction work.

A woman approached the piano and asked, "Excuse me, but do you take requests?"

"Sure," I said, "but I mainly do music I write myself."

She handed me a ten-dollar bill. "Play whatever you want, but will you please go play outside?"

Brutal, yes, but with a silver lining. Her table sat right next to the piano, and her guests couldn't hear each other over the din of the bar. She apologized for the request. Another piano was outside on the porch, cool compared to the stuffy interior. My two hours at the keyboard got happier with the fresh air and extra ten bucks that doubled my pay.

Life got better as I embraced my inner eccentric child. Initially, my performances were mostly music, but while touring throughout the USA, the stories between the songs lengthened, and my comedy slide show reared its humorous head. I'm sure you've driven down the highway, seen something strange, and thought, "I should stop and take a picture." Well, my camera was always ready, and I always stopped. Nothing I could make up was as ridiculous as the surrounding reality, but without evidence, no one would've believed me! This decision to bring the visual proof into my show has influenced my writing for decades.

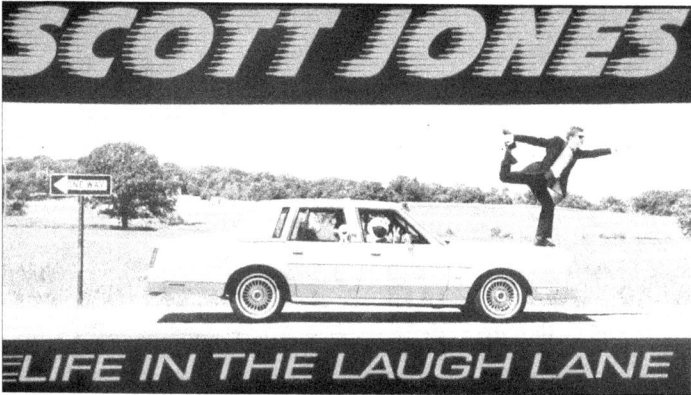

SCOTT JONES

LIFE IN THE LAUGH LANE

Working part-time as a hood ornament to make ends meet.

"Music, comedy, and stand-up photography!" This catch phrase drew people in, and the concept allowed me to shorten set-ups and jump right to the punch lines.

Feedback became more civil when bar gigs gave way to concert tours in colleges, but went beyond brutal as comedy shows increased. If comedians chose the "wrong" topic on

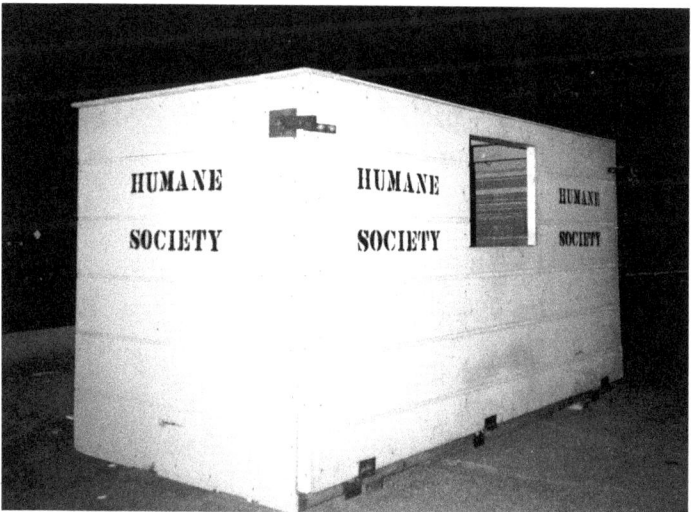

The Humane Society Drop Box:
"Got a puppy? Leave a puppy. Need a kitty? Take a kitty."

OPEN 24 HOURS sounds convenient, but check out the fine print:
"8 a.m. MON thru 10 p.m. SAT., 9 a.m. to 6 p.m. SUNDAY."
It's open 24 hours, but not always in a row.

Some pics included the punch line. I didn't have to say a word.

the "wrong" night, they might enter the No Joking Zone and suffer wild consequences. I was the headline act for the weekend at a major comedy club in Denver. On night one, the opener made a joke about clubbing baby seals, the kind meant to disparage the clubbers. Nothing about this topic was remotely humorous to the woman at a front table who stood and flung the contents of her wineglass up into the comic's face. He couldn't continue with burgundy dripping through his sinuses into his brain and bailed from the stage.

On the second night while I held forth as the headliner, raucous noises resounded from the rear of the room interrupting my set and the entire audience. An irate cowboy was beating up the middle act and hurling him around the dressing room. I never found out why. They evicted the cowboy and took the comedian to the hospital. I felt lucky to escape unscathed and vowed never to return.

I do not miss the miles required to chase the smiles or the pressure of live performance. Writing in the comfort of my home is a pleasure, and I find odd photo ops right in my backyard. I glanced over at the garage one night and freaked out upon seeing an erect dark shadow on the wall. No one else was outside. I wasn't naked. *Ah, it's the new porch umbrella folded up for the night.* This strange visage reminded me of the little known fact that celery is the world's best aphrodisiac… but only when used as a splint.

~ ~ ~

Not Quite Right

PEOPLE TELL ME, "Whenever I see something stupid, I think of you." I hope the comment means they know I collect stupid photos, instead of "Scott is stupid." I'm always amazed by businesses whose English is not quite right on a sign or a product label, which completely alters their marketing message, or makes the very name of their company sound downright silly! One mistake in the office becomes a million mistakes in the field.

Oops! Hair Salon: "Oops" is the last word you want to hear from a stylist who snips off a major lock so your hair looks like it was cut with a weed whip. "Oops! Sorry, ma'am. Here's the rest of your earlobe and a discount coupon for the cosmetic surgeon next door. Would you like your hair dyed red to match the blood on your neck?"

LIFE TIME WARRANTY

DJ-12

SOSO ®

SYMBOL OF QUALITY

SOSO: "Soso" may be the owner's actual name, but the English dictionary says that so-so means "neither very good nor very bad." Their "symbol of quality" is definitely suspect. I found this brand of tools, right next to "Nice Tools," a name which would sound quite complimentary: "He has a nice tool." A so-so tool is definitely a no-no.

กล้วยกวน

INTEGRATE WITH BANANA

ผลิตและจำหน่ายโดย

บริษัท สำรับไท มาร์เก็ตติ้ง สำกัด

Integrate with Banana: I doubt the newspaper would print much I'd write while imagining the possibilities the name of this product brings to mind, but at my next party I'll definitely hand out some and ask, "Wanna integrate with a banana? Can I watch?"

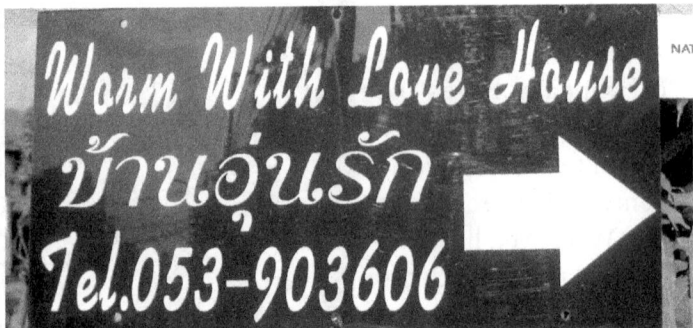

Worm With Love House

บ้านอุ่นรัก

Tel.053-903606

NA1

Worm with Love House: Any worm involved with love should be prevented. Worms with houses mean termites. If you can read Thai, the translation could be, "warm, loving house." But no read Thai, no stay here.

Supper Glue and Hiway: Do you add it to make meals that stick to your ribs? Do you put it on the chair so your kids can't leave the table? Can I use this at lunch? Is it legal to eat this glue while driving on the Supper Hiway?

The Moral: Be a hero instead of a zero. If you think you'll lose face with your colleagues because your English is weak, go find a friendly Farang (foreigner) who would likely give you a private reality check for free. It's better than losing face with millions!

P.S. Excuse me, Daiso Industries in Japan who manufactures "Getting damp taking of residence" in China, but exactly how do I use this product? Your instructions are a word salad tossed by monkeys. Try to read the fine print on the packaging back without laughing. Dare a guest to read it out loud at your next party. Hysterical!

Getting damp taking of residence

Use: It is possible to break in, and the dress chest of drawers, the storage warehouse, and the shoe cabinet, etc. will be dehumidified.

Handing Method: Please take a cover, peel off only the dampproof seat, and close it again. Please substitute it for a new commodity when the collected liquids come to a changed standard.

Processing after it uses it: A white, transparent seat is broken with scissors etc., please process sink (Please do not put it on the plant etc.) container as a plastic garbage living drainage though the collected liquids are sinks as for water.

Caution: Please read before it uses it. Moreover, please keep it while using it. Please do not peel off and do not break a white, transparent seat. • Please note it fruitlessly about the child. • The thing is put on the container, and please avoid and use use [No, this is not a typo. Yes, it really says "use use" on the label.] by having fallen in the level place. An inside liquid leaks when using it while falling. • Please there must be a fear of damage and do not risk the container and do not throw it. Please do not use it when damaging or cracking by any chance. • Please gargle with the vomit water at once when you put medicine and the collected liquid in the mouth. Please do that it is washing in clear water well when catching one's eye. In both cases, please consult the doctor. • Please often flush at once in water and dry it when stained to the hand and clothes, etc. • Please repeat a water wipe and a dry wipe about the one that it is not possible to wash until not sticking. • The effect doesn't change even if the liquid level comes from the medicine up. • Some days until the liquid beginning collect on the condition change at the use time. Especially it begins to absorb moisture if the medicine hardens at the season when humidity is low though collecting of the liquid is late. • Please do not use it except an original usage. • We will substitute it in the purchase shop in case of the emergency defect. • Please acknowledge that our company can not assume the responsibility of any claim of damage, passive damages, and the third party caused by this commodity beforehand.

~ ~ ~

Book Report

Chiang Mai, Thailand, 2006, before publishing my first
book **Life in the Laugh Lane***, the "prequel" to this book—*

I F I DON'T GET MY FINAL MANUSCRIPT to the printer by
tomorrow, I might have to check into a mental ward,
though they'll probably refuse to accept me because my
hair resembles something between a compost heap and a
dense thicket filled with tiny creatures building nests.

"I'm sorry, sir, we can see that you are certifiably bonkers,
but your hair is over the edge. You'll frighten our patients."

A slave to my new book, I've neglected routine chores
like haircuts, washing my hair, cleaning the refrigerator,
eating, and looking in the mirror. I brush my hair furtively,
but never achieve a hair-do, only a hair-don't.

A month ago, my wife said, "You look like Einstein. Is
your hair trying to escape from your head?" These words
would be a compliment today.

Two weeks ago, she said, "You hair looks like broccoli." This observation might signal a serious issue since the
green color is undoubtedly due to multiplying mold spores
during the rainy season here in Thailand.

Yesterday she said, "Your hair looks like cauliflower."
Great. The stress is turning it white. I've heard of cauliflower

ears, but I now have a cauliflower head from beating up my brain until I feel like a vegetable.

The refrigerator door won't close because it cannot hold an expanding ice cube—the entire freezer, a solid block of ice with a narrow cave in the middle large enough to freeze one sausage—so everything inside is warm, except the ice cube, and the produce is mutating into a gelatinous sludge. The cleaning lady comes today, though the fridge will terrify her. Maybe she can do something with my hair, or I could wear the mop when she's finished.

For months I've been slaving over my first book, *Life in the Laugh Lane*. I'm terminally tired of reading one book, over and over, till death do us part. Some writing is from the distant past, but most comes from two years of my weekly humor column in *Chiang Mai Mail* newspaper: rewritten and augmented with words the newspaper wouldn't print, then fine-tuned because no one really edited my submissions. The managers, a German couple who spoke better English than the entire state of Alabama, trusted my work.

Several intelligent British friends edited my manuscript, while suffering through my plebeian American language and suppressing their innate urge to misspell neighbour, colour, and flavour by adding the unnecessary letter "u", or use strange Shakespearian words like "whilst" when "while" is sufficient. I chose one absent-minded Brit because he wouldn't remember editing it and think it's a completely new book when I hand him his complimentary copy.

Three scholarly Americans proofed my first draft in between absorbing their standard fare of literary works with lengthy words and no pictures, heavy books I'd only use to press wild flowers or stand on to clean tall cupboards. In spite of this painstaking editing, I've learned that words left alone switch places, disappear, or reproduce overnight, removing spaces and creating random baby letters while snuggling together during nocturnal intercourse sessions.

Very depressing! OPEN at 7:30 and LOSE by 11
Very impressive! Spelled "espresso" correctly. Get it HOT or CLOD.

Formerly Chief of the Typo Police at a design firm, I helped helpless clients purge errors from their projects. It's infinitely harder to proof your own work—you silently, efficiently, and mentally correct mistakes while you read because your brain knows what they *should* be. Like ordinary everyday life, you choose to overlook your own flaws. You miss one error, and after one day at the printer, you incur 4,999 more errors communicating to the world that you're mentally challenged.

A secret saying at our design firm was, "The job ain't over till you find the typo." After spending hours scrutinizing the multi-page CD liner notes for a new Celtic album from Willowgreen, group member Jim Ofsthun signed off on the proofs. Weeks later, upon receiving boxes of the product, Jim phoned and admitted timidly, "I found the typo."

My heart plummeted. "What is it?"

"My last name is spelled wrong."

"Blame your parents for saddling you with Ofsthun! They probably misspelled it on your birth certificate. The only time you see these letters together in English—fsth—is when you're explaining the sound of a dud bottle rocket, as in, 'We pointed it at my neighbor's open window, but it fizzled out with a feeble fsth.'"

Here's a horror story I didn't want to happen with my project. The New York office of Rollerblade, the mega-manufacurer of in-line skates, was producing their yearly, luxurious, six-color catalogue. Their design firm in Minneapolis delivered the final artwork to a large printer in a small town nestled in the pastures of rural Minnesota. The Fed Ex truck picked up the press proof to be sent overnight to New York for approval. After glancing at the package, Mr. Fed Ex turned around, drove back to the printer, and found the manager. "Are you sure you want to send it like this?"

The manager recoiled in shock when he realized the vibrant front cover read "OLLERBLADE." Six colors were there, but the "R" set in expensive gold foil was not. The manager was down-on-his-knees thankful for Average Joe Fed Ex who caught a mistake that could've turned his company and the design firm into livestock ready for slaughter.

My project would've been simpler had I collected the old newspapers, stapled them together, and created one book. If I can remain semi-sane, 2,000 copies should be available in three weeks, and soon after, become required reading in lit-erature classes throughout the known world, which brings to mind my favorite book report story shared by my friend Charlie.

The meekest person in his high school English class, who dreaded any form of public speaking, slunk to the front of the room, and delivered a clas-sic verbal typo.

"Today my dick report is on Moby Book."

~ ~ ~

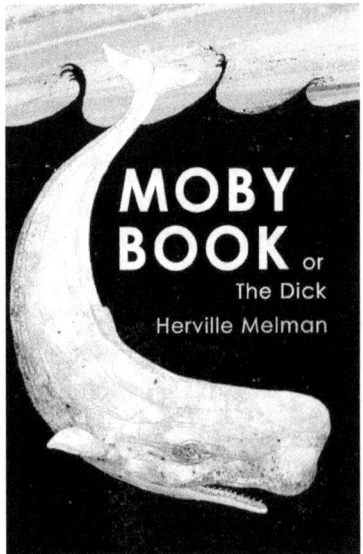

MOBY
BOOK or
The Dick
Herville Melman

SOB! Sell Our Books!

New York City, 2006, crawling the halls of a major literary convention after publishing Life in the Laugh Lane—

THE BOOK EXPO OF AMERICA (or BEA, perhaps named after my Aunt Bea, who has read several paperbacks) is a gigantic annual gathering of 40,000 people at the Javits Convention Center in Manhattan—1,000 publishers, subsidiary publishers, self-publishers, distributors, printers, literary agents, publicists, 9,000 bookstore owners and their worker ants trick-or-treating for free stuff, plus 30,000 struggling authors hawking, groveling, and begging with their two chapter drafts of the next great American novel.

After selling a copy of my new book to a Swiss publisher I'd met on the plane, I felt optimistic about my prospects at the Expo. Although he specialized in scholarly psychiatric works by and/or about Freud and Jung, I hoped he'd round out his catalog and include one title by an author who is clinically demented. I was also eager to practice handy phrases a buddy mentioned would be invaluable on the street, like how to ask someone for the time in New York.

"Excuse me, sir. Could you please tell me the time, or should I just go fuck myself?"

I'd arrived early to visit friends and prepare for a $200 Writer's Conference held the day before the Expo began. A model of efficiency and planning, I'd paid in advance. At 3:45 p.m., while relaxing with a beer and perusing the BEA website at my friends' home in New Jersey, I discovered the Writer's Conference had started at 8:00 a.m.—that very morning. If I survived the traffic, I might've been able to fight my way *in* through the crowds fighting their way *out*.

Feeling as though I possessed the brain power of an amoeba, I bussed in the next morning to attempt getting a refund and then attend the Expo, however, a lonely security guard at the front door of the uninhabited Javits Center informed me, "Sorry, Mr. Amoeba, the convention floor doesn't open until tomorrow." I had become the Official Village Idiot of New York City, having traveled 13,000 miles from Thailand to be there a day late and a day early… at the same time.

Lugging a backpack full of my *Life in the Laugh Lane* books, which weighed a bit more than a taxi, but cost less than the fare, I wandered the streets for hours testing my new chromium-cobalt, steel hip replacement installed three months earlier in India. [Gritty details later in "INDIA: a hip story."] The hip performed painlessly like steel should, but my neglected legs and feet became throbbing waste material, and the next morning I could barely walk at the Expo. I wished I'd gotten metal legs and feet, too.

Competition is fierce in the publishing biz, and I sought distribution with sufficient marketing so more people knew about my book than my Aunt Bea. *The BEA Expo Directory and Buyer's Guide* contained 126 pages of signing schedules with ten authors per page. That first day Alan Alda, John Lithgow, Mary Higgins Clark, other famous writers and celebrities—and I—autographed our recent creations. The famous folks were forced to sit in massive rooms behind tables and lengthy lines of bored fans who'd purchased tickets to wait hours to score their signatures. I was free to autograph anywhere for free.

That evening on the metro bus back to New Jersey, I met two cheery women carrying shopping bags full of give-away books, who still wore their Expo badges in case they forgot their names on the way home. One asked me, "Which book at the convention excited you the most?"

"Mine, of course," I said, and gave them a free auto-graphed copy on the condition that they'd email to tell me if it rocked, or if it sucked. I never heard from them. Obviously, they thought it sucked, but hey, I felt the same way about New Jersey.

Why would anyone care about my *Life in the Laugh Lane: facts, fiction, and photos from the USA to Asia* with others promoted at BEA like these? I did not change one word of their titles…

• *Touch Me There! A Hands-On Guide to Your Orgasmic Hot Spots*

• *Passing Gas and Getting Paid for It*

• *Don't Know Much About Anything,* "the latest edition in the million-copy selling series"

• *EEEEE EEE EEEE* (possibly a sequel to her debut novel *DDDDD DDD DDDD?*)

And three books destined to be chart-busters in Thailand:

• *Martina, the Beautiful Cockroach*

• *Woof! A Gay Man's Guide to Dogs*

• *Identifying the Wackos in Your Life,* which had a picture of my ex-wife in it.

My most humbling moment at the Expo? As I hobbled down an aisle on the last day, wondering why the hell I came in the first place, a pushy woman handed me a flyer about Adora Svitak and her new book *Flying Fingers.* From the photo on the flyer, I realized that author Adora stood right next to Mrs. Pushy, smiling up at me, bright-eyed and pony-tailed, her petite hand ready to pump mine.

"Hi! I'm Adora!" she exclaimed enthusiastically. "Nice to meet you what's your name do you want to read my book?" She was nine-years old. She'd written *Flying Fingers* at age seven, and her next title was due out soon.

Great. I'm 56. She published her first book 49 years before me AND has her own booth at the Expo. I'm still struggling with poverty, and she hasn't even reached puberty.

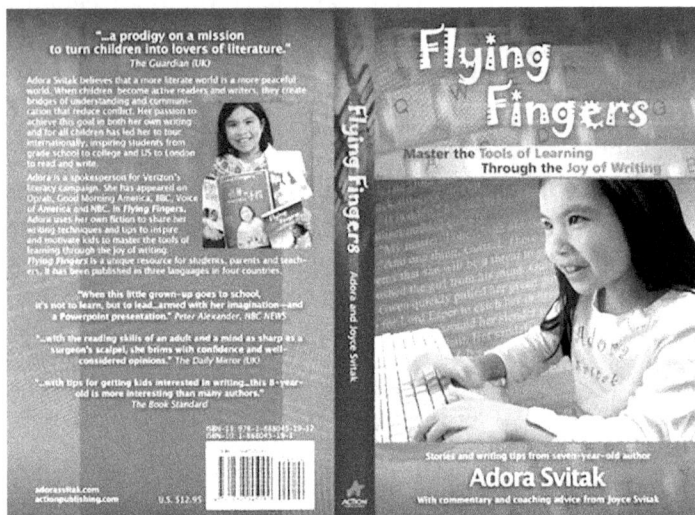

Adora and I traded books, while Mrs. Pushy Svitak, her mother and manager, hovered nearby like a vulture, probably with a bottle of adolescent amphetamines and a portable cattle prod concealed under her wing. As we chatted, I scanned Adora's flyer, which proclaimed: "*Flying Fingers*—a compilation of historical fiction and adventure stories, writing tips, her opinions on politics, religion, media, and education, plus a collection of her earlier poems."

What? Opinions on politics, etc? At age seven? At age 13, I still had a newspaper delivery route and no opinions. Her earlier poems? Written on the walls of her mother's womb?

I considered asking Adora for a few writing tips, but assumed she'd say, "Start earlier." Rather than sorting out the entire industry myself, I searched for a literary agent. On my final crawl through the halls with my one remaining book in hand, I met an enormous flamboyant lady dressed in what appeared to be medieval tapestry, who seemed vaguely interested while flipping through my paperback and laughing at the photos. I assumed she'd say: "This has potential, but it needs editing. Let's keep the pics and take out all the words."

Upon hearing I donated the profits to an orphanage in Thailand through my nonprofit organization, Give and Live, she chided, "I hate kids."

Could you please tell me the time, or should I just go…

I trudged out onto the streets of New York, convinced I'd have to sell my literary wares door-to-door, along with cosmetics and cleaning fluids, while employing techniques absorbed from that vaporous manual, *Passing Gas and Getting Paid for It.*

"I have a special offer for you today, ma'am. If you purchase at least $20 of goods, I will fart the song 'I Did It My Way' for free."

That was the 2006 BEA Expo, when self-publishing was in its infancy, and about 350,000 new books per year hit the shelves in the USA—40 books per hour, 24/7/365. I recently learned that, gasp, about 2,500,000 new titles are published per year! That's 6,849 books per day, 285 per hour, about five books per minute. My only experience with the number 2,500,000 is the amount of mosquitoes inside the hospital in India.

Target marketing is essential because most readers and book buyers are women—80% in the fiction genre. Writers must face the facts: men are primarily concerned with beer and sports, sports and beer, or playing beer drinking games in sports bars until they're too tanked to read.

"I've read at least 100 books in the past year, maybe 200," one user wrote on a literary blog. "My husband? I'm guessing zero, unless you count picture books and comic books he reads to the kids."

Hmm. Containing over 300 photos, my first book was remarkably manly. If its sales continue at the current rate, it should be a million-seller a few years after the universe has been sucked into a black hole.

My only hope for a best seller might be to display half-naked hulks and heaving bosoms on the cover, change my name to Scottina Higgins Clark, and get metal genitals in India when I return to re-place my legs and feet.

Maybe my next book will be a best seller if I steal this cover design?

The literary clock is ticking way faster than I am. At my advancing age, I'm trying to score a case of Adora's adolescent amphetamines to help me complete my second book, while she's pounding out her 20th. If I don't finish mine before I die, I'm going to kill myself.

~ ~ ~

Counter or Counterproductive Help?

I USED TO HAVE A HUNDRED MILLION DOLLARS, but I
gave them all away. Funny money starring the Statue
of Liberty on flimsy stock without the raised printing,
color-shifting ink, or mysterious watermarks of the real
deal, these million dollar bills became tickets into the lives
of everyday people. The busy bees in the hive of humanity
who I'd meet for a moment on the long and winding road
while performing across America were just working stiffs
like me. I'd hand bills to good samaritans—"Hey, thanks a
million!"—and buy a few smiles.

The funny money did its job, unless I'd entered a No
Joking Zone. At a convenience store somewhere, I grabbed

a coffee and set it on the counter with a million dollar bill. "Sorry, I don't have any smaller bills."

Surly counter help stood motionless with a blank look nailed to his face that silently screamed, "Think that's funny, eh? Hit the fuckin' road, Jack. I hate this place, I hate my job, I hate my life, and I hate you!"

When I did the same trick in a corner store run by a guy from Somalia (or Syria or a country I've never heard of that starts with a K and has no vowels), he gazed at the bill in a daze, momentarily speechless. His version of the American dream included the possibility that a white guy might have a million dollar bill in his wallet. Even after I explained it was fake, several times, he didn't believe me until I curled his fingers around the bill. "Here, pal. It's yours. Have some fun." He proudly introduced his new wealthy friend to the entire family lurking in the back... with a special focus on his two female, unmarried cousins.

In Wisconsin, the Dairy State, I stopped at a gas station/ grocery/whatever store selling large foam hats in the shape of Swiss cheese wedges, "Cow Pies"—the cheese heads' chocolate competition for Tennessee's "Moon Pie"—and bumper stickers proclaiming, "Wisconsin: Outdrinking your state since 1848."

I pumped his petrol, plopped a Cow Pie on the counter, and handed him a million. "Got change for this?"

He snapped up the bill. "You can have the whole place." Then grinned and walked out the door.

My kind o' guy. The admission ticket into their world might be a simple sincere question like "How ya doin' today?" And then listening instead of treating them like a vending machine.

Delving into the ridiculous can work wonders—people wondering if you're unhinged. Pull up to a turnpike toll booth, roll down the window, and say, "I'll have a big Mac, fries and a Coke. Supersize me! Wait... sorry. I must have fallen asleep."

Scrutinize a restaurant menu, then shake your head, and say to the waitress, "Jeez, I can't decide, so I'll have everything on page three and page five… to go… gift-wrapped."

At a rolling food cart selling smoothies for 30 cents in Thailand, hand the vendor your credit card. The look you'll get is priceless. Then say, "Poot len" ("Just kidding" in Thai) and hand over the cash. The second look when they understand you're joking is beyond priceless.

Deep in the flat heart of Texas, counter help was counterproductive. Traveling the thin blue two-lanes instead of the bright red four-lanes on the map, I stop in a speck of a town surrounded by short, scruffy trees wheezing in the heat and towering oil wells sucking the earth dry.

Visualize a counterfeit 7-11 store. I enter with my substantial thermos and ask Miss Counter, "Hi there. How much to fill this up with java?"

"We sell coffee by the cup here."

"Okay. Says on the wall over there, 'Coffee: 59 cents.' How many cups you think'll fit in here?" I set my thermos aka coffee mug on the counter. "About three?"

"Y'all gotta buy *ar* cups of coffee." (That's "our" pronounced "ar.")

"But I don't want the cups… only the coffee. You know, save the earth. Reduce, reuse, recycle." I could see she didn't know.

"We got procedures here."

"And they are…"

"Y'all can buy three cups of coffee an' pour 'em in yer mug there."

"But then I have to buy *three plastic* cups?"

"Yep. Um, nope. They're free with the coffee."

"What do you do with the cups when I'm done pouring?"

"Throw 'em away."

"You won't just pour coffee right into my mug?"

"No siree. We got procedures here."

Picking up my thermos, I attempt logic, reasoning, and marketing. "You know, some stores have mugs like this one with their name on it. Customers come back to have it filled, so they make more by selling the mugs, save money on cups, and help to protect the earth."

"We don' do that 'ere."

"No, you don't, do you," I sigh. "Your sign outside says 'Convenience Store.' It should say 'Inconvenience Store.'"

"Why?"

"Forget it." I am now pendulating between amazed and irritated, face-to-face with a minuscule slice of the redneck, environmentally oblivious, US population I've avoided for decades. An immobile, sturdy, thick slice. Let's just say she doesn't get out much, and probably doesn't want to, and if she ever gets out, she eats as heartily as when she's in. Her narrow blue tie and tight white uniform with horizontal red stripes accentuate her width. Flaccid hair hangs lifeless beside her ears, framing the acne blotches dotting her flushed face. If she'd remove her hat, I imagine her hair would come along with it. Time to ratchet up a notch.

"May I see the manager, please?"

"I'm the manager."

"I don't see 'Manager' written on your spiffy name tag."

"He ain't here. When he ain't here, I'm the manager."

"You mean, you're the *womanager*?"

"What?" The compacted folds in her brow look painful.

"Never mind. I'll bet he's a dick, anyway."

"He's my uncle."

"Ah, sorry," I sigh. "Uncle Dick. I've got one of those, too. Maybe we're related."

"What?"

"Nothing." My foreign North Dakota accent incriminates me. I am an alien dressed in black, trespassing in her southern domain. No way a million dollar bill will work here. Dollars to Dunkin doughnuts, she'd call the sheriff, another uncle. I tackle a new tactic: Partners in Crime #101. "So… since the manager's not here, how about if you and I common folks get together on this? C'mon, slip a little java into my mug. Your uncle will never know you gave it to me without the cups."

"He'll know. He counts the cups."

"People take away the cups. How can he count them?"

For the first time since I'd arrived, Miss Counter moves a muscle besides her mouth. She lifts a hefty arm and points to the coffee area. "He counts the ones leftover."

"But what happens when people *steal* some cups? Or take *two* and stack 'em to keep one coffee hotter longer?"

"I gotta pay for the missing cups." Her arm falls back into lethargy.

She is a stationary object in the world, like bedrock. I lean in, lower my voice, and press on with Extra Income Tactic #302. "Okay, I've got an idea. You pour the coffee into my mug and *hide* the unused cups. Then when three are missing, you can replace 'em, and *you* won't have to pay for 'em."

She pauses to let that sink in. It doesn't. No fertile soil. Impenetrable bedrock. "Can't do it. We got procedures here." Miss Counter points again. "An' a s'curity cam'ra."

After raising her arm twice, she must be exhausted, her resolve weakening. I deliver my final plea in her language. "Well, ah'm fixin' ta jes' mosey on outta here with nothin' but mah principles, so y'all'll get no cash a-tall and have ta keep y'all's precious little cups and coffee. How zat?"

She shrugs off my nightmare. "Suit yer se'f."

I give up and lay two bucks on the counter. "Ah surrender. Y'all got procedures here. Three cups o' coffee, please. Keep the change, darlin', even though y'all don' like change."

She pours three cups of coffee. I pour the coffee into my mug and set the cups on the counter. She throws them away. I lose, along with the world, and leave.

At a recent job interview, The Powers That Be and Interrogate sprung a surprise question on me, the prospective employee. "What really bothers you or makes you angry?"

I didn't even have to think. "Little people enforcing their petty little rules which make no sense whatsoever." I got the job, but that became the main reason I quit a few months later.

Challenging the rules in that one-off, Texas Stop 'n' Squat store paled compared to my trial at Subway, the international fast-food franchise I'd visited countless times, on tour and off, all over the America. A recent Subway slogan: "Enjoy your sub the way you say."

One day after work in Minneapolis, the largest city in the state of "Minnesota Nice," I attend my ten-year-old stepdaughter's softball game. When she tells me she's hungry, I leap into action. "There's a Subway a couple blocks away. How's that?"

Her eyes light up. "I'd like that. You know what I want?"

"Of course! Whole wheat bun, turkey, cheese, and black olives, hold everything else."

"That's it."

"I'll be back in a flash. Don't get any home runs until I return."

Visualize a standard Subway. I'm in blue jeans, tweed sport jacket, and a button-down, pin-stripe shirt with a festive tie. No one is in the room as I enter.

"Hello? Anyone here?"

From a doorway to the side, a hulking dude struts up to his position behind the work station laden with fresh ingredients. He's wearing the classic Subway-green polo with "Sandwich Artist" embroidered above the pocket. "Wha'd'ya want?"

"Hi, there. How are you?"

"Fair," he mutters.

"Okay…" I point to the menu on the wall. "I'd like the carved turkey on nine-grain whole wheat."

"Foot-long?"

"Sure. For my little daughter. It'll last three days."

"Toasted?"

"That'd be great."

"Cheese?"

"Monterey Jack, please."

Silence, except for the hum of the oven. Toasting completed, he asks, "Wha'd'ya want on it?"

"Just black olives, please. That's the way she likes it."

He sprinkles about six slices of black olives on the turkey—and I'm not making this up—*slices* of olives, not *whole* olives. He raises his eyes and mumbles, "That's it?"

I glance down at the sub, which looks like six beetles with bullet holes shot through the middle have crawled onto the turkey. "Yeah, but could you please put more olives on it? Seems a little sparse…"

He grabs three olive *slices* and drops them on the sub.

I wait for him to grab and add more. He doesn't. With a wry smile I say, "Cute. A few more, please."

"No."

"No?"

"No."

"But I'm not even getting any other items." His pursed mouth does not move, nor do his lifeless eyes. I am not upset—yet—only confused. *Is he giving me some of my own medicine? Is he yanking my chain, and a grin lurks behind the inert mask balancing on top of his shoulders?* "You're kidding, right?"

"No."

I begin to unravel, but eke out compliments as I ramble on. "You know, I love Subways. I've must've eaten in a hundred of 'em all over the country. 'Eat fresh. Enjoy your sub the way you say.' Those are *your* slogans. Sandwich Artists everywhere fill up my bread with whatever and however much I ask for, including black olives." I point to the individual bins of ingredients as I list them. "I don't want your lettuce, your tomatoes, your red onions, your cucumbers, your spinach, your sliced carrots, your pickles, your green peppers, your jalapenos, or your shredded purple cabbage. Just black olives. Can I trade *every one* of those ingredients for a healthy serving of black olives… for my hungry little daughter?"

"Not here."

"So this is unlike any other Subway in America, or maybe on Earth?"

He's silent, a breathing wall of lead bricks. Magma is rising from the core of my soul, coursing through the mantle of idiocrasy. *Ratchet up.*

"I'd like to see the manager, please."

"I *am* the manager."

Holy fuck, I'm in hell. "Okay, Mr. Manager, my mistake. I thought you were a 'Sandwich Artist' like your shirt says. It should say, 'Sandwich Asshole.'"

I immediately regret saying this for several reasons which hurtle through my head. *I am a miniscule minority of one in the neighborhood. I'm not young; he is. I'm reasonably strong, but humble and wiry with glasses; he's a couple pounds short of Goliath with shoulders as wide as my office desk. Decades ago I dodged the Vietnam War for medical and ethical reasons; he probably single-handedly exterminated stampeding enemy platoons in Afghanistan… last month… and thoroughly enjoyed it.*

Staring at me like a cobra with its head raised, flared, and poised for a strike, Goliath the Manager knows he could disable me with a flick of his pinky. "You want it or not? There's nobody else here."

That sounds like a threat, but imagining my starving daughter, weak on the softball team bench, I risk death. *I'm on a mission and must deliver the goods. New tactics: Fake Humility Plus Alternative Action #207.* "Okay, I'm sorry. I apologize. Please forgive me. Can I possibly *buy* some more olives?"

"How many d'ya want?"

"How much are they?"

"10 cents apiece."

My voice elevates a minor third. "One olive for 10 cents?"

"Per slice."

Approaching the temperature of the sun, the magma seeks escape through the earth's crust to fulfill its destiny in an erupting volcano. "You're going to charge me 10 cents a slice?" I inspect the sub closely. "Let's see… including those puny slices on each end, that's about five per olive. 50 fucking cents for one fucking olive?"

"So how many d'ya want?"

"When I asked you how you were when I came in, you said 'Fair'. This is *not* fair."

"It's fair to me."

"I could go to the grocery store next door and buy a can of a hundred olives for a buck."

"Go ahead."

I'd have to buy a can opener, too. A plate and napkins. And a knife. Hmm… I could come back here with the knife… no, he has many knives, heavy pans, and an oven. Once again a vision of my daughter creeps in, faint from hunger, collapsing in the dust during her final dash to home plate. I do not speak the first six words of my response. "*I hate you, you despicable prick.* Okay, fine. Give me two bucks worth. Count 'em carefully. I'm gonna check your work."

With a sadistic sneer, he adds twenty olive slices and holds up the sub for my inspection. I nod. He wraps it in wax paper and drops it into a plastic bag. Like in a tense drug/money deal, I fork over my cash as he hands over the bag, though he makes me tug it out of his tight fingers.

In the sarcastic tone of a triumphant warrior towering over his victim, standing calmly with his spiked leather boot buried deep inside the hero's chest, the Sandwich Asshole taunts me. "Have a nice fuckin' day." And gives me the finger.

Hovering at the exit with one hand on the door and the other clutching the frame, ready to launch myself toward the curb and into the safety of my car, I deliver my curse. "I will *never* come here again. I will tell *all* my friends, relatives, and random people on the street *never* to come here. I shall contact the main Subway office and apprise them of your actions and location. I write for a national magazine that will publish my scathing review of your pathetic macho antics. Have a nice fucking *life*."

I told my friends, but they never shopped in that area, anyway. I never contacted Subway. I didn't write the scathing review until now, twenty-five years later. Nice guys finish last, even in the Land of Minnesota Nice.

Nine out of ten times, the reason I request the manager is to praise their establishment or employees. Managers advance with hackles raised for battle or wearing knee pads ready to grovel since nine out of ten times they are the chosen ones summoned to deal with disgruntled customers. I smile, stand up, and shake their hands.

"I just want to let you know your food is marvelous, the atmosphere is charming, and your employees are splendid. Our waitress is a star. Don't lose her. You should probably pay her more."

If you plan to return to a restaurant, this tactic is better than storming out as an irate ogre, setting up the inevitability that the chef will spice your next burger with his spittle and freshly ground cockroaches.

At an upscale but casual French café in Minneapolis while dining with a close friend plus our two dates, I did *not* call for the manager. My friend was also my boss, the president, who'd run several major companies and been an interim president for new ventures acquired by a wealthy investor. He had decades of experience deciding what was good, what was bad and needed trimming, you're fired.

Following his advice, we ordered four foo-foo chicken dishes called Poulet Beret or Poulet Guillotine or Chicken Checkered Tablecloth. I don't recall; it sounded authentic. Our entrées arrived lukewarm and overdone. The Prez immediately demanded to see the top of the food chain: he knew how to manage managers.

Soon the maître d' appeared, nattily dressed and professionally meek. "Good evening, folks. I hear you're not pleased with your dinners?"

"I've eaten here many times." The Prez gestured to everyone's plates. "We all ordered the same dish, and they're all overcooked. The chicken's cold and dry."

(I'd have been a bit gentler. "Hey, thanks for coming over. If you don't mind, I'd like your opinion. The food's normally delicious here, but maybe your chef left the chicken on a little too long. How about tryin' a bite and telling us what you think?" Then I might step into the ridiculous, take a sip of my drink, and ask, "And would you try this, too? It tastes kinda funny, but feels good on my cold sores.")

The manager groveled graciously. "I'm so sorry you're not satisfied. I'll get you new entrées as soon as possible."

I wasn't in the mood for this. Four new meals seemed over the culinary edge, even though the boss had spoken. He was president of the company, not the table.

"Thanks for the offer," I said, "but mine's fine. I'll keep it."

Chin lowered and eyebrows raised, the manager asked, "Are you sure? I'll be glad to replace it with another one."

"Get a new one," the Prez grunted.

"No, it's okay." I grabbed my plate, set it in my lap, and hunched over it like a refugee protecting his bowl of rice. "I'm hungry."

Replacements were served promptly, perfectly prepared. The Prez' poulet was moist and tender. Mine was like chewing chicken gum… or a beret. When the waitress brought our check, she announced, "Your meals are on the house!" Except *my* meal. The complainers' three meals were complimentary; I had to pay for mine. Nice guys not only finish last, they're punished, fined, and chewed out.

Sometimes you *must* rouse the manager as a community service and to protect humanity in general. On an Oregon vacation with the family, we stopped at popular cheese factory on the coast, took a self-guided tour, and saw the production of cheese from windowed hallways. The final elevated walkway led us above the packaging and shipping process. Cheese wheels emerged through plastic curtains on conveyer belts like luggage at the airport.

We focused on one rotund, bald worker in a wife-beater t-shirt—white and sleeveless with low-cut armholes. The size and shape of his distended belly suggested he'd eaten an entire cheese wheel in one bite. We watched as he took wheels off the conveyer, inspected them for a second, and placed them in a shrink-wrap machine. When the belt paused, the man leaned back and folded his hairy arms by sticking his hands into his hairy armpits. We recoiled in horror in unison, internally vowing never to eat another morsel of cheese.

I felt it was my duty to uninformed customers to inform the manager and found him shuffling papers in his office. "Hi. Sorry to bother you." I could see he wasn't used to hosting visitors. "We just finished your factory tour, and I'd like to show you something."

"What is it? Is something wrong?"

"I think you need to see for yourself."

Curiosity piqued, he followed me up to the walkway.

When we reached our previous outlook position, I pointed. "Watch the worker in the wife-beater t-shirt."

"It can get hot in there. We let them wear what they want."

"Sounds humane, but that's only part of your problem. Check out what happens when the conveyer belt stops." He intently focused on the man, and then the belt stopped. I put my hand on his shoulder. "Wait for it."

The worker did his armpit trick again, and the manager recoiled in horror, a rewarding déjà vu for the family. "Oh, my god! This is terrible! Totally unacceptable. Thank you so much for showing me! It will never happen again."

"You're welcome," I sighed. "Well, he *is* wearing rubber gloves to assure that his glistening pit juice doesn't absorb into his hands. Does this underarm marinade enhance that pungent musty flavor of your blue cheese? Natural fertilizer for the mold, perhaps?"

The manager brown-nosed us out of the building while offering us large amounts of cash and prizes and a lifetime supply of free cheese.

"Thanks anyway, but we'll stick with Wisconsin cheese… *after* we've thoroughly inspected their facilities." As he pampered us to our car door in the parking lot, still apologizing profusely, I couldn't resist saying, "Maybe you *can* help me. I'm considering the concept of selling a line of Israeli dairy products called 'Cheeses of Nazareth'. What d'ya think?"

Responses vary to my day brightening or—depending on the mood or moment—obnoxious quips. My favorite reply of all time came in a health food store managed by one of my dear friends, a genuine Minnesota Nice woman. I've learned that one Law of the Universe states: "Nice managers hire nice people; asshole managers surround themselves with a shitload of assholes." A staunch vegan, my friend meditated routinely, fasted one day every week, chose not to speak on Sundays, and consumed copious amounts of beer—technically a liquid medley of vegetables.

The store sold a plethora of natural lotions, potions, and pills, salads made from imported Japanese tofu and pesticide-free grass clippings, products no one pronounced correctly like quinoa (Keen! Wha…?) and 25-grain, gluten-free bread that could also serve as roofing shingles when toasted. The atmosphere: calm, quiet, and contented. Chill out, dude. Comatose is politically correct in this serene celestial setting.

I enter unobtrusively. No one asks what I want or shadows me like I might shoplift their Korean ginseng and other ancient remedies guaranteed to keep me alive forever. New Counter Help I'd never met is wearing a vegetablistic yoga shirt and a flowing rainbow skirt—no leather or animal accessories allowed. I assume she'd been harvested from the same Minnesota-nice organic garden as the manager.

A few minutes later, I approach this fresh comedic challenge ruminating next to the cash register, wholly at one with her new age paperback. "Excuse me, ma'am. I'd like one of everything, please."

Without batting a makeup-free eyelash, she peers through her waist-length locks, and asks, "What size?"

My kind o' woman.

~ ~ ~

Good News

BAD NEWS IS EASY TO FIND. Open a newspaper, made by one species (homo sapiens) destroying another species (trees) in order to report on how humans are destroying themselves: the USA vs. some random country; any Mideast country vs. one of their neighbors; Myanmar dictators vs. the Karen, the Shan, and anyone else that has lived in their country longer than they have; rich vs. poor, terrorists vs. the world, this religion vs. that religion, mankind vs. Mother Nature; rape, murder, bombings, genocide, etcetera, ad nauseam. Has humanity progressed at all in the past five thousand years? We seem to be the same marauding hordes with higher tech hatchets.

I prefer to read local newspapers in Thailand where front pages present a gentler life amongst the mayhem and are often devoted to respect for beloved royalty or charitable projects. Murder occasionally makes the headlines, but recently in Chiang Mai the victims were 200 chickens, which is pretty much par for the course of any chicken's destiny.

The alleged perpetrator, a Canadian gray wolf on the lam for a month from the Night Safari zoo, was "alive, though weak, and has injured its leg and genitals," which sounded very similar to the physical state of human Canadians after a wild night at Spicy's nightclub. While the wolf devoured juicy chicks, jealous roosters must have pecked his cock-a-doodle. "The starving animal was shot with a tranquilizer gun," though "starving" seemed a bit of a stretch considering it had feasted on 6.66 chickens per day for a month.

The Night Safari Director accepted that they had made mistakes in allowing the wolf to escape, and the police vowed that if negligence was discovered, "the people responsible will be punished." Following the strict law of karma, something would undoubtedly happen to the director's legs and genitals involving drugs and poisoned darts.

I'm glad to be a Good News Reporter to counterbalance the bad—no belly laughs intended, just a smile in your soul and a hint of hope for humanity.

Mentally Challenged Foreigner Saved by Good Samaritan. When I first arrived in Thailand with a marginal concept of the actual value of multicolored baht bills as opposed to boring, monochromatic American greenbacks, I purchased a pair of flip-flops for sixty baht on the tiny divers island of Koh Tao. I gave the sales woman three blue-greenish bills sporting pictures of the King of Thailand and walked out of the shop. A few minutes and two blocks later, she ran up and handed me 2,940 baht: my change. I had given her three thousand-baht notes instead of three twenties—$90 dollars instead of $1.20. I asked her to marry me, but she didn't want to spend her life with an idiot.

Mentally Challenged Foreigner Saved by Flock of Good Samaritans. On a motorcycle trip through the mountains, my wife Joomi and I chose a route via a state park, but upon arrival at the gate, were told that the road didn't continue through the park to our destination. The Thai park ranger showed us an alternate route on our map, thirty kilometers back down the road, and onto another highway from there.

An hour later, on the ridge of the mountains, police officers waved us over. You never really know what they'll want, and I was ready to reach for a wad of baht. A gleeful policeman beamed and said, "You left your wallet at the state park!"

Another hour later, we were back at the park, surrounded by a bevy of happy officials, women, and children who were honored to return my wallet, intact, filled with credit cards and baht. They cared enough to call and find Thai officials to help strangers they'd met for only a moment. We wanted to take them all home with us, and though they would've been comfortable on the Harley, I can't quite do Thai-style with seventeen riders plus two dogs.

Vigilante Committee of One Springs into Action. While parked at a turnpike rest area in Ohio, a friend saw a family get out of a car and dump their garbage on the grass. Appalled, she jumped out and gathered up their trash as the family drove away. She pursued them on the highway, exited when they did, and followed them through town to their home. As Mr. and Mrs. Litterbug and their kids walked from their car in the driveway to the house, the Vigilante Committee of One scattered their garbage in the center of their yard, stomped back to her car, and drove away. No words or weapons necessary. Action screams louder than words!

Read the Signs. While stopped at an intersection in Minnesota on her drive home from work, alone, a forty-something friend noticed a disheveled man holding a sign. "Will work for food." Her heart took her beyond the fear of the unknown as she rolled down her window and held out a twenty-dollar bill. The man looked her in the eye, folded her fingers around her twenty, smiled, and said, "Thanks anyway, ma'am. Have a nice evening." Then he walked away. He didn't want her money; he wanted to work for food. That's what the sign said.

Do Unto Others... Market Street in San Francisco is a hodgepodge of streetwalkers, street-talkers, leftover freaks from the sixties, homeless beggars, shell-shocked Vietnam vets, preoccupied purveyors, snappy accountants, and bustling stockbrokers. While waiting for a bus, I watched a few moments in the lives of two wizened comrades, their hard times written in wrinkles on their faces. The black guy rode in a wheelchair; the white guy leaned on it and pushed. The ambulatory man asked passersby for a cigarette and got one on his third plea. He fired it up and gave it to his buddy in the wheelchair. Then he searched the gutter, found a half-used fag, and smoked it as he rolled his friend away. He didn't have much, but he had a wealth of compassion.

Good news if it's Sunday but very bad news if it's Monday, and you have to wait six days while keeping your legs crossed.

Grampa couldn't wait for the toilet to open, and he's never been quite the same after using this porta-potty.

~ ~ ~

A Chance Encounter

I F YOU EVER HAVE THE DESIRE to get a Siberian husky, read this first, and learn about the breed before you've fallen hopelessly in love, become addicted to its quirky personality, and spend the next decade suffering through its naturally adorable yet challenging traits. Had I been half as intelligent as our husky or done the slightest bit of research, I'd never have gotten one. *I'm so glad I didn't do the research!*

A few years ago while shopping for garden plants, my wife Joomi and I happened upon a dog market in Chiang Mai, Thailand. After cuddling a six-week-old German shepherd, she widened her eyes to full

Day One

One Year Later

moon proportions, summoned her four-year-old baby voice, and pleaded, "Can we pleeease get a puppy?"

I've always loved dogs. My overdeveloped heart melted immediately, but my mature manliness prevailed. I replied, "We'll talk about it."

Our talks narrowed the dog desires to "big and intelligent," most likely a shepherd which each of us had previously owned and cherished, or a husky which we'd mainly seen in movies or met in cages. We mutually agreed on a timeline of "let's wait awhile." A month later on Christmas Eve after serious scrutiny of the existential question—*What if today was the last day of my life?*—I returned to the dog market with full intention of purchasing a surprise German shepherd puppy. Sigh, they'd been sold.

Destiny turned my head. Across the lane, I beheld a litter of four exquisite husky pups, one with nearly the same black-and-white markings as Marcus, the shepherd who had been my constant companion for 13 years. With these words blaring in my mind—*I might die tomorrow! Who needs a German when an Asian Marcus clone is standing by? I'll be a hero!*—our lives careened down another path.

Well, I became a hero, except for the "mutually agreed time line" part, and puppy love ruled the day. Joomi suggested the name "Einstein" as an option, but the inevitable edited version of "Einie" didn't cut it, so we christened him Chance. Soon the unedited version "Chancellor" appeared, and depending on the moment, is firmly in place because he now rules our personal universe. The name Chance is nearly impossible for a Thai to say, as is my name: Scott. To the local guy who helps around the yard, no matter how many times I give him explicit pronunciation lessons, I'm still "Suck Kah" with a dog named "Cat."

After a memorable eve of infatuation, with visions of a guard dog for Joomi when I'm not home, unleashed cavorting through the neighborhood, domestic tranquility in our yard, and a new being in the bedroom, I awakened Christmas morning to an odd odor. I rolled my head to see a dozing puppy head next to mine on the pillow, its baby breath flavored by goat milk recommended for his diet. We fell in love all over again. That afternoon I checked out more info about huskies on the web.

"Huskies adore everyone. They are not watchdogs."

"These dogs will dig to Australia… if you truly love your yard, don't get a Siberian."

"If huskies are bored, they'll howl forever and tear apart your house."

"This breed should **never** be off the leash!!!"

"Huskies are magicians at getting over or under the fence, on the roof, out of the yard, and into the next county. They love to run and will be gone if they have a chance."

Gasp. We have a Chance. All of these traits are accurate, but we've learned to cope with them while reveling in his affection, his talkative ways, and his ability to change directions at full speed, spring upward, and momentarily hang in the air like a high jumper suspended above the bar.

Chance is an intelligent watchdog and intelligently watches everything… trees swaying in the breeze, a bird on the wire, the flossing of teeth and clipping of toenails, or any people anywhere doing anything. He craves company.

If a burglar approached our gate, Chance would wag furiously and howl in Siberian, "Hey, come on in and let's play! We got some really cool stuff in the house! Want me to help you load up your truck? If you've got a sled, I could pull it!"

The only hope of Chance thwarting a thief would be if he licked them to death. Fortunately, most folks don't know this and are terrified of those big teeth making up that big bad wolf grin behind the gate. The locals have another name for him: "Phi Na" in Thai. *Ghost face.* The house is safe.

I've changed our garden greenery from small delicate plants to tall large-leaf varieties, cacti, or Thai vines more durable than leather that can grow on concrete and sprout again from chewed bits. Chance's excavation attempts have mainly been confined to his substantial pottery water bowl, which he frantically flails, digs, and removes all the water while filing his nails so they don't trim the skin off my arms while we're wrestling.

Because Joomi and I have become hermits, the three of us hang out constantly. Chancellor doesn't get bored, and our couch is intact, unlike grim photos on the web of husky owners standing knee deep in stuffing. We distract him from the heat with air-con, strategically placed fans, routine ice cube delivery, and by locking him in the refrigerator.

Outside our walled yard, Chance is on a leash. Period. I don't want to revisit the traumatic times he slithered through the open gate and sprinted down the street in unbridled ecstasy as I hobbled in pursuit wearing flip-flops while suffering minor heart attacks or major nervous breakdowns. So far, he hasn't loped happily back to Siberia, via Switzerland, Finland, or China.

During his middle age of six years, Chance evolved from a lean leaper into a husky eighty-eight-pound fullback. His latest moniker is "Nong Mu" or Little Pig, because he eats anything in sight or smell. We wouldn't be shocked to return home and find the couch gone. My favorite snack, Ovaltine cookies, have become his favorite snack. I sneak into distant rooms like a closet alcoholic, silently open the package, and chew with my mouth closed. Even during a snoring nap attack, his nose will catch that one Ovaltine molecule wafting through the air, and Piglet will sleep-trot over to claim his fair share.

When we're out and someone calls, he might answer the phone and leave the receiver on the floor. One day my cell phone disappeared. I found it in the yard with teeth marks on the keys. We suspect he tried to buy a ticket to Siberia on Air Asia to escape the heat.

**Stressed middle-age Alpha Dog staring at front door for four days
and nights waiting for his Alpha Human to return from Malaysia**

Some dogs don't obey because they're too stupid to learn. Chancellor knows what "come here" means, but his independent streak resists immediate compliance. He might leave his preferred post at the gate on my third command, in his own sweet time.

Me: "Chance, c'mon."

Him, motionless: "I hear you. Chill out."

Me: "Chancellor, come here!"

Him, still a statue: "Whatever. I'm busy."

Me: "Damn it, Chancellor! Get over here! Now!"

Him, plodding toward me at the speed of a two-legged chihuahua: "Jeez, don't pop an artery, dude. My ancestors ran thirty miles an hour for forty miles at fifty degrees below zero. Fuck *that* shit."

These days my wife delivers a new plea in her baby voice: "Can we get another one, puleeeease?"

"Honey, I'd love to have ten more, but I'm the sole dog walker. If my eyes aren't focused solely on Chance when he spies a cat, dog, or invisible alien, my limbs are in jeopardy. His sudden charges have taken me to the ground and nearly yanked my arm out of its socket."

"I could help," Joomi begs.

"Hmm. Ninety pounds of delicate Thai tethered to eighty-eight pounds of sprinting canine. I imagine you flying horizontally through the air behind Chancellor like a scarf in a stiff wind." *Were I to attempt walking two huskies, the authorities might discover them heading north through Tibet sporting two leashes dragging two detached arms with frozen fingers still clutching the handles.*

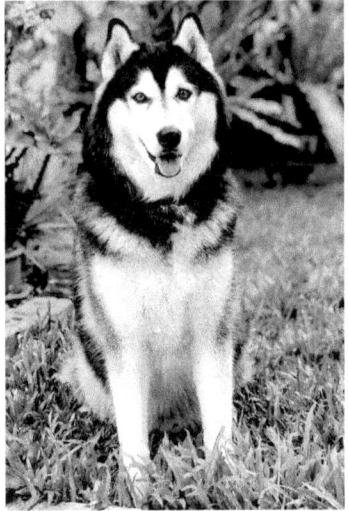

If you…1) live in a tiny apartment or sanitary house with immaculate gardens and are allergic to mounds of shed hair everywhere (including dangling from light fixtures on the ceiling) plus dark outer fur covering your light clothing and light undercoat covering your dark clothing…

or 2) work all day and don't have time to love, exercise, and play with your best buddy…

or 3) fancy a one-man, vicious guard dog barking and lunging toward strangers at the gate…

Do not get a husky!

Either man's best friend will soon be for sale in a cage at a pet shop, or you'll soon be in your own padded cage at the psychiatric hospital, right next to my room.

~ ~ ~

Finger Bananas and Mango Rain

ONE MINUTE, OR LESS. That's how long it took this American to fall in love with Asia when he first stepped out of the Hong Kong airport into the warm January atmosphere. Mmm. Thick, moist, and exotic. I could almost roll the air between my fingers.

On the flip side of the temperature scale, I once stepped out of a hotel into thin, Canadian, January air for a morning jog at 30 below zero, layered with as many clothes as I could wear and still move my legs. After two kilometers, my fingers, toes, and nose ached from the cold, and I realized I couldn't feel those valuable, soft appendages hanging below my torso. Frozen fingers plunged into my sweat pants to protect the Jones Family Jewels and stayed there all the way back to the hotel, as I ran for my potential family's life, kind of like a duck, a lame duck, speed waddling along and trying not to get arrested for disorderly conduct.

I loved China for three weeks, then loved visiting Vietnam for two months, though thirty years earlier, I'd have done anything to *not* visit it during the war, including, gasp, move to CANADA, which stands for Cold Arctic North America Desolate Area. Then Thailand stole my heart and won't give it back to me.

Folks in America wonder why I love Thailand, and ask, "So what's the big deal about Taiwan?" (Those who might have heard the word Thailand think it must a store at the mall called Tie Land that sells neckties sporting Mickey Mouse, the Playboy bunny, or your favorite fishing lure.)

"Because it's beautiful, the food's scrumptious, and I can ride my motorcycle, wear sandals, and plant flowers any day of the year." No one quite gets it. The real reasons I love Thailand aren't "a big deal." They're the little things, the sights, sounds, and smells that don't exist in America, the ones folks won't understand until they experience them.

Finger bananas. Tiny, delicate and delicious, big as your thumb, a buck for a bunch, you can't eat just one. I remember seeing a sign in a 7-11 in America: "Wow! Bananas! Only 90 cents each!" I thought, *Wow. Only? For one banana? In Thailand I can get an entire bunch for that much, unlike these hard enough to use as a hammer.* In the USA, if I ever said, "I ate an entire bunch of bananas," I'd be talking to an emergency room doctor, who'd raise both eyebrows, cautiously step back from the bed, and quietly instruct nurses to transfer me to the loony bin after a stomach pump.

The 80-year-old wizened woman who floats by, pedaling just fast enough to keep her bicycle upright, who lives at home with her 100-year-old mother and her 60-year-old daughter, none of whom had been prematurely embalmed in a nursing home with their knickknacks and left alone to slip into Alzheimer's.

The basil plants I love, I don't even have to plant. They appear here, there, anywhere, growing in the dirt/gravel of the driveway, well on their way from plant to bush status.

"No, thanks. I don't need any water. Had some a couple months ago. Sorry to block your driveway. Mind going around me if I let you have a few tasty leaves?"

The sweet mango rain. I woke one morning to the strange pitter-patter on the window panes in January. *Rain? In the middle of the Non-Rainy Season? Did I sleep until May?* Oh yeah, the mango rain, the perpetual phenomenon that magically happens as the mango trees bloom. When they need it, the sky provides.

Markets and street stalls, open day, or night, or both, that sell everything—in combinations you've never considered. The Computer and Pomelo Store. The Bulk Eggs and Used Shoe Store. The "We Buy EveryTING Store." *Ha! I'll bet they wouldn't buy the motorcycle I rented right around the corner!* On Khao San Road, a three-hundred-and-three-ring circus of travelers, goods, services, and sustenance thrives in Bangkok next to the police station. Score a diploma from Harvard for a couple bucks instead of $200,000, a driver's license from anywhere in the world, or a student ID, even if you're 103.

Kaleidoscopic butterflies that flit through

the yard and sometimes land on my hand. In my old hometown of Fargo, North Dakota, butterflies were mainly white or boring brown or in between. The only multicolored varieties available were expensive, had been murdered, and came in the mail, shriveled under glass.

Those singular, unforeseeable, exquisite life moments. Sitting outside in January eating Burmese food in an Indian restaurant in Thailand, surrounded by people chattering away in their native languages from countries that didn't exist when I was a kid (like Katchascatchcanistan or whatever it is), while listening to live musicians perform "Rocky Mountain High" (better than John Denver ever did), with my beautiful wife and Siberian husky at my feet, (the husky, not the wife), I think, *I love this. As a kid, as a teenager, hell, as an adult, I couldn't even have imagined this would ever be happening!*

I even love things I don't love. The incessant tuk-tuk of the tuk-tuks, motorcycle taxis with three-wheels and an enclosed double seat in back that delivers you and your lungs through the traffic and exhaust fumes. Metal accordion storefront gates rolling up at dawn, screeching like fingernails on a blackboard. These minor irritations transform from noise into music after I return from a trip to America.

After nearly two decades of living in and loving Thailand, I'd feel very insecure going back to my old homeland, now fiercely guarded by Homeland Security. If the Fate Police ever came up and demanded, "Sir, you'll have to move back to America," I'd look them in the eye and reply, "Just shoot me now." *No, no, that sounds too painful.* "Let me amend that request, please. Just take me to Canada for one last frozen run until I'm numb, *then* shoot me."

~ ~ ~

Thailand's Hidden Hazards

TRAVEL GUIDEBOOKS WARN YOU of exotic diseases that melt your brain, shopping scams that gut your wallet, and cultural no-no's that could send you to the slammer, but seldom cover the day-to-day, life-threatening hazards you only learn about if you survive them. On my first day in Thailand, I almost died just trying to walk.

Uneven Floors and Teflon Tiles. I didn't notice the one-inch drop when I went into the guesthouse bathroom. On the way out, however, with wet feet, I smashed the toes on one foot into the imperceptible step up, and catapulted into the next room, as my other foot slipped on the smooth tile coated with Teflon to assure that the maids can remove the caked blood after tourists land, slide, and die. While airborne, I somehow avoided the sharp edges of the teak furniture heading toward my skull. Wear socks, or step on a throw rug, and it's like sledding down an icy hill. Add water and you might as well crawl.

Dangerous Doorways. A bumpy, black-and-blue forehead is the badge of courage worn by foreigners trying to negotiate low doorways. The midget portals, where you obviously have to stoop, are not the problem. Door frames one centimeter lower than the top of your head—depending on which sandals you're wearing—are deadly, especially the ones with rough plaster that will peel off a lengthy strip of scalp. And, of course, you don't notice the height of the doorway when you're focused solely on the height of the step up to exit the toilet.

A slow but safe prevention for the above hazards is the Centimeter Shuffle, which I learned from my 93-year-old stepfather. His feet never left the floor, nor moved ahead more than a centimeter at a time. I'd wake him up and say, "Time for breakfast!" Then I'd shower, go to the market, prepare a meal, mow the lawn, and read the Encyclopedia Britannica, Volumes A to F, before he reached the kitchen.

Don't touch this!

Bare-naked Wires. Neither safe, nor technologically sound, Thai electrical wiring is more like a surrealistic painting by Salvador Dali, where reality stretches beyond the absurd. You can marvel from afar at the deranged maze of cables out of your reach, but it gets personal when the bare, live wire lurks in the bathroom, or under your feet at a street market during a downpour. Electrical Tape 101 is apparently an optional course at Thai Electrician Tech. I don't know how many times I've gotten a full dose of 240 volts, but I'm definitely half-baked and probably sterile.

Absolutely do not touch this! Just don't touch anything!

Cute Caterpillars. In America, the friendly reputation of hairy caterpillars comes from the familiar, red-and-black, Wooly Bear caterpillar, forerunner—well, forecrawler—of the Isabella moth. We'd gather them up, stage races on our bare arms, and mystically predict the length of winter by the width of their stripes. Not in Thailand. Think of the Thai varieties as grizzly bear caterpillars with poisonous hairs instead of teeth, hairs which reportedly can kill a small dog. Welts swell, spread, burn, itch, and drive you crazy. You might not even see the caterpillar that stung you, because some eject their hairs into the wind. Treat them as you would a grizzly with cubs, or someone playing Britney Spears hits from the nineties: Run away!

Issan Cuisine. Issan is a large, flat, oven-like area in northeastern Thailand near Laos, where they eat most anything raw, and have to add things besides heat to kill the germs and worms. If you see the word "Issan" on a menu, know that it stands for "It's Severely Spicy And Noxious." A typical Issan recipe must say, "Add the same number of hot peppers as you have added grains of rice." If you survive eating one or two of these tiny Thai peppers—called *kee nuu* which means "mouse shit"—and want to remove the rest from your plate, do not use your fingers to pick them up, then rub your eyes and scratch your crotch. You'll go blind, and your pubic hair will be on fire, but that's just the beginning. You'll soon be aware of other parts of your body, specifically, the entire food processing system and exit tunnel. The next day you'll be howling, "Where's that ice cream I ate? Send down the ice cream!"

Teflon Flip-flops. Like the tile in Thailand, most sandals are also coated with Teflon, so Thai folks can slip out of them while deftly flowing into one of the countless No Shoe Zones in stores, temples, and homes. Balancing a plethora of packages on both arms and shoulders which block the view of the floor and their feet, Thais can somehow slip one foot backward out of the sandal as the other foot miraculously holds its position for a micro-second before similarly shedding its sandal while their entire body levitates above the threshold. Apparently unaware of this dexterous "sleight of foot," soft-shoe shuffle, the 10-, 50-, or 100-year-old Thai lands inside, intact, and upright as the sandals are deposited outside. Do not try this in public until you've had at least a decade of practice, alone at home. Remember: Thai people have this skill imbedded in their DNA and come out of the womb wearing flip-flops, while simultaneously riding a motorcycle, cooking, and playing the guitar.

User-loser Errors. Sometimes you can't blame anyone, or anything, but yourself. A snow-white friend from frozen

Minnesota came to visit the islands during January. After a couple days he complained that his suntan lotion was weird, and more like sunburn lotion.

"Here's the tube I bought when I got to Thailand. It's not working. And look, it says 30 right on the label. Sun Protection Factor 30."

I tried to break it to him gently, but couldn't help but do it hysterically. "Actually, that's the price—30 baht—not SPF, and this is not suntan lotion. It's Thai shampoo that you've been spreading liberally on your body." Although his skin was the color of a burning ember—red underneath with a white coating—he was unquestionably clean.

It all comes together… or apart. Sunburned to a crisp, you sample an Issan dish from a street vendor to take your mind off the pain, but the peppers become a bonfire on your tongue, which sends you scampering across the sidewalk to the snack store for a cold Coke to douse the flames. You prematurely try the Thai flip-flop removal flick, but the sandal sticks to your lagging foot which snags the uneven floor, launching you over the 103-year-old store owner. While careening down the aisle during a useless attempt to right yourself, your flailing arms sweep goods off shelves and disrupt a family of hairy caterpillars, who eject a cloud of poisonous hair into your nostrils, escalating your panic, causing you to crash through a rack of potato chips, and smack your skull on the low door frame. Life slows to snapshots as you lose consciousness, slip down Teflon tile into the split-level toilet, grab a bare live wire for support, and finally collapse headfirst into the dark water trough, which looks like it's used for baptizing rats. Game over, man.

Well, I guess not. It's the Land of Smiles. Everyone is laughing and clapping. They want you to do it again!

~ ~ ~

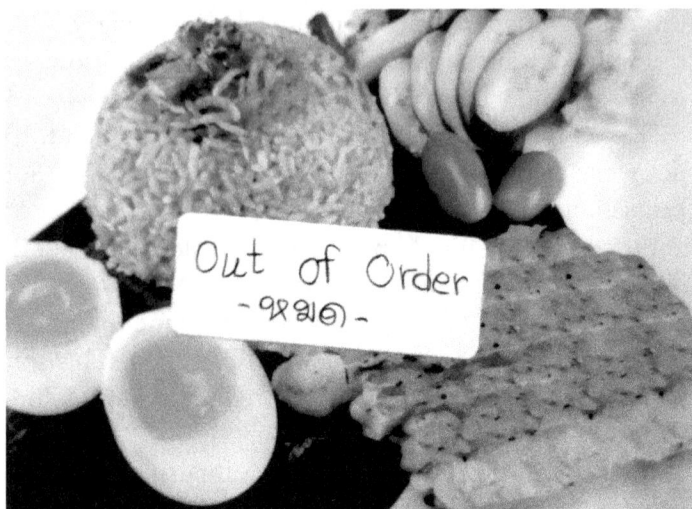

ปลาฆู่ฉี่ (ราคาตามขนาดปลา)   230 B.

Fish pisses.

ปลาผัดผงกระหรี่   230 B.

Fish cooks whore dust.

ปลาผัดพริกเผา   230 B.

Fish cooks the chili burns.

ปลายำมะม่วง   200 -230 B.

Fish mixes the mango.

ปลาลุยสวน   200 -230 B.

Fish wades a garden.

Exotic Entrées Etcetera

I DIDN'T DARE ORDER THE ENTRÉES on the previous page. If "Fish" were the cook's name, these titles might have made more sense, but I didn't want he or she pissing near my table or anything to do with whore dust.

Thai menus can be exactly descriptive. If you read "Scorpion on a Stick" in the USA, you might think, "Hmm. Spicy Corn Dog, maybe?" In Thailand, it means "Scorpion on a Stick." Spelling issues are rampant, so you assume "Fried Beep" is beef, but "beep" could be the last sound made by the original body-part donor, or the beep of the truck that ran over the donor. Pictures in menus don't help when they're blurry and look like the road-kill burger they probably are.

Fried Beep with oyster sauce

Street food and market stalls present the safest method for accurate entrée identification. When you gaze at piles of fried grasshoppers, worms, and giant water bugs, you can immediately make your decision. "No, thanks." You might be tempted by "Grilled Water Buffalo," but when you see and smell the burning hair on one side of the meat slabs smoldering on the grate…

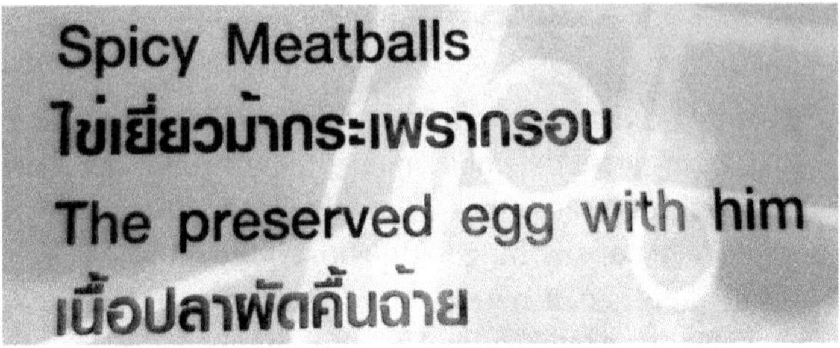

Spicy Meatballs

ไข่เยี่ยวม้ากระเพรากรอบ

The preserved egg with him

เนื้อปลาผัดคื้นฉ่าย

I've never experienced "the preserved egg with him"?
Is he here today? Will I be required to eat it with him?
Is it a rooster, the father of the egg?

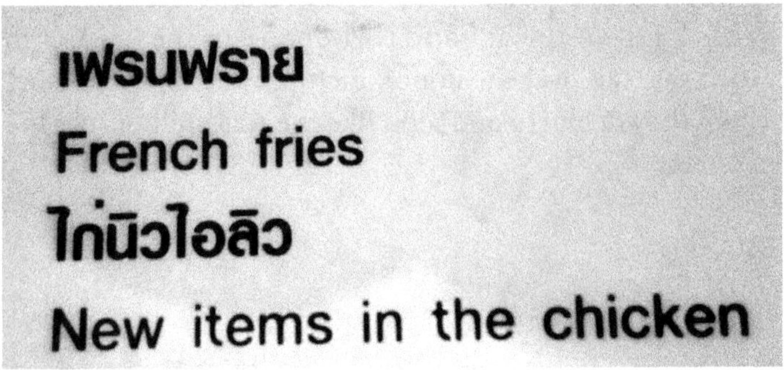

เฟรนฟราย

French fries

ไก่นิวไอลิว

New items in the chicken

New items in the chicken? I'm hoping these are eggs.
Or did the chef misplace a few utensils today?

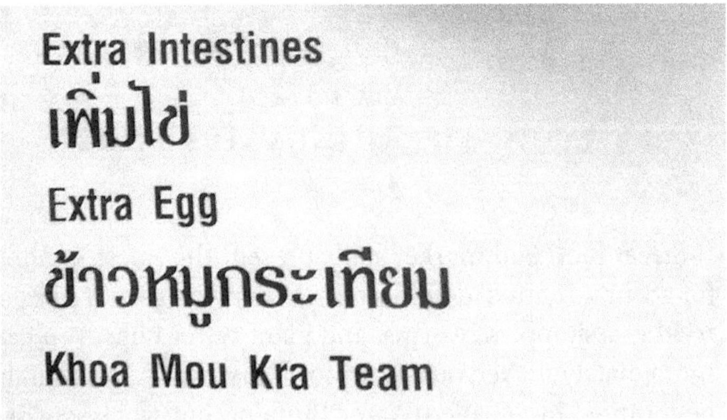

Extra Intestines

เพิ่มไข่

Extra Egg

ข้าวหมูกระเทียม

Khoa Mou Kra Team

I was born with plenty of intestines, thanks, but I'll take the whole
Khoa Mau Kra Team to go. They can help around the house.

ราดหน้า Topping

เย็นตาโฟ Prison Break Trailer

ต้มยำมะนาว Spicy lemon

ต้มยำน้ำข้น A thick soup

A topping? Chocolate? Ranch Dressing? Ranch Chocolate? And do
we get to see the entire Prison Break or only watch the trailer?
FYI, a thick soup is called a stew. So what flavor is this one?
Spicy lemon? Or is that another topping?

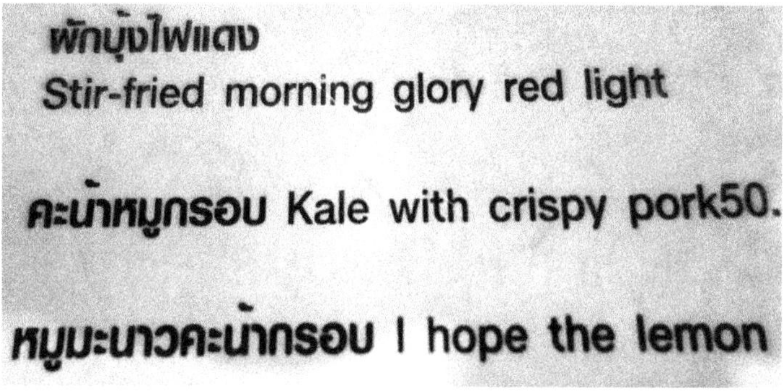

ผักบุ้งไฟแดง
Stir-fried morning glory red light

คะน้าหมูกรอบ Kale with crispy pork50.

หมูมะนาวคะน้ากรอบ I hope the lemon

And I hope the lemon is not spicy.

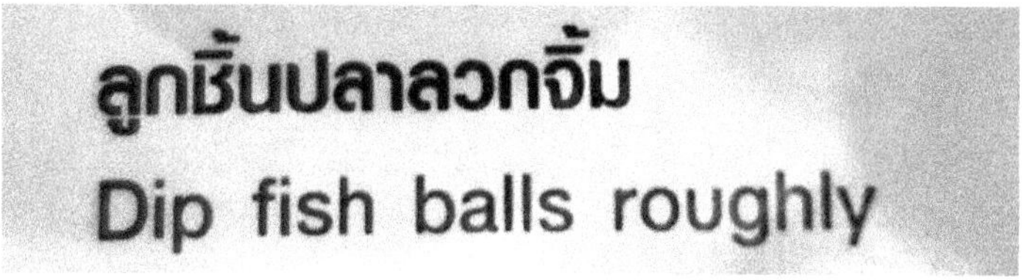

ลูกชิ้นปลาลวกจิ้ม
Dip fish balls roughly

Dip fish balls roughly? Hmm. I didn't even know fish had balls.

พระกระโดดกำแพง   600-1,000.-
佛跳墙
Monk Jump Over The Wall Soup

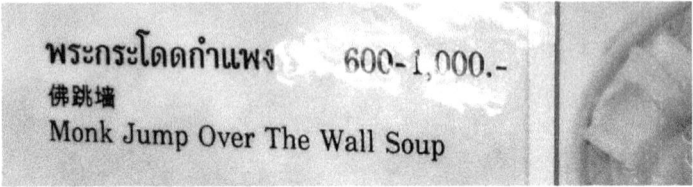

For thirty bucks, it better be a big bowl.
And no spilling when the monk goes over the wall!

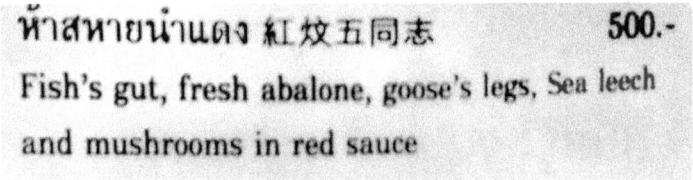

ห้าสหายน้ำแดง 紅炆五同志   500.-

Fish's gut, fresh abalone, goose's legs, Sea leech

and mushrooms in red sauce

This sounds like a bad accident at the beach.
Local critters got caught in the boat propellers?

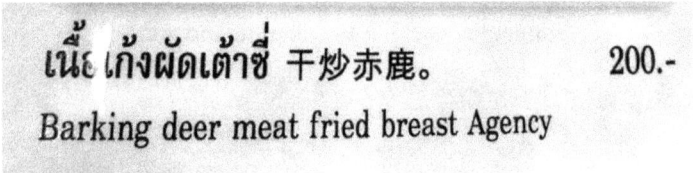

เนื้อเก้งผัดเต้าซี่ 干炒赤鹿。   200.-

Barking deer meat fried breast Agency

Did your chef throw darts at a dictionary
to determine the words for this dish?

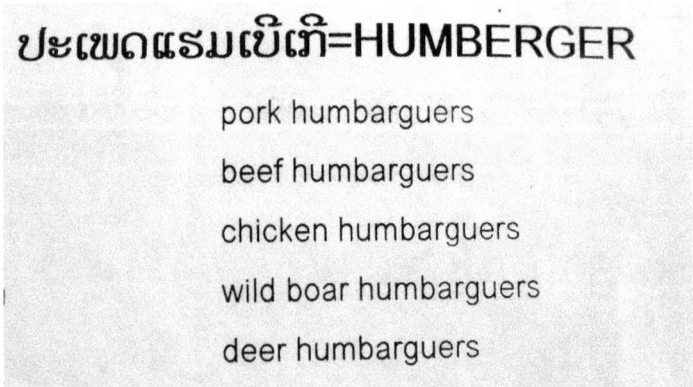

ปะเขดแธมเขิเกิ=HUMBERGER

pork humbarguers

beef humbarguers

chicken humbarguers

wild boar humbarguers

deer humbarguers

Make up your mind. Are you only going to spell English wrong
or pretend you're spelling French wrong, too?

FRIED HEAD FISH WITH SWEET & SOUR SAUCE

หลนปูเค็มทรงเครื่อง

BOILED SALTED GRAVE WITH MINCED PORK

**You only fry the fish head?
Then boil and salt your dead diner's grave with pork?**

Pork with… with… With what? The suspense is killing me!

**Some stores stock plain old aged cheese. Boring!
Our cheddar is very, very old, eccentric, seriously mature,
and we won't sell it to anyone under 21.**

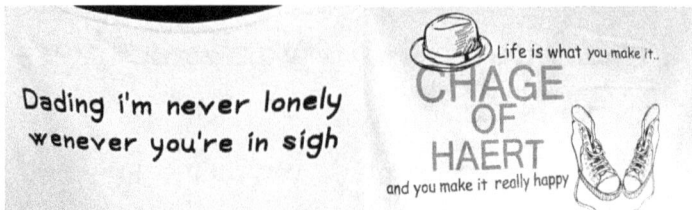

Dading i'm never lonely
wenever you're in sigh

Life is what you make it..
CHAGE
OF
HAERT
and you make it really happy

Above: t-shirts to wear while in the Confusing English World.
Below: athletic bags to differentiate you from people sporting
other fake Adidas products. Hmm. Are those Power or Mower
Rangers? Lower? Tower? Flower? Big decision—do you want a
Puma logo on your fake "disada" bag? Reality check for purchasers
of the "ediads" brand—It's Greek for "Idiots."

Rabbit & Carrot Service Center in the airport. No clue what it means.

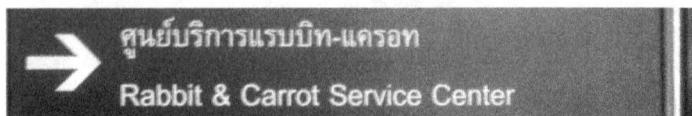

ศูนย์บริการแรบบิท-แครอท
Rabbit & Carrot Service Center

~ ~ ~

An Ignorant Non-immigrant

DISCLAIMER: This column contains time-sensitive material regarding immigration procedures that change yearly, daily, or moment-to-moment, depending on the new Director of Immigration assigned yesterday, or the indigestion ruining the day and demeanor of the officer in front of you, or the price of tea in China.

Though you might find astute advice here on how to save time during your next trip to the Thai Immigration Office, your success will depend on whether you deal with a 1) Friendly Worker Ant or 2) a Rubber Stamp Fanatic, who essentially wants to leap across the desk and pound an indelible **INVALID** stamp on your forehead that can't be removed without a skin graft.

Residence Certificate

1. **2 Color Photos**
2. **Copies of Passport**
   - **Picture Page**
   - **Visa**
   - **TM6 : Departure Card**
3. **Copies's Documents of your Residence**
   - **Rental Contract**
   - **Hose Registration**
   - **Letter from House Master**

Sign on wall of Immigration Office: Don't forget to bring your "Hose Registration." Better yet, just bring your hose.

A decade ago, you could saunter into the Immigration Office, lean on a counter, and someone might help you, expeditiously, with a smile. As traffic increased, a self-service, number-dispensing machine appeared on the counter, one with obscure directions about which buttons to press for what. They soon replaced the self-service system with a live, uniformed Number Guardian pressing buttons and giving out numbers, probably because unsavory entrepreneurs were self-stealing low numbers and selling them outside in the parking lot.

About five years ago I arrived at Immigration at 10 a.m. to learn that no more numbers were available for the entire day in the visa renewal category. A mild inconvenience for me since my due date was the following week but quite disturbing to an ancient English lady I chatted with. Pale and frail, she seemed to have stumbled in from the hospital to renew her visa for a few more hours until she passed away later that evening.

When I came back the next day at 7:30 a.m., I noticed they'd moved the number dispenser to the back corner of the cramped lobby. The door opened at 8 a.m. and scores of impatient immigrants streamed in, immediately formed an impenetrable gridlock around the machine, forcing the Number Guardian to coat himself with palm oil to slip through the crowd to dispense their indispensable numbers. An hour later I got my precious life destiny number, but didn't get my visa prize until 3:30 p.m.

A tad smarter the next year, I arrive at 7 a.m. one day before my deadline, ready to battle the Immigration Mafia and Lobby Mob. My friend Jiggs had come at 6:15 and snared the commanding chair next to the main door, guarding his precarious position with what appeared to be an electric cattle prod up his pant leg. (I'm not sure if he'd come at 6:15 a.m. that day or at 6:15 p.m. the previous evening.) A caring humanitarian, Jiggs says, "Here's the sign-up sheet! An immigration evolution! This year you sign up to get a number to get a number!" I use my whiteout to remove his name and write mine in his space.

An inconspicuous English-only sign on the door mentions the new sign-up sheet, which eliminates comprehension of the process for half the people descending on the building who can't read English. As the office opens at 8 a.m., the double-wide line snaking through the packed parking lot slithers inside until it fills the lobby. The atmosphere is tense, and the tourists are sweaty. The Number Guardian slowly, ever so slowly, shouts out numbers as the respective number holders fight through the morass of humanity to get their new numbers.

Since the entire left half of my body presses into the entire right half of the tall guy next to me, and we're not moving anywhere, I strike up a conversation.

Me: "Do you have a number?"

Tall guy: "I thought I'm in line to get a number. Why are they already calling out numbers?"

Me: "I guess you didn't see the list to get a number to get a number."

Tall guy: "Nope, I missed that. We're trying to extend our tourist visa for a couple days before going to Malaysia."

Me: "Be careful of little elderly ladies in this mob. Some of them carry sharpened knitting needles."

An hour later as he leaves the parking lot with a very high number, he says, "We're outta here. It'll take less time to go to Malaysia now and get an extension visa there."

My new number is 402, but no numbers show on the LED screens above the Rubber Stamp Fanatics' desks. A half-hour later, one screen reads 200, which seems to tell me that 202 people are queued ahead of me. Another LED reads 500! If they must count **UP** from 500 till they reach 402, I'll spend the rest of my life here. My goal? Change my retirement visa to a marriage visa. My wife Joomi is on her way, but I still need a formal letter from my bank verifying sufficient funds in my account. After a hectic bank trek that's worthy of another column, I scamper back to the Immigration Office, meet Joomi, and enter the lobby as Number 403, *not our number 402, sigh,* blazes on a screen.

Quite harried, we go for it, enter the inner sanctum behind the counter, and position ourselves in front of the desk under Number 403. As Joomi pleads with Miss Strict But Friendly Worker Ant to honor our number 402 that has become INVALID ten seconds earlier, I set my Big Cola bottle on her desk. OMG, it tips over, spreading its contents over Miss Worker Ant's papers, letters, completed visa applications, knickknacks, family heirlooms, etc, gasp, oh, no, I think I might need a Divorce Visa!

While Miss Antagonized Worker Ant quietly screams, "Get a new number!" the expanding Flood of Big Cola oozes underneath the glass desk protector, drowning her personal photographs. Joomi futilely wipes the mess with three tissues from her purse, which promptly turn into blobs of mush. I consider sitting on the desk to soak up the liquid with my butt or whip off my shirt to use as a rag, but luckily execute neither of these maneuvers. I expect Miss Worker Ant would have torn up my passport on the spot and directed the beefy uniformed gorilla in the corner to escort me directly to the border.

A new number and an hour later, after praying feverishly that we get sent to any other person who handles these visas, we slink back to the same Strict, Unforgiving, Tense Worker Ant. At first she's surprisingly nice to us, but after scrutinizing my passport, exclaims, "Mai dai, mai dai!" (Cannot do, not do!) For some unintelligible reason in fine print on a Nonimmigrant B Visa, *which I thought stood for Business or Baloney,* the only way I can change from Retirement Nonimmigrant O, *which I think stands for Old,* is to leave the country and get another B, *which now stands for Bullshit,* from another Thai consulate, which I can then change to M for Marriage, so I could have a Non-Immigrant BM, *which stands for Bowel Movement or Big Mouth, which I do not mention that I think she is, or has.* I realize Miss Crafty Worker Ant has become extraordinarily genial because she's figured out how to remove me from the country without summoning the gorilla and intimidating the remaining applicants. While I'm absent, she can leisurely change my immigration computer profile to INVALID and prevent me from returning.

Joomi and I brainstorm in the parking lot before getting into the car. My current visa is due to expire the next day. Thai consulate choices in our Asia-Pacific neighborhood are Laos, Vietnam, Cambodia, or Malaysia. Kuala Lumpur (KL) is the least expensive with the best flights, and we secure a seat via the web. The next morning I'm off on my four-day visa adventure.

Taxi to airport, fly to KL, twenty-mile taxi ride into KL, locate hotel, find Thai consulate, fill out form after form, leave essential documents (passport, Thai ID cards, house registration, marriage certificate, etc.), find hotel again, wander around KL, have a discussion with a large leery inmate at the bird sanctuary, return to Thai consulate in two days, check out from hotel, reverse taxi ride to KL airport, fly back to Chiang Mai, realize I'd left every one of our essential

Big bird seemed to listen to my complaining about the visa predicament, but I think he just wanted me to crack open my Pepsi can.

documents in the safe in my KL hotel room, scream and panic, contact friend of friend who lives in KL, grovel, beg, and plead that she'll go to hotel, gather documents, express them to Thailand, or I won't need a marriage visa since my wife will kill me. Cost? $1,000 and a new swath of grey hair.

Joomi and I return to Thai immigration with the "correct" visa so I can switch it to the required marriage visa. After the Getting Our Number Marathon and the Endless Déjà Vu Waiting Forever Trial, we meet with the Official Worker Ant at the desk *right beside* our previous Big Cola Worker Ant who had sent us far away.

Our new uniformed helper is courteous and friendly, and after shuffling through our documents and forms says, "Oh… you didn't have to leave the country. We could have done the paperwork here."

Needless to say, we are speechless while imagining the $1,000 which should still be in my bank account and the dastardly things we *cannot* do to Big Cola Worker Ant unless we want to celebrate our legal marriage visa in prison.

What can you learn from this?

1) A flash flood of Big Cola onto an official cluttered desk does not make a good first impression.

2) Go to Immigration a day or two before your deadline, preposterously early in the morning, or better yet, go right now.

3) Sign the list to get a number to get a number, but check carefully if you might first need to get a number to sign the list to get a number to get a number.

4) Bring a bottle of palm oil to ease the pain when the Immigration Officer tells you to bend over.

5) If you plan to drive to the consulate and attempt to find an empty parking space, first try Malaysia. Perhaps I can help, since I'll probably be living there.

~ ~ ~

Plastic Baggage

IN AMERICA, YOU MIGHT FIND the following ominous items in a plastic bag—severed pig snouts, miscellaneous worms, an excrement-brown casserole of malignant gooey stuff containing vaguely familiar shapes that, upon closer inspection, you realize are chicken feet. That bag would likely be a black garbage bag in a dumpster.

Here in Thailand, you can take each of these splendid entrées home for dinner from the market in separate, clear-plastic, doggy bags. Most anything is available in plastic bags of all sizes, including miniscule ones that hold a quarter teaspoon of monosodium glutamate. Although the unofficial symbol of Thailand is the elephant, it should be the plastic bag. (If you look closely at the official symbol, the elephant is actually in a plastic bag.)

When I first arrived in Thailand, I ordered a Coke and received it in a bag with ice and a straw. This was new to me, since their marketing slogans never mentioned, "Coke is it! Pick up a refreshing bag today!" It worked okay, but I couldn't sit down and set it on a table without the Coke creating an embarrassing wet spot in my lap. I had to finish it before tackling my next novel activity, trying to decide which insects to eat, which was quite simple—none. I had yet to learn that I could buy 150 bagged Cokes, 75 sacks of complete meals, plus an unlimited amount of exotic brooms, stuffed animals, and used car or squid parts, hang them all over my motorbike, and sell them in the streets.

Motorbike grocery store with customized plastic baggage

After seventeen years in Thailand, I still haven't mastered the art of removing the steel-belted rubber bands used to close the bags with a complex series of mystical twists and knots, a slight-of-hand trick deftly performed in one second by vendors. I need knives, scissors, or sharp keys to puncture these bulging, pressurized bags, which invariably send instant-staining chili sauce spurting onto the whitest part of my shirt. (This taught me to dress in black clothing, or multi-colored, which will soon be crusty with dried food, but at least you can't see it.) I want to master this remarkable binding maneuver, so I can quickly bag the head of the rooster that wakes me every morning at 2:30 a.m. or the next motorcycle mechanic who returns my bike disassembled in a bag.

Recycling is approaching official religious status in America, although my grandmother had indoctrinated me decades ago. She carefully washed, dried, and reused the few bags that appeared in our home. In her honor, I try to alter the behavior of the natives in Thailand.

With my marginal Thai language skills, I politely try to convince counter help that I don't need *another* bag for the bag of peanuts that are *already* in a bag, thank you very much, "I can just put this bag in my handbag." They look at me as though I'm deranged, as if the sale isn't complete without the final redundant bag, and they have failed to do their job. They put the bag of peanuts in another bag anyway, which I remove from their bag and hand back to them, which they throw away, foiling my useless attempt at saving the environment.

Three cheers for Rimping Market and their proactive program: for every bag you do not request, or use, or something, they'll give a charity 50 satang, a mythical denomination of Thai currency—nothing costs 50 satang. (It's like donating a penny in the USA.) You only get these coins as change. If you try to spend 'em, vendors look at you like you're cuckoo, as if you've given them useless items you found under your sofa cushions like faded plastic buttons, seven-year-old popcorn, and moldy jigsaw puzzle pieces.

Years ago in America, my modest recycling efforts helped the world a bit, but ruined my reputation in the neighborhood. By separating my garbage, I got a break on the trash collection bill from the city. So I divided my trash categories into individual bins—colored glass bottles, clear glass bottles, plastic bottles, newspapers, cardboard, and takeaway boxes with unintelligible classification symbols printed under decaying food stuck to the Styrofoam.

The apartment building across the alley had no recycling options, only one huge dumpster. A few concerned tenants clandestinely dropped their hodgepodge of garbage onto my segregated trash behind my garage, including enough liquor and beer bottles to host a block party. I posted signs requesting them to stop, which only seemed to alert other residents to do the same thing, so I accepted my duty to a higher cause. I systematically combined their garbage with mine, on Sunday night at 30 below zero, while battling blizzards and snowdrifts. Whatever. They're trying; I'll help.

Years later, while chatting in the alley with my neighbor, I asked if she ever got bags of trash from the void flung onto her property. She didn't, so I shared my recycling mission.

"Well, that's good to know," she said, "cuz every Sunday night I'd wonder about your piles of liquor bottles. I knew you liked to party, but never had major bashes. You went to work daily and seemed to lead a normal life, but I couldn't believe how much alcohol you put away every week!"

Okay, back to Thailand and my latest recycling conflict. An older guy used to stop by every garbage day, balance our huge bag of recyclables on his bicycle, and ride off. I felt good, helping the little people sell it for extra cash, instead of letting random city workers take it. One day while walking the dog on an off-road path just down our street, I noticed piles of trash along our route through the trees. That pissed me off. I bent down for a closer look. *Hmm. An assortment of fruit juice containers, polyolefin yogurt cups, collapsed cardboard boxes... What the...? This is our garbage!*

Mr. Nice Local Bike Guy only wanted the aluminum cans and clear plastic bottles. He dumped everything else in the woods, turning us into second-hand littering low-lifes.

Sigh. Another setback, but I will continue my mini-quest for the Thai environment. Every week I wait patiently for the official garbage men to arrive like clockwork—Thai time, which means sometime between eight a.m. and two p.m.—so I can hand over my recyclables through the gate. And today I am responsible for Rimping market's contribution of 50 satang to a charity, which should provide one person with a microscopic bag of fish sauce, one dried baby squid tentacle, or three peanuts.

~ ~ ~

Western Toilet Instructions

In a Thai petrol station toilet, this poster on the following pages is prominently displayed to educate the locals about the solitary, raised Western toilet recently installed, complete with a seat and flushing capability. For foreigners like me, no instructional pictures are posted near the standard squat toilets—ceramic bowls and their holes sunken into the floor, two porcelain footprints on the sides, and a hose or bucket of water—only the guidelines below which remind you to "enjoy to see it flow."

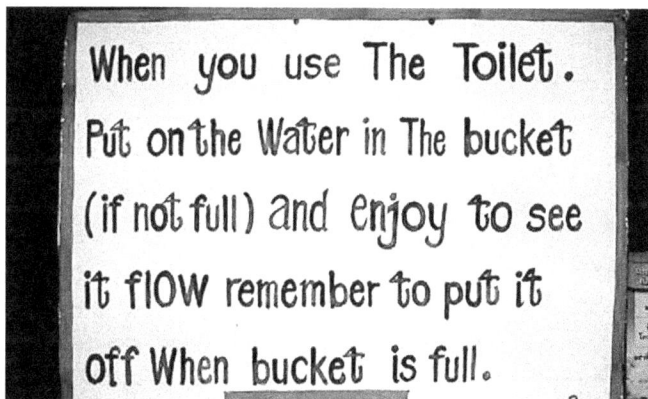

When you use The Toilet.
Put on the Water in The bucket
(if not full) and enjoy to see
it flow remember to put it
off When bucket is full.

I'm still not sure how to deal with the absence of toilet paper, with ladles in water buckets, or the correct direction to hose my butt, from the front or the rear, so I don't emerge from the stall with soaked shoes and embarrassing dark spots from the waist down—as if I'd just gone to the toilet without going to the toilet. Though some stalls have flushless varieties with a seat, there's no toilet paper, so I use a shiny, non-absorbent, magazine ad for the required cleanup while trying to avoid paper cuts in vital areas.

Because the instructions are in Thai, the letters of which I haven't learned (except the one pronounced "gai" that looks like and means "chicken") I can only guess what each drawing is attempting to teach. Here are my fictive translations of the Thai words accompanying each picture which is worth a thousand meanings.

Hee, hee. I'm alone here in the stall, and if I wear rubber waders, I can do anything I want!

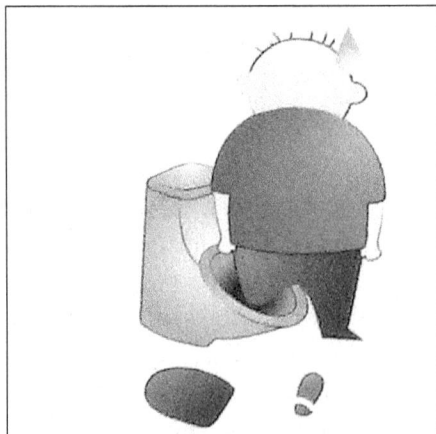

Cool! I can clean my shoes in here with this neat lever that moves the water.

Wearing my weird glasses upside down, I can't tell where I should do what! Is that a tall toilet or a sink?

Wow! It's a birdbath for cute little flying white cuckoos!

Don't add any more of your own little white cuckoos unless you can swim!

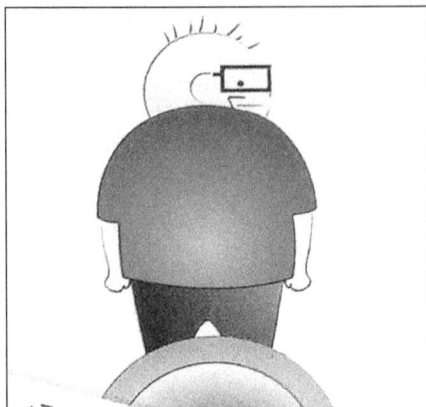

Maybe this thing will work even if I don't pull down my pants.

Help! The Toilet Spirit is angry! Gimme a squat toilet any day. I'm never coming in here again!

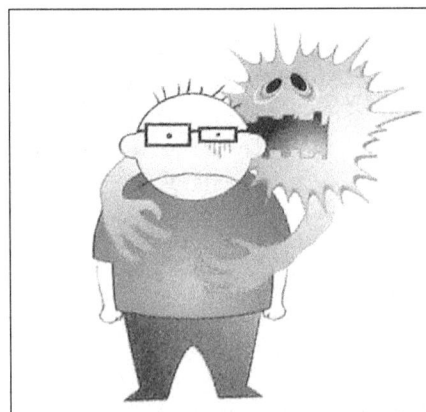

If I get rid of these stupid glasses, maybe the Toilet Spirit will leave me alone.

~ ~ ~

FLICK it!

URING THIS RELENTLESS RAINY SEASON in my soggy corner of the world, the Land of Smiles has evolved into the Land of Snails. Hundreds of them devour my plants, poop profusely, and make slime trails everywhere. Suicide snails crawl into my path on a jihad missions to infect and cripple me by jabbing shell fragments and flattened body parts into my bare feet.

I experimented with an extermination technique I'd used in America: put beer in bowls in the garden, like filling your swimming pool with whisky if you wanted to attract Irishmen. Useless. Too many snails and too many bowls. Too much rain diluting too many beers. Why not drink the beer until I'm oblivious to the snails? No, not good, I'd start seeing double the amount of snails and go insane before I went blind.

For a week I fought back with daily squashing sessions, until one day before another massacre, I thought, compassionately: *FLICK YOU.* Now I just flick them over the fence. Flicking is a politically correct, humane method because snails have strong, protective shells, land in soft plant matter, and have the opportunity to fly once in their lives, though not exactly to the vacation spot they might've imagined. Since they're some of the slowest creatures on earth, except for my waitress in a local restaurant last week, I thought they'd be gone for life—my life, I had hoped.

Before my recent snail removal research, I didn't know much about them, other than what snails say while riding on turtles: "Yay! Oh, boy! Wheeee!"

I'd also heard of a collision between a snail and a turtle in the road. The snail was knocked unconscious, and the turtle left the scene of the accident.

When the snail woke up in the emergency room, the doctor asked, "What happened to you? Who did this?"

"Jeez," the snail sighed, "I don't know. It all happened so fast!"

I learned these amazing snail facts on the web. The snail has been evolving on earth for 600,000 million years, which is even longer than the vegetables decaying in the bottom of my refrigerator. It's body has only one foot which is so tough, a snail can crawl across a razor blade, which negates my plan of lining the yard, driveway, and fence with millions of razor blades fastened to boards. Snails can't hear, so my screams and threats don't faze them. Their slime trails, similar to those behind lawyers and politicians, provide the suction enabling them to hang upside down, which can also cause me to slip on the walkway and hang upside down in the air before smashing onto the cement driveway.

Snails are hermaphrodites, organisms which have both male and female sex organs, so dating and mating are very open-minded and expeditious endeavors, unlike humans with all their gender issues. A single snail might produce 10,000 little girl-boys in their lifetime, and hordes of them want to rear their gigantic families in my yard.

"Honey, which sex you wanna be today? I'm feelin' kinda female."

The average snail moves at a rate of 12.2 meters per hour, only a tad slower than any workers I've employed to help around the house. It's apparent why the Olympic 100-yard Snail Dash is not a popular TV event, since it's nearly seven hours long. "They've been at it for five hours now, folks! Look closely at the eyeball protruding from his head, and you'll see Shelly Slimeberg is a millimeter ahead! Oh no, a crow plucked Sluggo Gastropod from Lane Number 6!"

I assumed the return crawl time after flicking Mister/Miss Snail on their one-way flight was similar to the story of the snail sitting on a porch, minding his/her own business. Suddenly the door flew open. One monstrous hand picked up the newspaper as another threw him/her across the road into a lake. Months later, the snail made it out of the lake, through the grass, across the busy road, along the sidewalk, up the steps, and onto the same porch. The next time the door opened, he/she looked up and said, "What the hell was that all about?"

Hmm. The distance of my snail launch might be ten meters; a snail's pace is an impressive 12.2 meters per hour. Even considering the dense grass/bush terrain and formidable two-meter wall, he/she could be back in a few hours. Internet says: "A snail never gets lost because instinct guides it back to its hiding place, no matter how far away it wanders." (Or has been flicked.) "Snails normally live at least 15 years."

These facts make me realize the whole flicking situation is FLICKING hopeless. I'll bet they even like my little launches, and those tiny noises I've heard as they fly into the distance are the snails shrieking with joy, "WHEEEEEEEEE!" My snail tenants probably invite friends they meet along the way to follow them back to the Exotic Land of Snails.

"Hey, guy/gals, come with us! Free beer, great food, lots of dark, damp bedrooms, and you get to fly every day!"

My current fantasy is to ship a 40-foot cargo container of snails to France, where chefs will christen them "escargot" and seal their fate in style. If they escape and make the journey back to Thailand, the 9,600 kilometers should take them 90 years, and I'll be long gone.

~ ~ ~

Crash Course in Computers and Harleys

THIS CHAPTER OF THE LONG AND WINDING ROAD comes to you from the complimentary computer in the comfortable coffee/wifi lounge of a massive motorcycle dealership in Staunton, Virginia, USA, where I'm uncomfortably waiting and paying for repairs, surrounded by a hundred sparkling new Harley-Davidsons and most everything else imaginable that can display the Harley logo: several million chrome accessories, pinball games, pool tables, popcorn machines, garage floor coverings, wind chimes, and a catalog that touts a Harley-Davidson vault for $12,000, which is probably in the office right now, filling up with my cash. You can even set up your own mirrored mahogany Harley bar with matching stools and cocktail tables for about $20,000 so you can drink heavily before you ride out chewing on Harley Beef Jerky, which is what your head will look like after it hits the pavement because you didn't wear your $500 Harley helmet.

The pet section has "fashion dog wear" t-shirts for $30, canine rain gear, barking puppy chews that say "Bad to the Bone," and little leather caps guaranteed to embarrass any dog meek enough to let its master dress it. Within the unending clothing department, the Kids Korner is laden with propaganda material—shirts that say "50% Mommy,

50% Daddy, 100% Harley," a picture book entitled *Why Grandma Loves Her Harley Too*, and to promote the cult at birth, quilted booties for "Age 0–3 months" sporting the slogan "Born to Ride." I'm surprised there's no Harley Viagra for brand marketing that targets sperm.

For two days, I've been trying to ride my Harley Sportster 1,200 miles to Minnesota, but am trapped in Virginia, having traveled about 200 miles forward and 200 miles backward. Before departing my friend's house in Charlottesville on a lovely Sunday morning, I related a recent forgetful tale. A month earlier, I left my charger in San Francisco, which is like that familiar song and too familiar in my life. Last week I left another cellphone charger in North Carolina. Within the year, I won't need to carry one because my friends around the country will have one traveling exhibit of my National Charger Collection.

First stop on the way out of town: Radio Shack. As I walked out the door after purchasing another charger, the checkout lady summoned me back to the counter. "Y'all want this or not?" she asked, handing me my cellphone.

In the parking lot, I put on my sunglasses, but they felt very weird under my helmet. I'd forgotten to take off my regular glasses, a new meaning to the term "old four-eyes."

Five miles down the road, marveling at how lightweight the backpack carrying my laptop felt, I realized I wasn't wearing a backpack. *Shit, it's back in the driveway.* I raced back to my friend's house, imagining my confession. *As an English tutor in Thailand, I learned that demonstration is a more powerful teaching technique than explanation. So instead of merely telling stories, I thought I'd show you what an idiot I am.*

To my horror, I returned to my friend's driveway to *not* find the backpack. I'd put it on my back seat, not on my back, and it had fallen off somewhere along the road. The laptop was worth a couple thousand dollars, but the two external hard drives had my entire virtual life—files that would take months to reconstruct, irreplaceable photos from around the world, passwords for the bank, for credit cards and Web accounts, etcetera forever. I didn't care about the dollars, only the ones and zeros, my precious digital info. For hours, two friends, one policeman, and I scoured the road sides—deep ditches tangled with poison ivy, nettles, and blackberry brambles, some leading twenty meters down into streams.

A pickup truck stopped, and a semi-toothed head stuck out the window. "Y'all lookin' for this?" The driver held up my backpack, which looked like rabid bears had fought over it. "Y'all's computer was pretty banged up. Ah couldn't find any names on it, and since Ah dunno much about 'em, Ah left it at a buddy's place in the hills."

We drove into the hills which are home to primitive tribes that speak a different language, then down a dusty road into a "holler," and found the house, a testament to the traditional riddle: "What's the most popular color to paint a house in the Appalachian mountains?" (Primer.)

We retrieved my mutilated laptop before the trucker's friend's son could locate my bank account passwords with his Ouija board and a divining rod.

Back at the starting line in Charlottesville, I discovered that one of the hard drives was undamaged. *Oh, thank you, Ruler of the Universe and God of Karma, my digital life is intact from the day I left Thailand!*

While copying the data from my drive onto his computer, my friend asked, "Do you have a warranty?"

Brilliant idea! I'll send the crushed pieces to Sony with a letter lying, "I was calmly sitting at the table when the laptop suddenly exploded, shooting the LCD screen into our wall, which is made of rubber tires as you can see by the black marks on the case. The letter 'E' flew off the keyboard and blinded my grandmother. Please send me a big check or, in true American style, I'll sue for millions."

I rode out of town again at 5:00 p.m. As the sun set, my Sportster backfired majestically and expired on the interstate highway, somewhere in the mountains. No cellphone signal. No highway patrolmen. No Good Samaritan drivers or bikers. No Good Samaritans, period.

After cooling off, the bike started and limped along the roadside until it again overheated, limped, died, then overheated, limped, died, then... Two hours later, I crawled into a dinky town somewhere between Boondocks and The Sticks, and found "cheap" lodging priced lower than the Best Western but higher than the adult No-tell Motel.

"We'all gots wireless internet," the check-in guy said with a grin, "but y'all probably ain't packin' a computer on yer bike anyway! Ha ha!"

I leaped across the desk and strangled him. After hiding his body under the cubes in the ice machine, I checked out my dingy night's digs—vintage '60s, avocado green, burnt orange, and cigarette stench. Traveling salesmen had chainsmoked four packs a night in the room for the past fifty years. I could have lit up the pillow and smoked it. Monday morning I learned the only motorcycle shop in town, of course, is closed on Mondays.

The Harley dealer eighty miles back down the road in Staunton sent a truck and trailer to pick me up. My comatose Sportster entered their emergency room around noon and emerged at 4:30 p.m. Doctor's bill? $225. I rode out of town, and my bike died again... 30 miles later.

Luckily I had a cellphone signal and rang my new buddy, Mr. Service Manager: "I got a question fer y'all. Did ya disrepair mah bike 'cause ya miss mah wallet or 'cause someone saw me steal y'all's Harley ballpoint pen offun the counter?"

Mr. Déjà Vu, the same trailer man I'd met that morning, arrived in an hour.

"Hey, Déjà," I drawled. "I like you fine, but y'all're the last person in the world I wanted to see again today."

Before walking to the nearby Hampton Inn that charged a hundred dollars per night, I told Mr. Service Manager in plain ol' Yankee speak: "Perhaps you work for the Chamber of Commerce and think I should buy a house here, get married, and have a few kids, but I'm going shopping now and will return tomorrow morning with a chain saw, three Doberman Pinschers, and a flamethrower. God bless you and good luck with my Sportster."

So today, wearing black leather gear from neck to toe on an already-scorching-at-nine Tuesday morning, I began my interminable journey by walking a mile back to the Harley dealership—not a good omen, but infinitely better than walking the last thousand to Minnesota.

While waiting for the repair bill, I peruse the Harley paraphernalia, coveting the $10,000 Harley jukebox, but since it won't fit on my bike, I settle for a Harley wind chime. And a t-shirt that fits little ol' me, hidden amongst the thousands of choices in the XXXXXXXL size designed for average Harley riders and Japanese sumo wrestlers.

Owning a Harley automatically puts me in an exclusive club of large friendly brothers with whom I have only two things in common: 1) we ride Harleys, and 2) we breathe air. Two of my brothers are milling around the lobby, and the t-shirt I'm wearing grabs their attention. A black shirt with their beloved orange logo on my chest, but "Harley-Davidson Motorcycles" is written in Thai, strange foreign symbols possibly illegal in this red neck of the woods.

"Where y'all from?" one asks.

My standard answer: "Thailand, right around the… globe."

The other brother says: "Y'all don't look Taiwanese, ha!"

(I want to say, "That's Thailand. Pull up your shirt and let me tattoo the earth on your world-class belly!" I don't because I also want to remain alive.)

$300 dollars poorer for repairs, plus hotel and meal charges, and minus two days, I hit the highway at noon with a lack of confidence in my steed and humble expectations of getting to the next state of West Virginia instead of being stranded in the states of shock, confusion, and chaos. If Mr. Sportster does his fucking trick again, I'll ride the shoulder at 15 mph and make it to Minnesota by Christmas.

For some insane reason I fell in love with the classic vibration of a Harley, but all of its, and my, screws seem to have come loose. Able to efficiently forget most anything at any time, I forgot the advice given to me before I bought one: "You'd better tow a big magnet behind your Harley to pick up the parts as they fall off."

My mind races ahead of my bike and into the near future. *Ten miles up the road, my new Harley wind chime blows off the handlebars, flies through the window of an eighteen wheeler, and impales the driver in the neck. Handbills taped in truck stop and on post office walls warn: "Vicious terrorist attack on driver! Suspect believed to be Taiwanese with a light complexion and slight Norwegian accent."*

Terrorist arrives alive with dead computer

~ ~ ~

The House Rules

A THREE-MONTH TRIP BACK TO AMERICA: fifteen states, twenty homes… and only four motel rooms. I'm lucky to have friends and family scattered over the landscape who will put me up, or more likely, put up with me. Some folks have lived in the same home for 40 years, so even when they've tried to lead me astray by sending fake email addresses, bogus phone numbers, and faux PO boxes in foreign countries, I still find them lurking in the same place with the lights off.

When you're a guest in a home, common hospitality might say anything goes, until the second day when you have to learn the house rules. Sometimes the rules are unspoken, and you must discover them by trial and error, unlike motels that list them on the wall.

Check-out time: 11 a.m. (Unless you convince counter help of a greater need.) "Congratulations! You've been chosen to star in a new reality TV show called 'Motel Hell.'" I need to wait in the room for the Hollywood producer who's coming at 1 p.m. Are you free to travel?"

No motorcycles in the room. Unless you distract the staff by setting off car alarms in the front parking lot with your 130-decibel Harley and then ride into the rear elevator.

No sex in the hallways, with someone, or alone. "Does that include animals and inflatables?"

One unwritten rule puzzled me at my first home stay in San Fran on the left coast. My graphic designer cousin's abode felt more like a work of art than a house. Elegantly decorated, the bathroom had ultramodern or fashionably antique fixtures, black-and-white photos mounted as if hung a chic gallery, towels matching the rug matching the curtains matching the Italian tile matching the imported soap... and a plain ol' clear plastic quart bottle for a doorstop. Once you close the door and do your business, you put the bottle back to hold the door ajar. High concept art? Advanced Feng Shui? I didn't ask why; I just did it.

One rule at House Number Two near Nashville required men to sit while doing Number One, which is a good thing, because every once in a while, without warning, *two* separate streams burst out requiring that you quickly adjust for one while soaking the toilet paper, then swing to adjust for the other and hose the hand towel, unwilling to experience the grisly pain of stream stoppage.

This rule also reduces the Yosemite Falls Effect, which causes thin streams of water falling from great heights to widen, to drizzle and sprinkle to the sides, to splash into a pool of water at the base, and coat the surrounding area with a mist of yellow droplets. Add beer to this equation and the Seated Number One Rule becomes geometrically beneficial. You invite three guys to your home for beer and a baseball game on the tube. Three guys times five beers equals fifteen trips to the porcelain throne. By the fifth beer, your Captain Beer Trio, collectively nine sheets to the wind, sways without a breeze, sees two or three thrones, no longer aims to please, and saturates your entire zip code.

At House Number Three, a three-story mansion on the right coast in New Jersey, locks and security codes were in place but never used because of their three vocal dogs, two of them psychotically affectionate Old Yeller labs, who, if you dared climb over the fence, would cavort merrily, fetching balls and stuffed animals for you to throw while barking madly in Dogspeak.

"Oh goodie! A marvelous person has arrived! We have a new buddy who will throw the tennis ball into the pool forever, unlike our masters who are totally sick of it! Yay, bark, yay!"

After an extensive history of six kids with hundreds of friends coming, staying, and hardly ever *going*, the parents had to accept one unwritten rule: "This is the neighborhood refrigerator." They'd posted other guidelines on the walls.

• *No outfit is complete without dog hair.*

• *We never really grow up—just learn how to act in public.*

• *If you're pushing fifty, that's exercise enough.*

• *I'm having a CRAFT moment: Can't Remember A Fucking Thing.*

Attempting to find peace beyond the urban throngs during their twilight years, my friends told me they purchased another home in the Vermont mountains. They've given me an address, although I suspect their *actual* address is somewhere in New Hampshire.

Before hitting the highway from House Number Four in North Carolina after my friends had gone to work, I meticulously locked every door, but forgot my shaving kit inside. When I stopped by the office to ask if the missus would send it to me, her jaw dropped. "You locked the doors? We don't lock the doors. I wonder if Ed has a key?"

I know they got in, or broke in, because a few days later I received my kit, its contents coated in sticky white goop. I'm pretty sure the slit in my toothpaste tube was intentional.

The single house rule in Wisconsin was simple. "Drink as much beer as possible and pass out in the hot tub."

We only have four house rules in Thailand.

1) Chance the Siberian Husky must never escape.

Therefore, guests do not get a key to the gate. We'll let you in or out when you please, or you can climb the fence. It's not that we don't trust you; we don't trust him. He's way too intelligent and has a vast English vocabulary. Chance hasn't spoken to us but he's waiting for you, the innocent by-the-gate-stander. He'll blink his big browns, put on his irresistible persuasion face, and say, "It's okay! They let me out all the time! Don't worry. I gotta poop. I'll be back in a minute."

Chance has a terminal case of DADHD: Dog Attention Deficit Hyperactivity Disorder. If he escapes, he might chase a cat into Myanmar, where he'll be distracted by another cat, which he'll follow north into China, and eventually arrive in Siberia. My wife would demand that I find him, a useless endeavor since I can't even find my glasses, keys, or phone when they're laying next to me on the desk or on top of my head—the glasses, not the phone. I would spend a fruitless year in Siberia, end up empty-handed and empty-pawed, then commit suicide to save my wife the trouble of killing me when I returned.

2) Please remove your shoes before entering the house. Nothing personal; it's a Thai thing. And we want to keep the latest pandemic outside.

3) Do not disturb the hundred-plus geckos living on the walls, floors, ceiling, or in your suitcase. They eat mosquitoes and termites. Thais say it's bad luck to kill one. Consider gecko poop on your shoulder a free exotic souvenir.

4) I haven't seen one—yet—but if you witness a king cobra slinking through the yard, please alert me as soon as possible by tapping me on the shoulder, screaming hysterically, or cell-phoning from the top of the nearest building… or the airport.

I *never* tell friends about these rules before they arrive at our gate, otherwise they'd cancel their flights.

~ ~ ~

Now Meets Then

MY STEPFATHER WOULD SAY at the ripe age of 94, "I still feel like I'm 17, until I look in the mirror in the morning and gasp, 'Gadzooks! Who the hell is that?'" I experienced this at my 40th high school reunion. I remember my classmates the way they used to be in 1967, but when I looked around the room, I'd seen younger faces on cash.

In a moment of insanity, my wife Joomi agreed to travel with me to Fargo and attend this two-day ritual of mortality, against the advice of my "friends" who had warned her. "Are you sure want to hang out with Prehistoric Man?"

As we walked across the parking lot from my Harley Sportster to the designated reunion restaurant, several full-figured white-haired citizens waved exuberantly from arriving cars bigger than our bungalow in Thailand. I thought some high school friends had sent their grandparents to take their place. Another full-to-overflowing-figured woman wearing a flowered dress the size of a king-size bedspread emerged from a passenger van into the brisk wind. Not one hair stirred in her semi-tall, very rigid hairdo, perhaps kept in place with Super Glue.

At 88 pounds dripping wet with clothes on, Joomi might have weighed as much as one of this woman's thighs, concealed under her bedding. Most folks were larger than their former lives. Joomi and I panicked, ran behind a pickup truck, and each smoked a carton of cigarettes before I dared trespass into the past.

Our confidence bolstered, we entered the Mexican Village, now transformed into the Village of Scandinavian Vikings, where people had continued to grow in every direction: older, taller, and wider. One couple must've had to ride separately to the third floor because together they'd have exceeded the load limit of the elevator. Emcee Stan Grimm's comment tickled everyone, no matter what size funny bone they had. "I don't remember the bra sizes of the senior girls being quite so substantial."

Several women were taller than I, but Dick Hanson still towered above everyone at 6' 7"—the former center of our football team and current college president, who undoubtedly had no problem with discipline.

I looked up at Richard, and said respectfully, "I thought people we're supposed to shrink as they aged."

He replied, "Only you."

Joomi—comparatively short, perhaps even wee, definitely closer to the ground—appeared to be a lost tourist, head back, gazing up at skyscrapers in New York City. Though she would've preferred to be invisible, I convinced her to get a name tag. Considerably more complex than the Scandinavian surnames Olson or Swenson, "Joomi Benjapa Tewintarapakti" required three separate tags, but no one tried to pronounce it, anyway.

Besides being the shortest person in the room by a foot, she was also the youngest by twenty years. Her smooth Thai skin and youthful smile fools the camera. Friends had seen photos that took off another decade, and one commented, "When we saw photos of you and heard you had two kids, we thought they must be eggs."

We just didn't look like other couples. Sun-baked Joomi had recently come from two-months of hanging with her kids on the beach in Florida, and her tan had gone beyond bronze into the dark mahogany spectrum. Mixed marriages are infrequent in homogenous Fargo, where terminally calcified conservatives might disapprove of a couple comprising a Norwegian and a Swede.

Some didn't even try to be friendly, just ALOOF, which

stands for "A Lot Of Old Farts." Damn, even though I still felt 17, this fun house room of living mirrors forced me to remember that I, too, had become an old fart.

Joomi took me aside and suggested, "Stay as long as you want. I'm gonna take a cab to the airport and wait for you back in Thailand."

Although the attendees looked like they came from the Land of the Giants, we were the last graduating class of the Fargo Central High School "Midgets." Because the first basketball team was short, they named all the athletic teams "The Midgets." Since their legacy had been around for decades, we never considered the ridiculous nature of our moniker or how it might *not* have struck terror into our competitors' hearts. At their pep rallies, our opponents probably yelled, "Oh, no! The fighting Midgets are coming! Run away! Run away!" as they nearly laughed themselves to death. "Get out of here, you little Midgets! Gimme that ball!" I'm surprised we ever won a game.

Upon learning about the Midgets, and that I personally had created and starred as the mascot "Midgetman" in school colors costume—Batmanesque, purple, hooded cape, white shirt with purple "M" on the chest, purple shorts, tights, and ugly plastic shoes shaped like deformed feet—my non-Fargo friends ask, "They don't still use the term Midgets, do they?"

"No, our school burned down when I was a junior, and the fighting midget firefighters only had squirt guns." (Although our alumni newspaper reported that, as we watched flames licking the roof of our crumbling school, I ran back to the door and threw my books into the building, the rumor about soaking them in gasoline is false.)

Next comment from friends: "Midgets would be so politically incorrect today." So what? 1000 angry midgets might invade Fargo to protest? "Get out of here, you little midgets! Gimme those signs! Go to your hotel rooms!" If Walt Disney can have Snow White and the Seven Dwarves, Fargo could still have the fighting Midgets.

The second night at the reunion banquet in a Radisson Hotel, the aging Midgetman appeared, bumping into walls, wearing glasses over his purple cowl and making a fool of himself, though secretly pleased he could still fit into the costume, and that the 17-year-old fool inside was still alive and well and NOT living in Fargo. (I may continuously grow old, but I can stay immature indefinitely.)

'67 School Mascot Sparks Pep Fests

Attired in his purple cape, purple tights and a bright smile, Midget Man, Scott Jones, floor, makes his eminent appearance at a pep assembly. The Illustrious figure, tipping across the gym historied gyrations, is interviewed by his announcer Clint Crowe. Midget Man after performing a series of produces Midget victories.

Joomi and I got the feeling that my classmates didn't get out much, since the "Traveling the Furthest to the Reunion Award" went to—and I'm not making this up—someone from Hawaii, which, to be further away than Thailand, would have to be a province in Australia or the South Pole. We didn't really care because the prize was a plastic basket bouquet of plastic flowers like you'd find at a Salvation Army store gathering dust next to rusting toaster ovens, cracked bowling balls, and other items no one snapped up during the last hour of a garage sale when everything is free.

All kidding aside, I didn't want it to end. I missed my dear friends and could've spent a year talking to each one of them. A few hours over two days only whet my appetite for more. Friends keep threatening to visit us in Thailand, but never seem to make it.

The next day I took Joomi on a tour of the countryside around Fargo, which is technically flatter than a linoleum floor, but not quite as scenic. After passing several subdivisions of new homes painted in every shade of color imaginable between taupe and slightly off-taupe, designed in a wild myriad of styles from square to very square, she fell asleep and missed the two curves in the road that offered dramatically different views of the surrounding four taupe fields of wheat, wheat, wheat, and wheat.

Honoring Joomi's fervent pleas to be rescued from North Dakota and taken anywhere else, even if it involved jail or discussions with door-to-door Jehovah's Witnesses—pleas she delivered by shouting to passing motorists, calling random phone numbers on the wall in the women's toilet, or even responding to email spam notifications that she had won the lottery in Nigeria—I duct-taped her to the Harley and dragged her 50 miles into neighboring Minnesota, which has a few miniature hills, vast forests swarming with mosquitoes, and a state bird: the loon. This neighboring state was also the location of my family reunion, attended by twenty members of the aforementioned bird species.

After Joomi chatted with three of my cousins' children who have mental challenges referred to by odd acronyms and are possibly hereditary, she said, "Now I understand," referring to *my* psychological eccentricities.

We heard a fascinating story of a hyperactive son, once discovered on the kitchen counter hurling flour and sugar into the air, then, as Mom cleaned up the mess, yanked pots and pans onto the floor, before scampering away from Mom's screams to pull out books from the shelves, and was cornered on a chandelier hanging from the ceiling. The son's age was 2 or 3 or 23. I don't remember which, but it sounded like great fun, and reminded me of Stupid Human Tricks from high school.

A refrigerator had been delivered, so two of us took the empty packing box downtown on the top of Dad's Pontiac Bonneville. My friend, Ole Snake Miner—though I've rearranged the letters of his real name, Neal Eriksmoen, to protect the reputation of his current family—laid inside the box so it wouldn't blow off the roof. We took turns walking down Main Street, concealed under the box, bouncing off walls and bumping into signposts while frightening the locals. This activity prepared me for my future career touring the country as a comedian/musician where people willingly paid me to be mentally challenged on stage.

After leaving Reunionville, we stopped at an outdoor Craft Fair—Or was it a Crap Fair?—with booths selling fried mystery meat on a stick, crocheted proverbs only grandmothers would purchase, and household items made from deer antlers guaranteed to maim children.

A mile from the fair, we rode past three people sitting in chairs on the side of a country road, far from any town, next to a six-by-six-foot, hand-painted sign that read, in huge letters on both sides—and I'm not making this up—HONK. I considered turning back for a photo or to ask the burning question: "Did you take your medicine today?" But I decided against it because they were undoubtedly either a) human-like aliens with waaaaayyyyy to much time on their hands; or b) more of my friends and relatives.

~ ~ ~

Live Kids, Dead Teachers

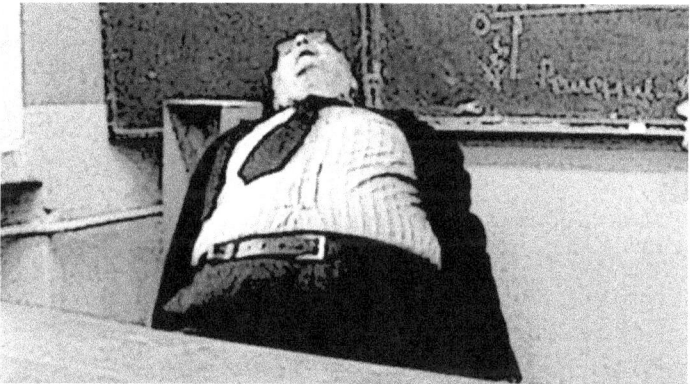

WHILE RESEARCHING the theme for this month's magazine (Education in Thailand, although DEADucation seems more appropriate), I conducted extensive interviews with a student, a teacher, a writer, and a house painter. Fortunately, they were all me.

One "learning problem" became clear after I took a TEFL course (Teaching English as a Foreign Language) and volunteered at a high school in a small but thriving town in northern Thailand. A Goddess of Grammar and head of her English department for nine years, the Thai teacher might have known everything about the Future Perfect

Continuously Confusing Tense, but she couldn't carry on an intelligible conversation with me. I wanted to quote George Bernard Shaw, "Those who can, do; those who can't, teach," but she wouldn't have understood, anyway.

My first task? Evaluate pronunciation as each student individually read the same paragraph to me. Littered with cumbersome, pretentious words like cumbersome and pretentious, the teacher's paragraph was one I would have stolen to use in an advanced sociology term paper—Greek to me and Gobbledygook to the kids. The students performed as expected: bored to death reading her boring, meaningless words.

What happens when a student ventures into the real world? Imagine Thai Lek visiting the USA and trying to chat with someone after nine years of this kind of "learning."

"Hi, there!" greets Mr. Whoever.

Lek doesn't speak while wondering, *I know "hi", but "there"? I'm here. Who's he talking to?*

"What's up?" he asks.

Lek looks up, expecting something to fall down, sees a chandelier, but doesn't know what it's called in Thai, let alone English.

"What's your name?" he asks.

Okay... Breathe... I got this one. "My name is Lek."

"How do you do?"

Lek is again speechless. *How... do... I... do? Do what? Talk? How do I talk?*

Noticing Lek's wide, clueless eyes, Mr. Whoever tries dialect. "Jeet jet? M'ungry! No'da'mean?"

Lek's tongue turns into cement. *I want my Mommy!*

"Jawanna? C'mon. S'queat!"

Lek's brain snaps, crackles and pops, her legs become wet rice noodles as she crumples onto the street, and Mr. Whoever calls 911.

In the TEFL course, which also means "Teaching English

For Losers," I learned this statement is false: "I speak English, therefore I can teach it." One of my classmates, Mr. Meek from New Zealand, had a camouflage personality—no one noticed he was there. His ever-present, wide-brimmed hat concealed most of his pale face preoccupied with staring at his feet. Mr. Meek talked so softly I could barely hear him. He spoke in thick Kiwi English, so the few words I heard, I couldn't understand. I hope he never inflicted himself on actual students, but he might be perfect in a School for the Deaf and Mute. They wouldn't hear him anyway, nor be able to repeat whatever he mumbled.

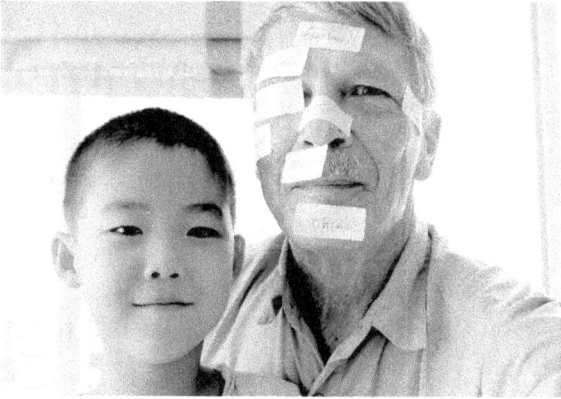

On-location English instruction of parts of the face
when student has no white board at home

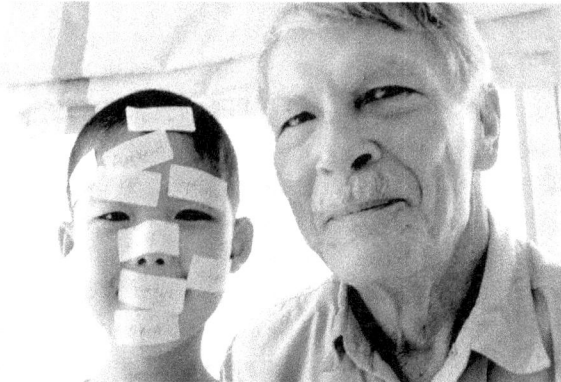

Some kids may have ADD, but many adults have TDD—"Teaching Disability Disorder." It's pandemic and has been around for centuries.

I remember my junior high history teacher, no matter how hard I try to forget him. Mr. Frizzell (we called him Mr. Fossil) was so old, he remembered when rainbows were black and white. He attended grade school with Socrates. His idea of learning history consisted solely of memorizing dates when men fought battles and died.

Our entire class practiced synchronized harassment. We'd arrive early, turn our desks backward, and he'd think he'd entered the wrong room. At predetermined moments, like when the minute hand on the wall clock clicked to 11:17 am, every student would drop their pencil; at 1:33, sneeze; at 2:51, fling open their desktop. One day he went into his closet and we locked the door. I don't remember letting him out. He might still be in there… a skeleton in the closet.

I liked math, despite my marginal instructors. Picture all the math teachers you've ever had and line them up in your mind. Don't they kind of look alike, like they're cousins or something?

You're sitting in class and a fully developed, adult geek plods into the room. His plastic pocket protector bulges with pens and protractors. Most folks consider complementary colors when they dress, but Mr. Math tries to match patterns, stripes, and plaids. His clothes look like they're wrestling with each other. You wonder, "How can this guy teach geometry when he can't even measure the length of his pants so we don't have to see the tops of his argyle socks, plus an inch of his hairless legs?"

Mr. Math launches into a tedious analysis of irrational numbers, as if anyone gives a rat's rectum, and you count sheep to stay awake. At my school, this math teacher was John Johnson. His name could even be reduced to a formula: John x 2 + son = ZZZ

Of course, I also had many great teachers—exceptional people with enlarged hearts full of passion for knowledge and compassion for their students, their educational partners. Great teachers live by this quote: "Give a man a fish, and he'll eat for a day. Teach a man to fish, and he'll eat for a lifetime."

Mr. Fossil never said this: "Give a man a fact, and he'll feel like a failure compared to William the Conqueror, who ruled most of civilization by age 26. Teach a man to learn, and he'll conquer the world."

One of my favorite authors, Terry Pratchett said this, although it has nothing to do with this chapter: "Build a man a fire, and he'll be warm for a day. Set a man on fire, and he'll be warm for the rest of his life."

So how do we weed out the weak ones? Teachers could be required to take Proficiency Final Exams administered by their students. If a 4th grade teacher scores a D, poor but passing, he's sent back to teach 3rd grade. If he fails, he's sent to the University of Kids, where every professor is four years old, so he can experience untarnished individuals, still curious and creative—before they're constricted in square classrooms and forced to think inside their teachers' boxes.

Years ago I spent a week painting a friend's house in America. Every day four-year-old Professor Mark would pedal over in his red fire truck and teach me valuable lessons about creative thinking.

"I painted a house before," Mark says smugly.

"Really? Where?" I ask.

"On paper."

Perfect answer! You got the concept, but a whole different scenario. We're bonding. "Wow. You drew a house and then painted it!"

"Yeah. I wish I had a ladder like that," Mark muses as he looks up at me.

"Why do you want a ladder?"

"I want to get high."

Cool, dude. You've already got an alternative to drugs.

"When I grow up, I want to be a teacher like my dad!"

"What does he teach?"

"Kids."

Of course he does! I'm the one asking the stupid questions. This is a crucial factor of the learning problem. Most instructors say they teach subjects, like science or gym. They've forgotten a simple fact. Teachers teach kids.

One morning Mark was picking up ants, squashing them between his fingers, and flicking them against the house. That bothered me. Somehow I wanted to convince him to stop by making him understand why he shouldn't do it.

"What's that tiny ant's mom gonna say when he doesn't come home for dinner tonight?"

"Nothin'," Mark replies.

"Why not?"

"I got her, too!"

You are way ahead of me! I'm going to nominate you for the International Director of the War on Global Terrorism.

The best teachers inspire students and then get out of the way. And learn from kids like the confident lass in this story—perhaps an urban legend, but she still inspires me.

A kindergarten teacher strolls through her class while the kids draw pictures. She peers over the shoulder of a girl working diligently and asks what she is drawing.

Shakti replies, "I'm drawing God."

The teacher pauses, then comments, "But no one knows what God looks like."

Undaunted, without looking up from her paper, Shakti says, "They will in a minute."

~ ~ ~

Mr. President? No, thanks.

I F THE PEOPLE CHOSE ME to be the President of the United States of America, I'd scream frantically, wet my pants, and flee to another country. Actually, I've already done that, without the screaming or wetting, just to avoid being a resident, let alone president.

POTUS sounds like the worst job in the world. Get hired and immediately half the country hates you; people around the globe want to kill you; security guards with necks wider than your waist surround your family; everyone dissects your life 60/24/7/365, watching for any mistake or strange behavior. You're chopped meat if you get caught with broccoli between your teeth, a booger hanging from your nostril, or your fly down.

I've lived through, gasp, 12 different presidents. From age 0 to 4, I don't remember Harry Truman, since presidents didn't say things I cared to hear like "goo goo da da frimp ga zoing" until George W. Bush took office.

In my pre-teen years in the '50s, former five-star general, "I like Ike" Eisenhower inspired me to build model navy ships and blow them up with firecrackers in the bathtub.

Brimming with charisma, JFK came on the scene and tragically left too soon, leaving probing questions like, "Did he really have an affair with Marilyn Monroe?"

With that titillating presidential possibility in mind, I dreamed of being POTUS. As North Dakota State Student Council president, I traveled to schools and gave a speech written by my ghost writer (*Readers Digest* magazine) called "24-hour Leadership," which must have included something about leading in your sleep, a skill perfected by Ronald Reagan during his latter years in office.

When the Cold War heated up in the late '60s, barren North Dakota became a center of mass destruction on the northern USA border. Hundreds of InterContinental Ballistic Missiles (ICBM or "I Can Bomb Moscow") were concealed in desolate underground silos and ready to launch. Why? If Russia vaporized North Dakota, no one would notice, or if they did, no one would give a shit. Fleets of B-52 bombers and fighter jets guarded us from imminent invasion by Canada and their Mounties, who might have ridden over the border to steal some of our wheat.

LBJ tackled civil rights, poverty, and disastrously, Vietnam. His Pinocchio nose was already formidable, but it continued to lengthen during his public downplay of the war, while he secretly revved it up. By the end of his term, he could wear his reading glasses, driving glasses, and sunglasses—all at the same time.

While in college at the radical hotbed of UW/Madison, visions of moving to Canada replaced my personal POTUS dreams. I disagreed with the Vietnam War, war in general, and the concept of visiting Southeast Asia to kill other teenagers like me. I only shot living things with my camera. Because of a congenital eye disorder requiring three operations and the wearing of glasses enabling me to distinguish living beings from inanimate objects, I was granted a deferment from the military. No one wanted a sightless pacifist wandering around foreign battlefields accidentally wasting his own comrades.

Enter Dick Nixon and the Age of Wiretapping, Watergate, and the War at Home. He wasn't your everyday Tom, Dick, or Harry—merely a impeached dick who resigned before being fired. I lost all confidence in the presidency when bland Fall Guy, Jerry Ford pardoned him. Then Jerry fell down exiting Air Force One, solidifying his image as a terminal klutz. LBJ once commented, "He's a nice fellow, but spent too much time playing football without a helmet."

I met Ford's son in my booth at an entertainment convention. As he perused my promo material, he lost his balance, collapsed my table, and sent my stuff flying onto the floor. I asked, "The apple didn't fall far from the tree, eh?"

Former peanut farmer Carter's term challenged Jimmy and the country, but he was, and still is, a good man. Visiting his tiny hometown of Plains, Georgia, I had a close encounter with his cousin. On the town square sat the Carter General Store, overflowing with household supplies and hardware, souvenir key chains, and jars of "Plains Presidential Peanut Butter." I carried a copy of *Turning Point*, "written and autographed by the author" to the check-out counter, and picked up a postcard next to the register of Jimmy shaking hands with his cousin, State Senator Hugh Carter. I looked from the card to the smile hovering above the cash register.

"Hugh!" I exclaimed.

"Yessir, Ah am," he replied proudly in Southern speak.

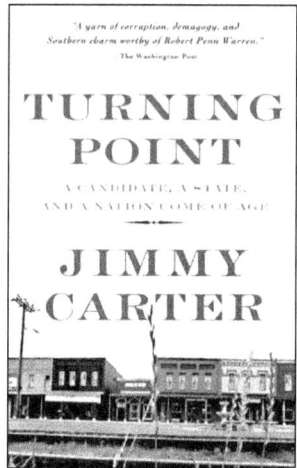

"I'm confused." I opened the book and pointed to the autograph. "Jimmy's signature looks a little weird, like it's blurry or something."

"Whale," Hugh drawled, which means "well" in English, "he came on by 'n' signed 'em with a pencil, so ah wen' over 'em with a pen."

The Reagan/Bush Years dragged on forever. The Clinton Risqué Era faded into another endless Bush Whack. To take on Obama, the Republicans could only dredge up another rich, old, white guy for their candidate. As his VP running mate, John McCain chose Sarah Palin, winner of the Miss Wasilla Beauty Pageant in Alaska, who negated any positives he brought to the position. Despite her dismal failure during the vice-presidential debates, she did defeat Joe Biden in the swimsuit competition.

Every president gave it their best or worst shot, succeeding or failing at exactly the same time, depending on who you talk to at what time during their reign. In my opinion, President Obama succeeded marvelously. If we have a few more like him, maybe they'll change the name of the official residence to the Black and White House.

I can't bring myself to refer to the current occupant of this venerable building as President except for the final four letters of the title—he's a wretched "dent" in US history which needs to be pounded out, sanded down, and repainted.

BREAKING NEWS!
POTUS Illegal Alien Born on Uranus and Expelled
THE US OF ANGST, APRIL 1ST, 2020: Today Men In Black revealed to the news media that the President of the United States, originally from Uranus, was exiled from his home planet and transported to Earth decades ago.

"Agent Orange was one of the first alien refugees our organization accepted," says Tommy Lee Smith, a Men In Black spokesperson. "99% of his native citizens voted him off the planet. His official classification on Uranus was also

POTUS, though on that world the initials stand for 'Piece Of The Universal Shit.' Most people referred to him by the shortened version: POS. He was nearly 300 years old, but could only speak and write like a third grader. After his businesses went bankrupt, he escaped to a remote swamp with several associates, and the Uranian International Congress sought to drain it.

"Over the years, they have flushed several of POTUS' cronies down to Earth. On Uranus, his President of Vice, Mikey Halfpence, had a private proctology practice at the Brown Nose Institute. Kelly Anaconda was a snake in the grass selling her own brand of snake oil door-to-door. Banned from the bar association, Billy aka "The Toad" became a bail bondsman for the USP, the Union of Swamp Predators. Jarred Kushnerd—a human, a robot, or some bizarre creature in between—worked as a model for plastic manikins because his expression never changed."

Extracting a pen-sized video projector from his suit coat and pointing at the white wall, Mr. Smith continued. "But Moscow Mitch is the weirdest varmint. He used to be a turtle on his own rotten log in the southern swamp. You think he looks strange now? Look at this footage when he sucks his head inside his body!"

When the tiny POS first arrived, the Men In Black felt sorry for him. In reality, he is only a half-inch orange worm with white circles around his eyes, but uses Uranian Hologram Technology to create the rotund behemoth his fans observe bulging around the podium. Critics have claimed he's daft because of his outlandish ravings, but Mr. Smith explained these statements verify his origins.

"Agent Orange spoke about injecting disinfectant into patients' lungs to kill the corona virus. That wouldn't hurt a Uranian. Their internal body components are more like porcelain toilet fixtures. Noise from windmills causes cancer? That's possible on Uranus. The average temperature's minus 360°F, and wind speed might reach 560 mph. You can't imagine how loud windmills are! Nuke a hurricane to stop it? Fallout that would spread across Earth couldn't hurt a Uranian. Everyone is naturally hatched in radioactive test tubes. Why do you think he's orange? Look closely and you'll see how he glows in the dark."

The Men In Back organization has concluded the time has come for the removal of Agent Orange, his associates, and his supporters. "We discovered the secret mission of this despicable POS. The letters in COVID-19 stand for Complete Oblivion Via Illicit Dictatorship. His minions created a vicious virus in the southern White House basement and smuggled it into China. His goal is to decimate humanity, then travel to Uranus via the Space Force, and enact final revenge on his home. We can't let that happen, so we'll be teleporting the POS and his swamp comrades to a sparsely populated planet called Narcissia in the Andromeda Galaxy. Lying is the Law of Land there, and Fake News is all they get. We told the whole truth and nothing but the truth about our POTUS to the Narcissia officials, but they didn't believe us. Agent Orange should feel right at home there, except they haven't discovered electricity yet, so without his hologram, he'll just be one more little POS worm destined to become a dung beetle."

The President Alien, Resident Alien Melanoma, and the concubines hiding in his bunker were informed of their imminent expulsion at a private White House meeting.

"The POS didn't take the news too well," admitted Mr. Smith. "He shouted 'Covfefe!'—the Uranian word for 'fuck you!'—blamed it and his hemorrhoid problems on Obama, fired everyone in his general vicinity, and trashed the Oval Office with a golf club. Melanoma remained benign with a smile frozen on her face and offered me a complimentary 'Morons Are Governing America' hat made in China."

~ ~ ~

Why White?

WHY DID BROWN RICE, sugar, and bread become white, robbed of many of their natural nutrients? Because of The Universal Law of Because, demonstrated in the following tale.

Mother is cooking, and her daughter Wynona asks, "Ma, why do you cut the end off the ham?"

"Because," she replies, "that's what my ma did."

Wynona phones Grandma and asks the same question.

"Because," Grandma says, "that's what my mother did."

Wynona rings up Great Grandma and asks, "Grandma said you always cut the end off the ham. Is that right?"

Great Grandma said, "Yeah, every time."

"Why'd you do that?"

"Because it was too big to fit in my pan."

Right. Monkey see, monkey do. Rice, sugar, and bread are white, because several hundred years ago, a bunch of rich old white folks liked white. They even made it a law.

In the 16th century, Elizabeth was Queen and white was king, because white signified wealth, class superiority, and purity. The color brown was for the poor peasants and those who worked the land. Liz's "Sumptuary Laws" regulated her minions' personal habits, clothing, food, and furniture on moral or religious grounds. If you were high class, everyone had better know it right away and remember it.

White products were harder to get and more expensive to produce. Back then a kilo of sugar—or "white gold"—cost a whopping $100 in today's dollars. A crazy contradictory circle started. The silver spoon citizens ate so much white sugar that their teeth turned black, which meant rich, so the poor spoon-fed citizens turned their white teeth black with cosmetics.

Another universal law applies here—The Eyes Are Stupider Than The Stomach Principle. To make these high-buck white products, merchants cleaned and polished the rice and wheat, probably while doing the same to their shoes. This removed the brown bran and germ, plus most of the vitamins, particularly B1. The refined nobles ate refined food, got beriberi, and very ill while merchants laughed all the way to their piggy banks.

The prissy well-to-dos who weren't well anymore wouldn't even touch some root crops because they came out of the brown peasant ground, or eat fruit, which prevented scurvy, because… they were stupid. Or… hmm, lemme guess… too busy keeping their skin fashionably pale and white, which is much easier to do when they're sick?

While visiting England, I toured several castles where spears, swords, hatchets, and paintings of pasty vampires hung on stone walls. To me, they looked like the undead nobility—cold-blooded creatures with no chins and curly white, slimy locks like salamanders in sheep's clothing. I thought, *these are the wimpy kids who got beat up on the grade school playground.*

"Ooo, scary, little fairy, Sir Prancelot from Whiningham. Gimme that sword!" taunts the neighborhood bully as he snatches away Prance's cardboard blade, gives him a laundry check, and shoves him into the moat.

White also meant holiness, and this was The Inquisition Era, when people were tortured if someone said they thought someone was even thinking about someone who was thinking something wrong, or something. Grilling out was common since you could always find a witch or two to use for the kindling at your BBQ, but you had to invite the entire village.

Peasant Percy and his wife Prim look over a fruit stand in the market. Prim asks her husband sweetly, "Pick out a watermelon for me, honey."

"Which one?" Percy asks.

"Ah, ha!" the merchant screams, arms flailing. "It's Witch One! Grab her!"

"He must be Witch Two!" the mob chants, lunging at Percy. "Let's fire up a couple of stakes!"

If a witch ever got to trial, the Men in White would decree: "Let God decide. Put rocks in their pockets and throw them in the river. If they die underwater, it is God's will. If they rise again, they are witches, and let the BBQ begin."

Underwear is the exception in the original color brown to white phenomena. Cotton is white in the first place, then made into white underwear, which soon turns multicolored with use. Why not make it brown in the first place? That would quell one of mankind's oldest fears: "What if I'm in an oxcart or automobile crash, rushed to the hospital, and my underwear is dirty?"

This reminds me of a story that might explain the use of the color white for medical convenience and diagnosis. Elderly Ernie and Nell are in the clinic. He can barely hear, so she has to translate.

The doctor says, "First we'll take his temperature."

"What'd he say?" Ernie asks.

"Put this thermometer under your tongue," Nell says.

"Now I'll check his blood pressure," Doc says.

"What'd he say?" Ernie asks again.

"Put your arm in this Velcro sleeve," Nell says.

"I'll also need blood, urine and stool samples, plus a sperm specimen."

"What'd he say now?"

"Just give him your underwear."

~ ~ ~

My Brain Is Full

THIS YEAR I CELEBRATED MY NINTH BIRTHDAY—in dog years. The other number was too gigantic to stomach. Last year I moved the decimal over to the left and celebrated 6.2, so it sounded more like an upgrade.

Thanks to Facebook, I received birthday messages from folks I haven't seen in decades, and from people who never remembered (or ever knew) the date before social networks and automatic computer reminders on the web. I posted this reply on Facebook: "Thank you for all the happy birthday wishes even though I have no idea who you are. I'm in the hospital recovering from first, second, and seventh degree burns from the fiery inferno on my cake."

The morning was splendid, with no planning whatsoever, except the plan to do whatever I felt like from moment to moment. I got up late, made coffee, swept bat poop off the porch, and then worked in the garden for a couple hours. I highly recommend this experience to any of you on your birthday, but please let me know in advance so I can leave the bat poop for you to sweep and find tasks for you to do in my garden.

My wife and I tried to reminisce about my past birthdays, and though we've shared the last nine here in Thailand, we could only recall three, with difficulty pinpointing the exact years or locations. Not an impressive average.

One was exact: my book release birthday party at a Chiang Mai restaurant, attended by a few friends and too many nameless vagabonds who straggled in for free food. Another was a cold day in the mountains near Pai, huddled under blankets, trying to warm our bodies with fifty-some candles precariously stuck in one cupcake, without setting our hair, the mosquito netting, or the entire bamboo guesthouse, on fire. Number 60 might have been a tiny gathering of four golfer friends, three of whom were older than me, when they undoubtedly discussed golf, personal ailments, golf, and more ailments.

Of my remaining 54 birthdays, I could only dredge up four for certain, a humbling display of mental ability only slightly higher than an eggplant. I have photographic proof of my first birthday—little Scotty sitting on the table with both hands buried in his cake—but I don't remember that specific moment. I do remember my 40th, which I celebrated as twenty-twenty, a culmination of a decade of not wanting to turn thirty and telling people I was twenty-nine, then twenty-ten, twenty-eleven, twenty-twelve, etcetera, and finally 20-20, when I could see perfectly. I will never forget my fiftieth birthday, gasp, a half-century, no matter how hard I try.

I recollect a twenty-something birthday lunch when my terminally festive father made a special cake for me, a festive failure. While whipping the frosting he'd dyed in his favorite color orange, Dad lifted the beater out of the bowl, flinging orange frosting in a thick line across his shirt, the fridge, and the kitchen wall, which he left to harden to honor the moment. It might've been the most rigid frosting ever created by man, and the only force holding the cake together. Dad had forgotten key cake ingredients like eggs and liquid, because once cut, dust poured out of the frosting. No one got a piece of cake, only a pile of crumbs.

Since it was inedible, and we were ridiculous, we stuck other things in the cake to "make it worth something": leaves for hair, a carrot nose, coins for eyes, an old pair of glasses, a shoehorn for the mouth, and a few cigarettes. As I was leaving, Dad poured the crumbs and all their accoutrements into a paper bag and said, "Don't forget your cake."

I left his apartment, then left the cake outside his door. At eight p.m. that evening at the hotel where I was performing, the birthday cake bag was waiting for me on the piano bench. At two a.m., I left it on the doorstep of my sister, who had participated in the cake torture at my party. Unlike father and son, she had sense enough to throw it away.

While I was feeling increasingly senile during this latest advanced birthday, my computer taught me a valuable lesson. For years, without question or pause, the remarkable program "Time Machine" has backed up everything on my Mac to an external disk with a terabyte (meaning: a shitload) of memory. Last week this message appeared on my screen: "Your backup disk is full. To execute the current backup, your files from April 9, 2009 will be removed. Click OK to authorize the deletion."

Since the underlying reasons for memory loss have been examined and accepted, I realize it's not a depressing problem. I've merely experienced so much that my brain is full.

Regrettably, when I was constructed back in 1949 with only 13k of memory, no fancy storage/notification programs were installed. Now when my mind reaches maximum capacity, random memories squirt out of existence without warning messages like:

1) "Your brain is full. The files from your 24th birthday will now be deleted, so you can continue to learn directions to the hospital."

Or…

2) "The file containing information that the eyeglasses you're currently looking for are sitting on top of your head will now be deleted, so you can remember the list of items your wife is currently telling you on the phone to pick up at the market."

Although this recent revelation comforts me, I fear the following story told to me on my birthday might be a harbinger of my future.

Two old guys, Ole and Sven, have known each other their entire lives and played cribbage daily for decades.

In the middle of their weekly card game, Ole tilts his head to the side as he looks up at Sven. "Uff dah, buddy. Sorry, but I forgot yer name. Wouldja please tell me what it is again?"

Sven pauses, then says, "How soon d'ya need ta know?"

~ ~ ~

Blue-eyed Monsters

ANSWERING A CRY OF DISTRESS, I find my wife Joomi, with tears in her eyes, pointing and shouting in a pinched whisper, "A blue-eyed monster!" My first mental picture is "Farang?" ["Foreigner?"] Me? Or a surprise visit from one of my strapping Norwegian relatives or a pack of those blue-eyed farang monsters who attempt to mate with the brown-eyed parasites on Chiang Mai's Loi Kroh Road, the Land of Ladies of the Evening?

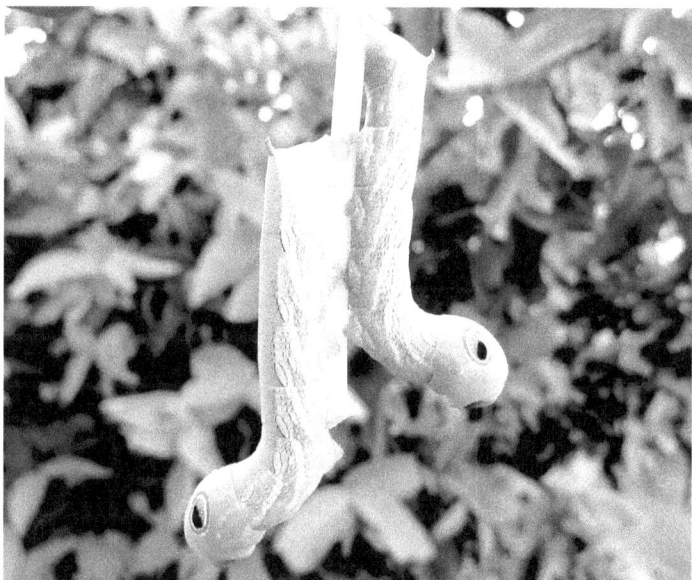

"In the second flower pot!" To warrant such panic, I think "Snake!"—the top entry on Joomi's terror list. Cautiously approaching our hanging periwinkle, I see nothing, and then, like every horror movie, I glance up expecting a two-meter, blue-eyed cobra to drop from the roof onto my neck. As I conclude she's lost her mind and head toward the house for sedatives, I spot *four* blue-eyed monsters—hefty, three-inch, green caterpillars with amazing eye-like spots, hereditarily developed to scare away birds and wives.

As a adolescent nerd with thick glasses in Fargo, North Dakota, I'd spent hours collecting insects, imagining one day I'd be an official entomologist, a bug scientist, a respectable nerd with thick glasses. I tended ant farms, raised caterpillars, and, sigh... netted butterflies and moths, mercilessly gassed them, and zealously mounted my innocent victims. It's time to atone for my sins.

After fifteen minutes of gentle coaxing and convincing Joomi that the blue-eyed monsters are harmless, while watching their cute little magnetic feet grab onto stems as they devour our pampered flowers, we transfer them into a plastic box filled with leaves and race into town. Now the new top of our task list—replace the shredded bed mosquito net that Joomi attacked with scissors to make a breathable cover for the monsters' new home.

Shame-faced Tigger caught in the act with geometric poop

Upon returning, we find lethargic caterpillars with nothing left to eat, their mass of leaves transformed into artistically shaped piles of poop. Joomi names the smaller yellow-brown guy (or girl) in his old age, non-green stage, Tigger, friend of Pooh. Considering his, or her, impressive amount of poop, I name his/her pal, Poopsie, similar to Pooh. The other two become Dumper and Crapula, and whew, can they eat! (And poop.) A leaf disappears in seconds! Picture a pizza half your size, your ten feet clutching the crust, then you demolish it in moments before moving on to your next fifty pizzas—while pooping them out the other end, but you don't have to dwell on the last part.

Caterpillars live on what they eat, often a single species of plant, and some eat nothing else, similar to my 30-year-old cousin who, at a Thanksgiving feast of turkey, herb stuffing, mashed potatoes and gravy, baked almond/green beans, cranberries, and Caesar salad prepared by his mother, demanded a hamburger and fries.

I put Poopsie on a stalk of impatiens flowers, and she remains motionless, as if I'd set her on, and requested she eat, a flagpole. Imagining an inexpensive food supply, I put a cabbage leaf in the Tupperware Monster Home. By morning, the four Blue Brothers are bored and lifeless on the untouched cabbage—which might as well have been a spare tire—surrounded by poop and no periwinkle leaves.

Proper identification is essential to determine and locate their diet, much more difficult than owning a dog, when the only action required is: find a pet shop and say, "Dog, old, big. Give me that bag." A butterfly/moth website helps—if you know the country and scientific name of the plant, it gives you bug options. Upon entry of Thailand and Catharanthus roseus, the scientific name for periwinkle, up pops a picture of the Oleander Hawk Moth and her blue-eyed babies! (I put in Mcdonaldus disgustus and a picture of my cousin pops up.) I suggest changing Tigger's name to "Ole" for Oleander, a Norwegian name honoring my heritage. She says, "That's not very Thai"—as if Tigger, Poopsie, Crapula, and Dumper qualify in that category.

We learn they also like to feast on their namesake—oleander plants—and although we can buy these cheaper than our cherished periwinkles, Joomi immediately offers up her former floral sweethearts to her new bug buds. The hanging pots become dining halls, covered with mosquito netting. (She's afraid they might get malaria?) We discover Monster #5, name him, or her, Cate—short for Defe Cate—and soon each of our honored guest have their own private periwinkle condominiums.

I'm hoping Joomi's fickle behavior doesn't go unchecked. A beautiful bird lands on Tigger's plant, gobbles him up, inspiring Joomi to sacrifice Dumper in order to keep her new bird (Swallow) happy. A cute Siamese kitten (Catula) chows down the bird, and soon a dashing puppy (Dogula) devours Catula. A handsome wild piglet (Boarzilla) takes down Dogula, and finally a magnificent tiger (named Tigger, in memory of departed Tigger) eats Boarzilla and me.

Our dream is to marvel at the wonders of metamorphosis from caterpillar to cocoon, and perhaps catch the brief moment when Mister, or Miss, Oleander Hawk Moth, enters the world, unfolds her or his lustrous wings, and flutters away to deposit eggs on our other periwinkles, which soon become dead stems.

If you don't see me for a while, it's because the internet states that the transformation may take days or weeks. You might catch me at the flower market, peeking through the windshield of a car stuffed with periwinkles. Or… if my wife takes a liking to termites, it's possible we'll have to sacrifice the house.

~ ~ ~

Rat Attack

I T'S THE YEAR OF THE RAT, specifically at my bungalow, and last week I officially declared war, although the rats attacked first. The death toll now stands at ten to zero, though countless cookies, crackers, cereal, and fruit have disappeared from my cupboards. I'm pretty sure they took a few cans of beer, too.

Half the bungalow, including the kitchen, is outside. The metal ceiling beams on the porch are custom-made highways which invite rats to scamper into the gaps between the roof and walls that have more holes than my Swiss cheese, which they also stole. At night they cavort above the ceiling, drinking my beer and fornicating, hissing, squeaking and running around like chickens with their heads cut off. I suspect they invite hens up there. Some of the neighborhood chickens have suspiciously beady eyes and thin grey feathers that might actually be hair.

I never remember seeing a rat in America, except in horror movies where they lurk in sewers, drop onto necks, slither underneath clothing, and eat the bad guy, though the word "rat" is frequently used to convey foul concepts. "Rats! [1] Did that ratty [2], rat-faced [3] ratfink [4] with the ratty [5] hair rat [6] on me because I was a rat [7]?" Definitions:

[1] a substitute for offensive words that start with "d", "s" or "f"; [2] bad-tempered, irritable; [3] self-explanatory; [4] informer; [5] teased, messy; [6] tattle; [7] non-union contractor, chiefly during a strike.

After a high-school session of kissy-face while parked by the river in Fargo, North Dakota, I had an embarrassing encounter with a muskrat, a marsh-dweller, four times the size of my nemesis in Thailand. Muskrat in headlights appears on the dirt road. Brave macho man jumps out to impress and protect date by frightening predator. Non-frightened, now raging, predator muskrat rears up on hind legs, bares sharp yellow teeth and screeches while chasing Mr. Macho, panting and sweating, back to the safety of his car and hysterical date, who nearly dies of a laughing attack, not of a muskrat attack.

Rat removal choices are diverse and dependent on the removers' personalities. I chose "catch and kill," purchased Rat Glue Trays, baited them with imported cheddar and peanut butter, and caught seven in two nights. Three more perished a few feet from the porch. I imagined they were seeking final refuge with the rat masses at my bungalow after being poisoned by my neighbors.

"Catch and release" sounds fine for folks with overgrown rodent hearts and a lot of extra time on their hands. I considered this variation: rip rats off the glue plate and stick them to the neighbor's auto tire so they're released a few miles away on the highway.

I've experienced the "catch and eat" phenomena a couple times—1) Outside Bangkok after a major deluge of rain when fried rat stands popped up everywhere next to the flooded lands, and 2) recently on the street in Chiang Khong, a Thai city across the Mekong River from Laos. I could never stomach a rat, but should have set up a stand selling my glue-tray rats with a sign heralding: "Fresh, home-grown rats that stick to your ribs!"

Thai delicacies: fried birds and rats harvested at home (not mine)

Puzzling to me is the "catch and train" option, which I learned about while viewing "pet rat" sites on the web. [A pet mouse, maybe. I had a pet hamster as a kid, but the cat ate it. Okay, I could live with a pet gerbil. But a pet rat? No.] People go on and on about rat care and delve deeply into their quirky behavior with FAQ sheets answering these pressing questions:

"Why do rats pee on each other?" This is a feasible query, but the next one?

"Should I pee on my rat?" [I'm not making this up.]

Or this one? [Look it up yourself if you don't believe me.] "Should I flip my rat over and yell at him?"

Here's a verbatim comment from a deranged ratophile: "Show the little thug who is really in charge. Put some of your urine in a cup and set it aside. Grab the little imp and flip him on his back, aggressively scratch his belly, and then brush your urine on his nose, belly, and sex organs. If he protests, yell: 'No!' Do this several times a day when you feel like it."

No comment. I'll stick with "catch and kill."

When I was planning to come to Asia and had no clue I'd be living in Thailand, my bedtime reading explored diseases to expect and thwart with vaccination shots of massive germ cocktails: malaria from mosquitoes, yellow fever from yellow things, Japanese encephalitis from day-old sushi that makes your brain explode, attornis affidavitis which causes you to yearn to become a lawyer, and, yes, the Black Plague. It still exists in some areas infested by rats. I pulled the covers over my head with a shiver and considered moving back to Fargo. Now I'm wondering if, near the Black Plague entry, there might've been a picture of my bungalow.

In case you're planning on moving here, there's another house for rent in the compound. When the previous tenants left, the landlord ripped off the roof, and found a ten-foot python. It helped control the rats.

~ ~ ~

Shaggy Soi Dog Stories

O F THE ESTIMATED 6,000,000 DOGS living in the country of Thailand, approximately 3,000,000 of them are within earshot of our bedroom. We hear them in the distance, any night, at any time, giving vocal support to the twenty-some hyperactive dogs residing in our general vicinity, who diligently attempt to warn everyone in our postal code of dangers lurking in the darkness: a neighbor returning home, an insect moving, the sunrise on the other side of the globe, or invisible aliens invading from another planet.

"Soi" means "street" in Thai, hence "soi dogs", ordinarily homeless though home-full, because our entire neighborhood is their crash pad. The entrance road to the bungalow dead ends at a circle surrounded by eleven other dwellings, a stream aka murky sewage ditch, exotic plants and trees, bamboo groves, gravel driveways, and no fences, where our own personal soi dogs roam, scavenge, and breed. Only two of these have official homes. An organic, self-sustaining security system, the POD—Pack of Dogs—subsists on buffets of rotting food from tenant garbage bags supplemented by miscellaneous leftovers from the landlord that didn't quite make it into their garbage bags.

Each dog is a father mother brother sister daughter son illegitimate offspring of every other dog and has at least one crippled appendage or visible scar from nasty brawls with the rest of the family. Their total combined brainpower is considerably less than one head of lettuce. I've lived here for four years, but the POD still doesn't recognize me and possibly thinks I'm one of the invading aliens who randomly becomes visible for a few moments every day.

Dead, dormant, or dropped into place from a helicopter?

Their sole remarkable trait is the ability to sleep in the sun when it's a hundred-plus degrees. Imagine putting on a fur coat and lounging on baking gravel or cement for hours, only hauling yourself up to move because the patch of sun you occupied, for some odd reason, slid over a few feet. This astounding skill is useful for a POD committed to harassing the tall, two-legged masters of their domain, because each dog must stretch out precisely in the middle of the drive, wait until a car tire is poised to crush its leg, then slink away while staring the driver in the eye with a pathetic but irritated scowl asking, "You gotta leave *again*? Can't you drive around me… *over there* through the bushes?

What breed are they? Hmm. To be very specific, I would suggest… "Dog." Further classification includes:

1) **Random short-haired "Brown Dogs,"** five severely meek creatures who are always groveling, whimpering, in heat, or recently impregnated by the POD;

2) **The long-haired "Leaf Dog,"** a shaggy lump who sleeps 23/7 while attracting leaves, pine needles, and debris which cling to tacky rasta fur so he, she, or it resembles a compost pile with legs;

3) **The landlord's "Beagle Mutation,"** stunted and stupid with deformed paws sticking out horizontally, which make him look like the ugly kid who always got beat up on the playground in grade school. This trauma created TOAD, or Terminal Ornery Anti-social Disposition. Symptoms: glaring, growling, and the propensity to bite the hand or ankles of anyone who doesn't feed him. Though named "Dang Thai," I call him "Damn Thai" or a raft of other four-letter words, which, unlike "Dang," do not mean "Red." Being the privileged landlord's pet, he's the short, snooty, rich kid on the playground now beaten up by the POD when the landlord's not looking. Damn Thai also hates my wife and I because his nemesis lives with us.

When our neighbors moved away, we adopted, or were adopted by, their adopted dog—a quintessential Thai breed: the "Default Dog." Lanky, sleek, and strong, the landlord never cared for him since he could whip Dang Thai anytime and frequently did. His name is Gluay, which means "banana" in Thai, and sounded cute until we learned he earned it because he likes to lick his banana, particularly when we have visitors. They ask with a WTF look, "Is this *your* dog?"

"No, no. Just a visitor like you." Distract, deflect. "He's his *own* dog, but likes our food and company. Like *you*." Divert. "Want some chips?"

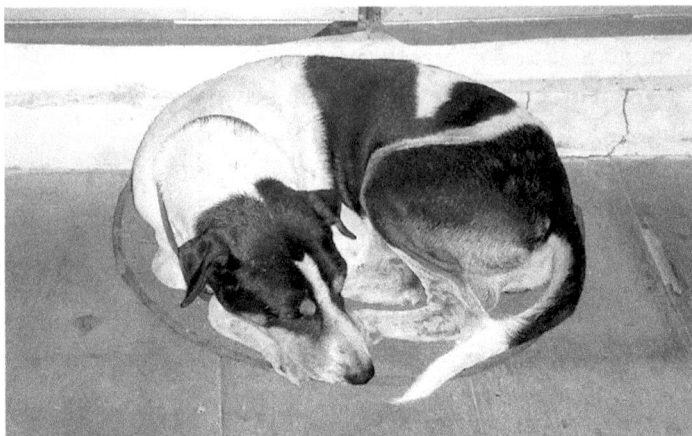

Gluay, our default dog, left behind by default neighbors. His name means "Banana" though "Log" would suit him better.

Gluay will disappear for days and return ready for hugs and pats, stinking like Roadkill Meets Rubbish, but a cool wash, shower, or sponge bath is unlikely. I've tried to coax him under the hose, but might as well attempt to bathe a random pedestrian on the street. He has learned to love us and would probably kill for us, however, the innocent victim might be the internet repairman while we're not home.

The good news? He's our Boss Buffer Dog and keeps the POD at bay. Bad news? Though faithfully alerting us at night of any inaudible sounds or invisible aliens, his bark starts the neighborhood bay, which sparks the village bay, which incites the city of Chiang Mai bay, which ignites the Lampang bay ninety kilometers south, which dominoes five hundred kilometers to Bangkok, etcetera, all night long.

Maybe I'll get some sleep during the day if I can learn the wearing a fur coat while lying on the scorching pavement in the sun trick.

~ ~ ~

The War at Home

PART ONE. BEWARE OF THE BIRDS. In Alfred Hitchcock's classic film *The Birds*, everyday birds begin to harass innocent townsfolk, then peck their eyeballs out, and attempt to eliminate the entire human race. It's starting to happen near Chiang Mai, Thailand in the tiny area of San Sai, specifically in our enclave of bungalows.

They're pretty, but I'd rather see them in the zoo or fried on a plate.

The Problem: My wife and I spend 90% of our home time in the kitchen, which is outside and open to the deck. The marauding band of twenty-some ragged chickens in the neighborhood would prefer to live there as well. Though profoundly stupid, they're getting smarter, possibly from their recent diet of human and dog food instead of their standard sticks and stones.

Besides their midnight crowing to alert us the sun may be rising in Italy, or at noon to remind us the sun is still up in Thailand, their main activity is the ingestion of anything vaguely organic in the general vicinity which they promptly poop onto the table. Too many times I've calmly entered the kitchen to confront a huge squawking, flying apparition above my head, causing me to nearly poop in my pants. They lurk in the ceiling rafters, and now, like the famous playground scene featuring the crazed crows in *The Birds*, they perch in the trees next to our bungalow at night, prepared to poop on my head, infect me with bird flu, and then peck out my eyes.

The Quick Fix: Slay them! Though I eat chickens and recently dreamed I ripped the head off the most obnoxious rooster, I'm totally uncomfortable with the murdering part of the process. I've only shot living creatures with a camera. *Face it, Scottie: you're chicken.* I've stooped to rock flinging, but I'm worried that, in an uncontrollable frenzy, I'll only murder my neighbor's car windshield. I didn't want to be like my former USA neighbor who snapped during his extended war with squirrels in his house. Enraged, he scrambled into the attic and blasted away with his shotgun. After his unbridled aggression, he still had squirrels who now had more entrances and exits, then a month later, a new roof and a bill for $8,000.

The Complications: No one I know claims the chickens—the landlord doesn't like them, but makes no move to remove them. The twenty-some ragged dogs ignore them because they could be distant relatives. I do not want to solidify my reputation as Demented Foreigner by demanding assassination or running around like a chicken with its head cut off trying to catch chickens with their heads firmly in place.

The Solution: Clandestinely, I must catch these chickens and release them in another location. I'd be willing to pay their airfare to India if I could indeed catch them. My web search for "catch a chicken" produced a popular computer game, a bluegrass picking tune, and strange snaring techniques used by farmers with relatively tame chickens and pens for them to go back to… the chickens, not the farmers. Bizarre farmer posts included—and I didn't edit this advice whatsoever—"sneak into the barn, cover yourself with straw, and make authentic chicken noises until a chicken is tricked into walking up to you."

Our local chickens are wild, Thai, and wily, and I'm not going to do this twenty-some times, besides, I don't have a barn. Though only possessing the birdbrain power of a fence post, these fine-feathered fiends have learned to sprint away frantically upon seeing me, even when I'm not screaming, flailing my arms, or throwing firecrackers.

Please contact me if you know of a local chicken SWAT team to remove the fowl invaders at night, perhaps Ninja warriors dressed in black, but definitely covert, non-violent, and Buddhist.

Lessons Learned Online: The splendid "Hummer EZ Chicken Harvester" will wade through a crush of chickens, sweep hundreds into a trough, and deposit them in cages," but it must cost four times as much as my neighbor's new roof.

The "eggs-citing" World Chicken Festival held in Kentucky features "Redneck Games." (Rednecks are American hill tribe members who burn their front yards rather than mow them, have family trees that do not fork, and live in states with laws stating: "When a couple gets divorced, they're still legally brother and sister.") Besides fowl events, you can enter the Watermelon Seed Spitting Contest, Blind-fold Bobbing for Pig's Feet, the Burping Contest (length and song recognition) and the Cornhole Tournament. (I won't attempt to guess the Cornhole rules nor is this respectable newspaper likely to print them.)

Back-up Plan: What do you get when you cross a chicken and a pit bull? Only the pit bull.

P ART TWO: ABOUT A YEAR LATER. In quintessential American style, we're engaged in a pointless war against a paltry kingdom of migratory natives. Our stern words have escalated to vicious threats; our guns have no effect; our recent bombing tactics seem fruitless. Fearless bands of guerrilla forces pillage our food supply daily while pooping strategically on the table, benches, chairs, countertop, and sink outside on the kitchen deck.

I'd never eat Chicken Feet Stew, but I'm dreaming of making some.

The Chicken War is still in full swing with thirty-some to two odds, with no help whatsoever from Gluai—Thai for "Banana"—our skinny multi-breed dog, who we should rename Log to match his mental capacity and military ambition. Immobile, as if bolted to the floor, Banana Log ignores the enemy and silently stares as his idiotic masters scamper around shooting massive squirt guns and embarrassing themselves in front of the neighbors.

Besides the blatant thievery of our rations and the psychological warfare of incessant clucking and cock-a-doodling at any time of the day or night—way before dawn, an inch from our window, one yard from our ears—the chickens' goal is to infect us with bird flu by surrounding us with gelatinous black poop, which we'll through the pores of our bare feet. I'm certain the Geneva Convention outlawed this form of biological warfare. Or was it the Swiss Army Knife Convention that proclaimed all wars must be fought with corkscrews, inefficient scissors, plastic toothpicks, and tweezers?

My mate gave up the gun for an arsenal of Chinese fire-crackers with impressive names—*Thunder King, Double Bangers, The Black Bomb,* and *Dancing Frogs.* At the slightest squawking sound, she flings these in every direction, terrifying Log the Dog, who flees the deck for the rest of the day to avoid being pooped upon by the Poulet Predators pilfering his provisions. Last week his orange dog bowl was full of dry dog food when we left the bungalow, but upon returning in the afternoon—and I'm not making this up—it was gone: the food and the bowl. A banana on the counter (the fruit, not the dog) had been pecked beyond recognition, and was covered with a thousand ants, although they weren't pooping anything large enough for us to see.

The chicken regiment is divided into three distinct battalions: the standard White Storm Troopers; the Checkered Metallic Marauders, whose cackles and screeches seem to emanate from unlubricated living machines; and the Giant Motley Fighting Cocks, standing gnarly and tall above the troops like basketball players.

One fact puts us at a great disadvantage during combat—no matter what brand they are, chickens only have five working brain cells, about four fewer than the dog who logs in at about nine cells on an abnormally alert day. These five cells control the birds' entire repertoire of bodily functions: 1) walk, 2) squawk, 3) eat, 4) excrete, 5) lay. Hens lay eggs; roosters lay hens. If you've ever seen a rooster perform its manly mating ritual, you know the act only lasts about three seconds because there's just not that much DNA information to transfer. Without an essential sixth brain cell to house a memory bank, these chickens have no recollection that our general vicinity is a danger zone inhabited by feral human maniacs. With typical Thai enthusiasm for fireworks, these cuckoo cocks appear to revel in the explosions, and I swear their cackling sounds like gleeful laughter as they sprint undercover into the neighbor's garden.

This Memory Out Of Order Syndrome (or MOOOS) reminds me of the night of heifer torture in my bright purple sleeping bag on a hilltop under the full moon at a friend's farm in Virginia. They had one young cow, who also had a five-cell brain, with each cell controlling one of its five stomachs. I'd wake to hot bovine breath on my neck, flail my arms to shoo away Bessie, and she'd lurch off to one side of the field. Again and again, while engrossed in serene rumination, she'd notice me anew, drool, and imagine, "Lookee here! A purple croissant! I bet it tastes good with grass!" Bessie learned nothing during that endless night of repetition of lookee here, hot breath, flail, lurch, ruminate, lookee here, hot breath, flail, lurch, ruminate…

My mate and I aren't violent killers. We're trying to find a gentler solution to this dilemma by considering alternative schemes: trade in Log for a fleet of pet foxes, build an electric fence around the entire bungalow, or duct tape a few hens to the landlord's back bumper. That last option isn't particularly humane, but you must realize what kind of barbaric beaks we're bearing arms against. I scattered barbecued chicken wings around the porch as a possible deterrent, but a rabid pack of live poultry picked Aunt Henrietta's bones clean. It's a chicken-eat-chicken world.

If I disappear, you might find me wearing a straight jacket in the Bird Flu Ward, tired and feathered, backed into a corner by the SPCA—the Society for the Prevention of Chicken Atrocities, a group of inmates on spindly legs craning their necks forward like birds and then stepping up parallel with their heads—as I clutch a handful of Dancing Frogs, (perhaps alive, perhaps fireworks), clearly demonstrating, as does the construction of and the mere existence of this final sentence (the words in this paragraph, not the court order committing me to the asylum), that I did indeed lose it (my mind, and the war).

~ ~ ~

Building Blockheads

THE SKILLS REQUIRED TO CONSTRUCT delicate, multi-roofed, exotic buildings in Thailand are remarkable, but these remarks are only about the semi-brainless builders regularly inflicted on me personally—blockheads. My dictionary says "blockheads" are idiots, but in Thailand, I prefer to go with the acronym **B.L.O.C.K.H.E.A.D.S.**— **B**asic **L**ack **O**f **C**onstruction **K**nowledge, **H**eavy **E**quipment, **A**nd **D**ecent **S**caffolding.

These workers seem to have vast pools of intelligence in their heads surrounded by black holes of ignorance. Coming from America where a raft of laws require steel hats, steel-toed boots, and steel scaffolding bolted together with steel screws, I'm in awe of the rickety bamboo nightmares loosely lashed together, several stories up the side of a structure, where sandaled laborers balance on bamboo beams instead of sturdy walkways or platforms.

Scaffolding in Asia tied together with twine and wires:
"Hey, bamboo's cheap. And it's easy to replace the dead workers."

A foreigner friend, new to Thailand, approached some workers and nervously attempted to communicate that their Tinkertoy framework looked unsafe. The foreman pointed out that they'd tied every joint together with 2, count 'em, *two*, thin strips of brightly colored plastic twine.

I marvel at the contractor who arrives with a truck full of random men who mix cement with their bare feet in a pool on the ground, erect an entire building, with no plans, while I'm taking a shower. And then leave a concrete abomination next to the door that invariably shreds skin from my toes.

With my financial help, my landlord agrees to enlist her personal blockheads to remodel a wooden shed into a modern office/studio. Because this will house computers and

Thai wiring is absolutely, positively, and negatively shocking.

music equipment, I request grounded, three-prong outlets to prevent lightning or rogue electrical surges from melting them into expensive metal blocks. Once my twenty-some, three-holed outlets are in place, I plug things in and receive a hair-raising shock. I summon a "real" electrician and learn the problem. Good news? Throughout my office building, I have three-holed outlets. Bad news? None are grounded. They are only "aired," as in "erred." Why?

"Foreigner like holes? I give him holes!"

While installing the telephone line, the landlord's block-heads drill several holes completely through the building wall, stuff a cord into one hole, and leave all the other gaping peepholes intact. *Natural lighting or air-conditioning, perhaps? Convenient passageways for mosquitoes to enter and harass me at night? No.*

"Foreigner like holes? I give him more holes!"

The metal door/window blockhead installs a sliding glass door and presents me with a miniscule key, almost flexible, like the tin forks in Thailand that bend when you stick them into Jello. The key locks it for a moment, but a slight movement of the door releases the lock.

He's quite perturbed when I complain how easily the door can be opened. After he "tests" it with two fingers, using about as much force required to pick up an ant without crushing it, he announces, "Door work good."

I give his "locked" door a medium shake, and it opens.

His nasty reply: "You do that and you break it."

Let's see now… thousands of dollars of equipment are in view behind a glass door, but a robber will gingerly jiggle it only once before giving up? Hmm, I wonder if my contractor's friend is the robber who'll be visiting later on tonight?

Considering the fact that a stiff wind could open my windows and doors, I find a contractor who is friendly, inexpensive, and supposedly competent, but only another blockhead in disguise. I select the color and a lovely pattern from his hundreds of designs for security bars; he measures and returns a week later to install the goods. Luckily, an hour after he arrives, I inspect the progress. His blockhead army is savagely hammering the ill-measured, one-centimeter-too-large, metal bars into the window frames, cracking the walls as chunks of concrete crash onto the floor.

"Yoot! Yoot!" I yell, "Stop! Stop!" though many other four-letter English words come to mind that I haven't learned in Thai. What did he use to measure the frames? A snake that grew by the time he got back to his shop? Savvy or stupid workers exist worldwide, but why do I only attract the morons? Like minds attract like minds? (Don't answer that.) When I was a kid, I had a fun game called "Blockhead": a bunch of multi-colored, weirdly-shaped, wooden pieces we'd take turns stacking, like Jenga in reverse. If you knock the pile over, you lose.

I still play this in Thailand, but now living blockheads stack their own blocks, secure them insecurely with duct tape, plastic twine, and sticky stuff, then leave, so I lose when I use, and the building falls down.

~ ~ ~

Painful Painting

D URING MY PREVIOUS LIFE as a painter, I learned the value of newspapers, masking tape, and plastic tarps to prevent destruction of my clients' goods, and the need for powerful solvents for routine or catastrophic clean up. Varsol was my personal favorite, respected for its power to remove paint from brushes or any surface, and to slowly dissolve skin attached to fingers.

The four basic categories of painters are the same in Thailand and America:

1) Real Painters, as in professionals wearing white uniforms, who understand preparation techniques, use Varsol judiciously, and, since they've been smelling spirits all day, drink heavily from dusk till dawn.

2) Construction Guys, as in burly men wearing low-ride jeans that expose their hairy buttocks, who can build whatever you want with no blueprints other than mental plans which you can't see, verify, or sign, who might have heard of Varsol, but use gasoline instead.

3) Human Beings, as in random people delivered in pickup trucks, whose only qualification for the job is the ability to climb into a truck, and have never heard of Varsol, or the words "clean up."

4) Sightless Morons, as in sightless morons, who *drink* Varsol for breakfast.

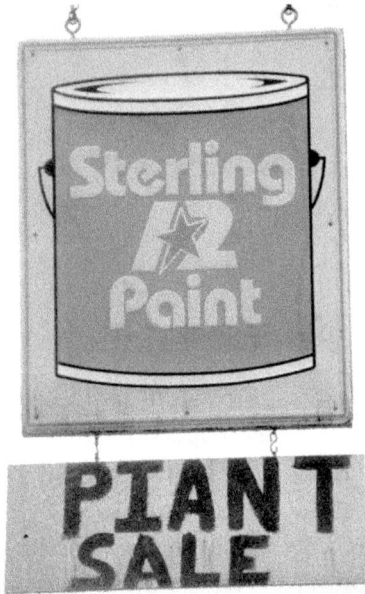

I can piant anything! Wait, y'all! What's that there rule again?
"I" before "A" except after "P"?

While I was away from my Thai bungalow for a couple days, the landlady commanded her horde of Construction Guys to remove a rancid smelling, unidentified corpse inside the wall. My bungalow had no walkways above the ceilings, only a trap door that allowed me to poke my head into the crawl space and peer timidly at dark, unreachable areas inhabited by spiders the size of auto tires. They tore apart the ceiling so they could look down inside the hollow wall and fish out the offending creature with hooks.

Upon returning, the odor had subsided, and the new ceiling painted, as evidenced by a thousand, hardened, white paint splotches on picture frames, tables, the couch, live orchids, and on the teak floor.

As an unwanted added attraction, she'd also employed Sightless Morons to smear paint in the outdoor kitchen and deck area. The patio ceiling now sported a coat of diluted white primer apparently applied haphazardly in eleven minutes. Some walls were covered, some not. The deck was dabbled with paint specks, and one poster mounted on the wall had a four-inch stripe of white paint *down the middle.*

After I showed Mrs. Landlady the devastation *her* minions had caused on *her* property, the Morons returned the next morning, again sneaking in while I was away. Standing on the teak bench, they must have flung paint toward the ceiling, right above several pairs of jeans and t-shirts draped over the back of the bench—not my personal choice for drop cloths. I strangled them with my jeans.

Varsol saved my professional painting ass twice in the '70s. I had a contract to paint a 48-unit motel, and my crew was a ragtag group of Category Three workers: artistic Human Beings, very clever in their own creative endeavors, but during those leisure days of their lives, mainly hungry, long-haired mavericks who needed cash.

Ernest, a phenomenal sculptor and former art director of the *Saturday Evening Post*, finishes painting the final panel around the second-floor balcony, using industrial-strength enamel paint, a vile liquid. With a victory cheer he leaps off his ladder—from two meters above the ground—which catapults his full pail of white enamel upward. It remains motionless in the air for a split-second before splattering onto the new parking lot, poured that very day.

As the paint spreads over the *black* virgin asphalt, I shout "Varsol!"

It takes gallons and brooms and hours to turn the entire parking lot *dark brown.*

My shoulder-length hair was unpopular with uniformed officials, and I had a job working right outside their newly constructed headquarters. While painting the railing by the handicap ramp at the new Virginia Division of Motor Vehicles, populated by an army of rednecks disguised as patrolmen, I was very uncomfortable—an alien. And my truck license plates had expired—an illegal alien.

I place a sizable sheet of cardboard under the railing, and meticulously inch it along while painting and attempting to be invisible. Moments from completion, a devil gust of wind lifts the cardboard and my gallon of paint into the air, spewing black enamel onto their snow-white sidewalk and newly laid sod.

I scream internally. *"Varsol!"*

I quickly turn the entire sidewalk grey, clean the innocent, but outraged blades of grass with toxic chemicals, and move to another state. Thirty-five years later, nothing has grown in that spot. I doubt Varsol is sold here in Thailand, but I'll bet the cheapest Thai whiskey you can find should do the trick.

~ ~ ~

Opening Axe

O PENING ACTS appear to have very glamorous jobs. They perform for a few minutes, watch the rest of the show for free, and then rub elbows with the star. *Wrong.* The audience comes to see someone else and the opening act just gets in the way. The promoter pays the opener as little as possible and only cares about the headliner. The star is an elite recluse who performs and leaves. The opening act is an unnecessary diversion, someone who hasn't quite made it, an insignificant person who only matters to his (or her) date, or mother.

Where opening acts end up after dying on stage: "We'all might could chop 'em up to fit in our li'l doggie caskets."

Once in a while, fate let me hang out with a few stars. I opened for Dr. Timothy Leary—the LSD guru of the '60s and '70s, a fiercely intelligent, pioneer and psychedelic psychologist, a globe-trotting character arrested often enough to experience the inside of 29 different prisons worldwide, and described by President Richard Nixon as "the most dangerous man in America." In the '80s he toured with his *Cosmic Comedy* show, heavy on the chemically induced theme very "in" in his day. Some drug culture terms are still in use, though the meanings have changed. In the '70s, "drug testing" was never something you feared at work, merely a recreational activity on Saturday night. "Hey, man, I'll test any drugs you got!"

Leary had a different slant and new punctuation on the slogan coined by First Lady Nancy Reagan: "Just say no to drugs." The doctor's irreverent slant: "When someone asks if you want a drug, just say, 'No, two drugs!'"

At a club in Milwaukee, Dr. Tim and I once shared a dressing room before the show. Many of his fans were Night of the Living Drug casualties stranded in the past. My job description of "opening act" broadened to security guard as I barricaded the door with my back. Tim's demented devotees—controlled by brains reduced to sludge stuck to the bottom of their skulls—pounded on the door, offering him psychedelic mushrooms in return for autographs on his books and record albums they'd brought with them.

An older man claimed to be his friend from their army days during the '40s, so Tim said, "Let 'em in." The rotund, suit 'n' tied, very straight, bald guy sat on the couch and explained how they'd met, etcetera, on and on and on.

Leary's eyes glazed over, but he clearly heard the dude was *Doctor* So and So. "Sorry," Tim said, "but I don't remember you... You're a doctor, eh? Got any ludes on ya?"

(For the uninitiated, that's Quaaludes: an addictive, central nervous system depressant that acts as a powerful sedative and hypnotic. A great sleeping pill, perfect for people who never want to wake up. Recreationally, it was fun to down one, sit in a chair, and try to get up again.)

The actual show that night was very strange: the first time I'd ever performed for vegetables. The motley audience members, several obviously in (or on) ecstasy, giggled too long at some jokes and guffawed at places where there weren't any. I imagine some laughed three times at a joke: once when they heard people around them laughing, again when someone explained it to them, and a third time at home puffing weed when they finally got it.

After the concert, Tim and I snuck away, sucked down spaghetti and Pabst Blue Ribbon beers, and closed down the restaurant. I poured him into a taxi. Getting lubricated with a legend was a memorable night for me, but I doubt if Dr. Drunken Leary ever wrote about, or even remembered, imbibing with one of the Jones boys.

Some nights were downright dangerous. A booking agent once sent me, the musician-comedian crossbreed, to a major rock club in the depths of Georgia to open for Leon Redbone near the height of his fame in the mid '80s. By nine p.m. the place was packed with 350 southern belles and good ol' boys drinking shots o' moonshine from bottles sporting hand-written labels that the bartenders kept hidden under the counter.

At nine-thirty, the advertised show time, I asked the owner if I should start.

He said, "Jus' wait'll Ah tell ya."

At ten-fifteen from somewhere behind stage, he welcomed everyone via the PA system. "We'll start real soon y'all, so jus' relax and drink yourse'f silly!"

This distracted the antsy patrons for a while, but soon their yelling turned ornery. A mammoth Neanderthal man with two or three very impressive teeth staggered toward the stage slurring, "Where's Leon? We'all wanna see Leon!"

It became apparent that the owner was postponing the show so he could sell more booze. Angry hordes drink more to quell their rage—a callous but effective sales technique developed during the Mid-Evil Ages. I also realized my name was not on the $20 tickets, the posters, the marquee, nor on the tip of anyone's tongues between their bouts with Southern Discomfort. Three people in the club knew about the opening act: Leon, the owner, and me. The only place I could find my name was on the Scott toilet fixtures in the men's room where it always is, and where my career would most likely be later on that night.

Around eleven p.m.—an hour and a half later than he'd promoted—the owner announced the show from the safety of the shadows offstage. The audience went berserk. They heard nothing above the sound of their own cheers until he bellowed, "Let's give a big Georgia welcome to Scott Jones!"

The room got quiet for a moment while the dumbfounded crowd tried to grasp what was happening. If any words still slogged through their dying brain cells, they must have been, "Wha' the fuck's a Scott Jones? I'll give 'im a warm welcome rope 'round his neck!"

As I skittered toward the stage, everyone chanted, punctuating their curses by slamming shot glasses and beer bottles on the tables. "Leon! Leon! Leon!"

I wished I were anywhere else in the universe—in front of a firing squad or underneath a safe falling from a tall building. *Lord, take me now! Quickly!* In show biz lingo, I wanted to kill, but was about to die on stage. I don't remember much about the rest of the night except: 1) only a couple of projectiles flew toward the stage, 2) none of them hit me, 3) the Neanderthal men let me live for the longest half-hour of my life, and 4) the owner said my check would be in the mail. It hasn't come yet, but hey, it's only been 30 years.

~ ~ ~

Police Farce

YOU MIGHT THINK THE PERFORMANCE is the hardest part of cross-country touring for an artist. *Wrong.* The show's a snap compared with trying to stay awake while driving through Nebraska, surviving New York hecklers, or avoiding policemen. Lawmen inherently don't trust entertainers. They might like a few, but preferably on TV or in another state. Artists in the flesh bring to mind nasty preconceptions—sex, drugs, and rock 'n' roll. Sex is something a father wants to keep from his daughter as long as possible. Drugs are bad unless enough are involved to warrant a mini-series starring the policeman. Rock 'n' roll is merely another way of disturbing the peace. Police enforce law and order—artists induce awe and disorder.

Entertainers are guilty until proven innocent. Some states are way too serious about their speed limits. Pennsylvania patrolman have the choice of sentencing speeders to the electric chair or shooting them on site. Okay, so I've broken the law for hours/days/weeks/years at a time. 68 mph in a 65 zone. *Or was it 78?* Artists must speed regularly to make up time lost trying to find concert halls at the end of the trip. The only place I never speed is in my garage. Speed Limit Zero. I haven't broken the law all afternoon.

Upon leaving my home state, I became a foreigner, a migrant worker… no, an alien life form. This bumper sticker did not enhance the impressions of me held by anyone wearing a uniform.

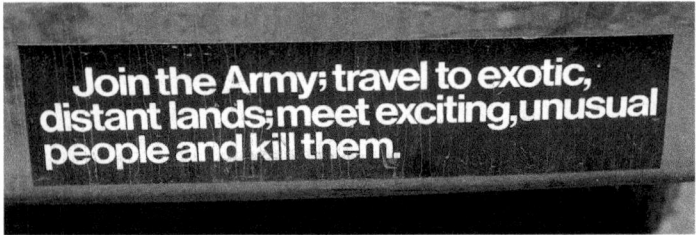

Join the Army; travel to exotic, distant lands; meet exciting, unusual people and kill them.

Pulling into a whistle-stop speck of a town with the one and only traffic cop staring out of a donut shop, I was an unusual person from a distant land, and he wanted a reason to eliminate me. Somehow he knew I'd been speeding or would speed sooner than later. These crossroads in the South, where star-spangled confederate flags yet wave in towns where everyone has the same last name, are home to the enormous policemen, larger than life because their office is the donut shop, and their sworn duty is to test every batch to protect the public from possible poisoning.

When I lived in North Carolina, I encountered an enormous sheriff named Bobby Bear. (His father was a grizzly, and his mother's name was Robert.) He had thirteen teeth, eight fingers, and about twenty hairs trying to escape from underneath his cap as if his scalp were unraveling. His well-fed head sat on a throng of chins, like a basketball dropped onto a stack of flapjacks. Bobby's jumbo belly protruded in *Guinness Book of World Records* style, barely restrained by the iron buttons and steel thread of his uniform. No need to pin his badge onto this prodigious ledge of flesh—he could set it next to the soda and Strawberry Frosted Cruller resting on his chest. His tremendous torso defied gravity, balancing precariously on top of two spindly legs, like a huge ham hock on Q-Tips. I doubt if he'd seen his feet for years.

We often debated this question. Does he have any bones in his body, or merely calcified fat? He could've been cast as the monster in *The Blob* movie. (His badge read BOB, but only because someone forgot the "L.")

Big Bob's duties didn't include running after criminals, only donut elimination and sharp-shooting speeders with his radar gun, both of which he performed simultaneously in the comfort of his patrol car. Bob didn't walk much, but when he did, he looked like water walking, and drifted forward precariously, his flapping thighs struggling to find their way around his liquid stomach.

A friend from Chicago stopped in town, bought a bag of donuts, and drove off. Within one block, he was either speeding or escaping with a couple of the Sheriff's favorites when the siren screamed. My friend pulled over to the curb.

From the opposite side of the street, Sheriff Bob motioned his prey over to the patrol car. "Where y'all from, boy?" Chief Bob slurred, then spit on the pavement.

"I'm all from Chicago," my friend said, ready to bribe him with the bag of donuts.

"Lemme see yer lahsense," Bob hissed.

My friend waited as the Sheriff scrutinized his license.

"Y'all said y'all's from Sheecahgo. What're y'all doin' with this here Ill-in-noise driver's lahsense?"

Would you laugh at Mr. Bob? I doubt it, but much holding of the breath and severe pursing of the lips would be necessary to stop your guffaws. Would you try to explain Chicago is a city in Illinois and not a state? Maybe, but you'd probably call him a butthead, or worse. This incident convinced us Bob only had one bone in his body... his brain.

As an unofficial representative for all drivers, I'd like to take a few moment and thank the creative officials with the law enforcement and highway departments who are responsible for these caring reminders along the road...

55 means 55. Thank you so much for clarifying that,
Mr. Policeman. What does 35 mean? And 25, sir?

7? Are you kidding? Please tell me you mean 70?
I don't even have a 7 on my speedometer.

Ah, yes. Forgot again. No driving in the ditch.
Thanks. This keeps slipping my mind.

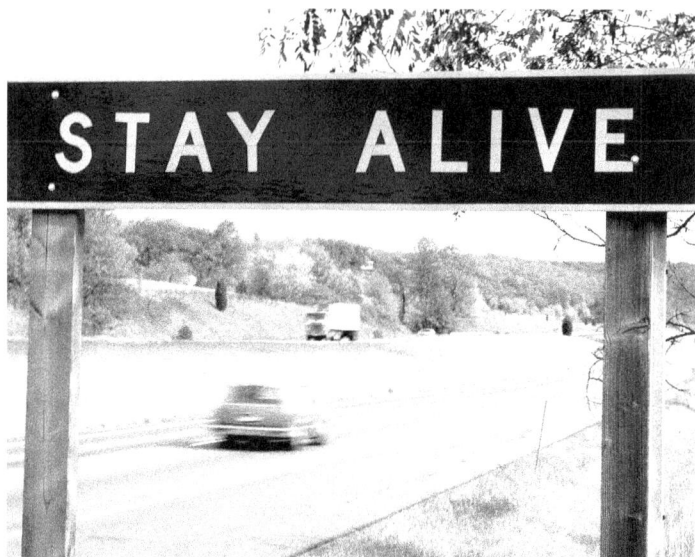

And damn! And I can never remember this.

If you come upon a man bouncing across the street on his head, stop and look carefully. He might not have any hands or feet.

NEXT
48 MILES

I've followed drunk drivers in the past, but for 48 fucking miles?

When you're walking on the sidewalk,
beware of people driving on the sidewalk.

I don't care how much you've had to drink!
You can't pee on the shoulder!

When you're driving up the roof of a house,
beware of cars coming up the other side.

If you're in a rest area and see a one-armed, 400-pound,
footless, hairless woman, walking a sausage on wheels
with a Pac-Man head, do not get out of your car!

~ ~ ~

Alarming Affairs

Your RECURRING NIGHTMARE: Dawn breaks and you don't want to face your stress-filled life, crawl down to your dead end job, and hang out with coworkers you hate. A monster alarm clock buzzes and blinks incessantly, has large wheels, a mind of its own, and scampers away from you. Naked and trembling, you chase it around the room, trying to punch it out to avoid punching into work on Monday, that grim day on which you must spend one seventh of your life. You can hear it, but you can't find it; your blood pressure rises; your screams wake the rest of the family…

For fifty bucks you can turn this horrible dream into a horrible reality, every day of your life with "The Runaway Alarm Clock" from Hammacher Schlemmer, the company that also offers you "The Synchronized Light and Sound Inflatable Holiday Carolers" for $390, and several hundred other exclusive items for the idle rich that begin with "The." You have to read the exact catalog blurb to believe it:

"This alarm clock rolls away and hides when you hit its snooze button, and continues to emit a random pattern of beeps and slashes, encouraging drowsy sleepers to seek it out in order to shut it off. Two rubber wheels allow it roll off

your nightstand from a height of two feet when it sounds its alarm, so there is no mistaking that it is time to get up. The wheels can move over wood floors and carpet, so the Runaway Alarm Clock can maneuver into unexpected corners, increasing the challenge to find it. Wheels may be disabled in case of extreme frustration."

Life contains enough uncontrollable stress without paying to add another dose, first thing in the morning. Who needs one of these? "Okay, my wife and I are sick of each other, and she's ready to leave me, so if I run around nude like a blithering idiot, this might put her over the edge!" It could be an effective deterrent in the guest room to prevent your in-laws from ever visiting again.

In quintessential American marketing strategy, the next product advertised in the catalog is the antidote to the poison. [*This technique is like your local drug salesmen selling crack with a side of Prozac.*] Does it comfort you to know these caring companies are trying to help you after trying to kill you?

"The Stress Relieving Wrist Band provides natural relief for stress without the use of medication [*unlike the valium you'll require to calm down after your naked romps*] because it gently massages and stimulates pressure points located at the inner left wrist, helping to improve sleep quality [*disturbed by the anxious anticipation of the next morning's bedlam*]. Similar to acupuncture, but without needles, the device transmits gentle electrical signals, convincing the brain [*or what's left of it after your self-induced dawn frenzies*] that all is steady, reducing stress [*caused by the runaway clock and your children disowning you*]. With a water-resistant band [*in case you're sleeping in the ocean*]."

I only remember four alarms when I was a kid. 1) Fire alarms at school when we'd race out of class, get rowdy outside at 20 below zero, and pray the school would burn down to warm us up. I never used 2) my wind-up alarm clock since 3) Dad's clock radio—volume set on Wake The Dead—would blare the local morning talk show three inches from his comatose head and jerk me into semi-consciousness in my bedroom down the hall. 4) Tornado sirens screamed several times during summers to trigger the recommended precautionary action: "Flee to the northwest corner of the basement, sit down, put your head between your legs, and kiss your ass goodbye."

Decades later, electronic alarms mushroomed. My Casio nerd watch had four alarms, but no way to record any associated events or duties, which I would invariably forget. I'd just know it was time to do *something*.

My Casio had a temperature alarm—for what? Hibernating bears? "Honey, what temperature do you want to get up tomorrow? 75? Come on, it's Sunday. Let's sleep until 80." This might have be appropriate for balmy Thailand, but in my home state of North Dakota, right next to Canada, if you set your alarm in September for 80 degrees, you wouldn't get up until the following June.

The watch also had a depth gauge, in case I found myself on the deck of a luxurious yacht trying to impress an exotic woman who would never ask even in my wildest dreams, "Hey, stud muffin. The water looks cold. I wonder what the temperature is at 100 feet?"

"No problem," I'd say, "I'll find out for you right now!" and jump over the railing, never to be seen again.

Cell phones took us to a new alarming era with rude boors in restaurants who select the Obnoxious Ear-Piercing Ring, then shout into the phone as if they didn't have a fucking phone, and their caller is on the opposite end of a soccer field. I loved the clandestine "Vibrate" alarm. I'd keep my phone in the front pocket of my jeans and tell my girlfriend, "Please call me whenever you want, sweetheart. If I don't answer, just let it ring."

Thank god I now have smartphone alarms to remind me I'm cooking or watering the lawn, otherwise my food and its pan would fuse into pure carbon and a seven-kilo water bill would be delivered in a wheelbarrow after I'd created the Bay of Thailand in my yard.

What I really need are tiny location alarms which fasten to the three things I lose daily—okay, fine, hourly—pens, keys, and glasses. I buy pens by the case, but might as well throw them out the car window so I have some idea of their general location. The key stall guy at the market loves me because I buy in bulk. "I'll need a box each of these four keys. Could I please have them tomorrow since I'm almost out of the boxes I bought last week?"

I'm farsighted, but see better without glasses for nearby things, so I constantly take the specs off and lay them down wherever, whenever. I have to rely on my own personal GPS—Gluteus-maximus Pulverizing System—which locates my glasses when I sit on them, creating a flattened style which might fit someone with no cheek bones and one ear sitting two inches lower than the other.

Personal computerized alarms have definitely gotten out of hand and can drive you out of your mind. A few years ago I bought a new Mac laptop during a trip to America. When I got back to Thailand, the computer chirped randomly, like that incessant, irritating sound when the batteries in your smoke alarm are fading. I checked the Mac trouble-shooting FAQs; I talked with friends who had Macs; I joined chat groups to find the cause. No one had experienced it. I documented which programs were loading when it occurred, but no pattern to the noise appeared. Months later I noticed a tiny throbbing icon in the shape of a ladybug at the top of my screen and clicked on it. *Great.* A program I'd loaded in America called "Weatherlite" was warning me of approaching thunderstorms, blizzards, and tornadoes—12,000 miles away in Minneapolis, Minnesota. No need to bend over and kiss it—I was a complete ass.

I Skype with an editor in the USA. Also a medium/psychic and bookkeeper/accountant, she's a living non sequitur/left-right brain paradox somehow balancing precariously between several worlds. Whenever we connect for our late night sessions, she has a problem with a chirping smoke alarm, and I watch her get up to check it.

"New batteries didn't help, so it must be my neighbor's smoke alarm," she reasons, "because I can hear them get up to fix their smoke alarm through these thin walls that consist of two coats of paint."

"Is your surge protector squeaking?" I ask.

"I checked it. It works fine." Perplexed, she tells me, "Nothing I do stops the noise. I can't quite place where the sound is. I stand over here, and it comes from over there, or vice versa."

I think, but don't say, *Well, that's what it must be like living in alternate dimensions.*

Yesterday she hears the sounds again and says, "It only seems to happen when I Skype with you."

As she gets up to pinpoint the problem, I imagine, *Somehow this is my fault. These days everything is my fault.* When she returns, I/we realize the sound is coming from *my dying smoke alarm*, squawking every few minutes, captured by my high-tech microphone and amplified through her high-tech speakers. I am the one living in another dimension, oblivious to this sound six feet from my ears! Mutual hysteria ensues.

I rip my smoke alarm off the ceiling and remove the battery. "Why don't you knock on your neighbor's door and say, 'Sorry. We've been hearing a smoke alarm in Thailand.'" More hysteria.

Soon she says, puzzled, "I'm still hearing the chirping."

I look around and see that my office window is open; two mynah birds sit on the sill, imitating my smoke alarm. Once more, I accept the blame. "It's two birds chattering away in the window. Why don't you call your neighbors again and claim, 'Now I'm hearing mynah birds in Asia.'" Our laughter becomes painful.

If the neighbors had heard she was a bookkeeper, they might have thought "zookeeper" instead and closed the door quickly. If they'd heard she was a psychic, they'd certainly think "psychotic" and soon a SWAT team of men in white suits would be knocking on her door.

I know I am a bad person, but I do get great satisfaction from riding my pounding Harley motorcycle through fancy hotel parking lots and setting off car alarms like in a movie when an alien force moves through the city. And I'm secretly tickled to know my smoke alarm annoys my friend's neighbors on the other side of the world.

I am thankful I don't have any medical alarms surgically implanted in my body like the guy whose pacemaker starts chirping. He races to the emergency room and the doctor runs some tests.

Nervous patient: "Doc, what's happening?"

Patient doctor: "I'm sorry to tell you this, but you've only got about 10 to live."

Patient: "10 what? Years? Months?"

Doctor: "9... 8... 7... 6... 5...

~ ~ ~

The Village Idiot

URING THE 17 YEARS I'VE LIVED IN THAILAND, I've visited "home" eight times, once for two months, which seemed to last a little longer than forever. The Boss Springstein wrote a song: "I'm a long-gone Daddy in the USA, born in the USA." Those words don't fit for me anymore. I'm a long-gone Expat from the USA, foreign in the USA. The longer I'm gone, the more I feel like an alien when I'm there. Or just the village idiot.

My last possession in America, a Harley Sportster, dictated my baggage requirements for a recent trip to the USA: riding gear and six bags for the bike. I chose my black leather jacket, chaps, gloves, and boots because they'll keep me warmer than comfortable mesh gear when it's only 45°F where I'm going. With tape, red rope, bathroom scales, lashing and cursing, everything fit in two massive, multi-colored, Thai plastic bags, the preferred style of refugees worldwide.

After my fifty-some hour trip to New York, Michael, my college roommate from a past life was waiting at the airport for me—a mentally challenged nomad with eyes like two burn holes in a blanket, smelling worse than a soccer locker room, smiling weakly while dragging my weird motley bags. I'm sure I tried to get into the driver's seat (the passenger seat in left-is-right Thailand) and scream in terror because Michael drives on the right, the "wrong" side of the road.

He poured me into his home where I collapsed for a couple hours before joining family and friends for dinner and drinks till two in the morning as my last three working brain cells devolved into sewage.

Twelve hours later, I partially revived one brain cell, and Michael helped me tackle two tasks: reactivate my USA cell phone at a drugstore and validate my ATM card at a Bank of America. A successful attorney in Manhattan, Michael probably earned more last week than I have in my entire life. As I pulled out my four-year-old, $9.95, decaying phone, the number two pad fell off the keyboard and onto the floor. My fingers stuck to other soft rubber parts that seemed to be melting. Michael was kind enough not to point at me and laugh, and politely said, "I'll get the car and meet you at the bank across the street," though he didn't finish his sentence out loud, "so no one else will see us together." I expect Michael later told the cashier that he was in charge of me for the day as VIP, the Village Idiot's Psychiatrist.

To validate my new card, the internet told me to stick it into the ATM machine. Easy! I put the card in the slot and nothing happened. I waited. Michael waited in his car. I took out the card, and the screen said I have to put it in. I looked at the drawing next to the slot to make sure I inserted it correctly. I waited. Nothing happened. Michael fidgeted in his car while considering the option of an impromptu trip to another state. After several attempts that exhausted my single working brain cell, I remembered that, unlike Thai ATMs that suck in your card, in America I have to stick in the card and immediately remove it. I withdrew essential cash and joined Michael, but made the mistake of telling the truth, instead of blaming the delay on the Bank of America.

After retrieving my motorcycle near Washington, DC, I set off to Minnesota, 1,500 miles west and north, dressed from shoulder-to-fingertip-to-toe in black leather, plus a black helmet, as a heat wave squeezed the thermometer up to 104°F. Harley riders I met in petrol stations wore t-shirts or sleeveless vests, shorts, definitely no helmets, and were solely protected from scorching pavement by tattoos that read, "Ride hard, die fast." Most of them were speechless, unable to process the concept that anyone would dress like me. I wanted to scream, "Brain damage! Bad bike accident! Gotta wear the gear! Scars all over! You don't want to see 'em!" but instead remained as speechless as my audience.

At dusk I checked into a cheap motel in a tiny town, which attracted professional axe murders, traveling sperm salesmen, and humanoids who'd recently evolved from reptiles, perhaps last week. People frowned or smiled nervously at the black-leather man in the scorching heat. They weren't surprised when I said I lived in Thailand, which they'd never heard of, but assumed must be a distant planet.

I made it to Minnesota where I'd lived for 20 years, but it had changed. New roads, new buildings, new news. I got lost, then I was late, and then lost again in conversations about how Obama saved (or destroyed) the country, about TV shows I've never watched, about the dangers (or benefits) of trans fats, and the latest sports events. The only sport I followed was my Harley Sportster, and I didn't do that well, either. While riding, I heard a high-pitched screeching sound and couldn't imagine what was wrong with the Harley. I stopped, shifted into neutral, and the screeching continued even after I'd turned off the bike. I removed my helmet and realized it was the tornado warning siren test that blares every first Wednesday of the month at noon.

At a fancy mall, I became transfixed by the bustling spectacle, like an immigrant oogling a new world. As a Godiva Chocolate sign caught my eye, a fancy woman in a flowing gown offered me a fancy green mint from her sample tray. I popped it into my mouth, and her mouth dropped wide open. The horror in her eyes explained why the "mint" tasted horrible, because it was a fancy soap chip from the Bed and Bath store next to Godiva. Should I have assumed it was soap? Did she assume I'd start bathing in the hall of the mall?

I'd rather be home in Thailand, where I can feel good about being a foreigner, because I am a foreigner. I may still be the village idiot, but at least I can't understand what people are saying about me behind my back.

~ ~ ~

Bear with Me

ITHIN FIFTY STEPS DOWN THE FOGGY PATH, the van and parking lot has faded out of sight along with the rest of civilization. The lush forest tunnel descends into a different dimension. A wild one. I'd been over, around, and through North Carolina's Great Smoky Mountains on roads, but this time, I'd hike into them on foot. Chances are we wouldn't see another human being for days.

"Are you sure this is the way to the Holiday Inn?"

I'd coerced my girlfriend, Cat Borreesha, into undertaking her first wilderness backpacking trip. Her true identity will remain anonymous since Cat Borreesha is merely a pseudonym formed by rearranging the letters of her actual name, Roberta Chase.

Born a northern lass, Cat had migrated south and morphed into the dignified proprietress of a lodge in an upscale, one stoplight town—a seasonal destination for folks born with silver spoons up various bodily orifices. She lived in an elegant mountain cabin and preferred to view the peaks from the comfort of her home, where the toilet was sturdier than a fallen branch or the precarious squatting position.

I had to twist Cat's arm and her lifestyle to persuade the woman to join me on a four-day wilderness trek. Unless you've recently visited a specific backcountry campsite, you're never really sure of its amenities, which range from none, to a circle of charred rocks, maybe a flat area, somewhere, and infrequently, a seat with a hole in it. From my mumbling about what a "wild holiday in the woods" might include, she probably only heard the words "Holiday in…"

My high-tech, $300 backpack can hold way more than my legs could carry. Cat lugs an ancient, borrowed, granny green, flimsy thing with a frail frame designed for deformed baboons or the Hunchback of Notre Dame. Her pack barely carries a sleeping bag, foam pad, wardrobe, and toiletries. Mine weighs a bit less than an oak armoire, and overflows with my sleeping bag, pad, clothing, and all the essential gear—tent, food, water bottles, purification filters, gas stove, fuel, pots, plates, utensils, lantern, contour maps, compass, plus survival necessities like my Camping Bible, cribbage board, playing cards, and several wine spritzers.

The first leg of the trip is scarcely six miles, but our wobbly legs on the steep slick trails make it seem like sixty. A wine spritzer becomes the mental mirage that keeps me going, whereas Cat envisions a more elusive oasis and mentions it repeatedly: "I'm pretty sure I see a Holiday Inn just up ahead."

Day One of our trek does not start, continue, or end well. Our rain gear never makes it off our bodies and into the packs. While selecting campsites at the park headquarters, we'd asked Mr. Forest Ranger about the weather forecast.

Through his tobacco chaw, he drawled, "Way'll…'round 'ese parts, y'all nevah know fer sure." [Translation: "Well, I have no clue."]

Throughout the day, rain waffles between drops, plops, and a splash, then hits official shower status, fades into a mist followed by countless dribbles, a torrent or two, then settles into steady sprinkles or interminable drizzles, and lingers throughout the night as indistinct combinations we name "sprizzles and drinkles" during a wine spritzer downpour inside the tent. Luckily the weather never hits the deluge category referred to by locals as "rainin' lahk a cow pissin' on a flat (pronounced "flay-at") rock."

Day Two begins with blue skies and a hot breakfast of eggs poached to perfection in a pan of brown rice. Our damp clothes and gear bake dry in the sun. Life is good for more reasons than the composting toilet with a seat right next to the campsite.

Cat wears a cashmere sweater, Versace scarf, and Armani slacks she'd scored for pennies at her department store of choice: the local goodwill store laden with designer clothing discarded by neighborhood blue bloods. My outfit is pure North Face—khaki pants, safari shirt, fleece vest, and gnarly boots. I look like the anal Personal Assistant's Assistant to an elegant actress on an adventure movie set.

Pampered, fed, and blond hair coiffed, Cat admits over her teacup, "Well, this is kind of nice, but you still owe me a night at the Inn."

With rested appendages and high spirits, we eat up the four miles toward the next site. I venture off the trail in search of free food from the forest, disappearing into a thicket of blackberries, brush, and brambles, picking berries until I can't move any farther forward. Nor could I move backward with a thousand thorns stuck in my pants, shirt, and skin. It's one of those "How the hell did I get in here if I can't even get back out of here?" places. I trade a bit of blood for the blackberries, and although my skin hates me, our tongues love me.

The final mile of the trail leads us down a steep ravine into a sweet, level campsite, nestled by a burbling brook, a wizened stone circle awaiting a blazing campfire, a toilet in the distance and, wait... lots of multicolored trash... no... shredded fabric, destroyed backpacks, crushed food containers... and... gasp... *Are those words etched in the dirt?* In huge hand-scrawled capital letters scratched with a stick, the earth screams, "BEWARE BEARS!"

Cat also screams in all caps, "OKAY, I WANT A ROOM AT THE HOLIDAY INN... NOW!"

Internally panicking, but outwardly calm, I stammer, "Be cool. Probably just an argument between some Chicago Bears and Detroit Lions fans."

Summoning any and all gods or goddesses in the immediate vicinity, we frantically inspect the site: no half-eaten human body parts or last wills scrawled in caked blood on empty granola packages. Pacing around each other, we consider our two options—stay or split—though the obvious cowardly choice has four complications:

1) the sun will set in a couple of hours;

2) the nearest campsites lay five miles ahead or back;

3) the van and park headquarters are at least ten miles away; and

4) neither one of us can fly.

I know the only bears in the Smoky Mountains are black bears, lots of them, about fifteen hundred, and recall some intimidating facts:

• *They can be over six feet in length and weigh 300 to 850 pounds, which is two, three, four, or five of me.*

• *Their diet is mainly nuts and fruits—which includes me, often a fruit who is nuts—berries, insects, and greens, but also carrion, deer, or small animals.*

• They can run up to thirty-five miles per hour, climb trees, and swim several miles. Their hearing is twice as sensitive as humans; their sense of smell better than dogs, perhaps better than any other mammal.

• Though not often, black bears maul or kill people, possibly both of us, soon after now.

My personal black bear experience is limited to watching them sleep behind bars in zoos, stuffed behind glass in museums, or alongside the road from the safety of a vehicle. Right now I want to get as far away from a close encounter of the bear kind as soon as possible.

About a half-mile back and up the ravine, I'd noticed a semi-flat area. Forty-five sweaty minutes later we stagger in as dusk descends. The "semi-flat" characteristic is the one and only amenity of our mandatory camp option—no toilet, no water source, no fire pit, no Holiday Inn.

We hastily set up the tent, cook a meal, scour the pots, and then separate our gear into two categories:

1) edible and attractive;

2) inedible and boring.

Bears are attracted to food, cooking utensils, trash, perfumes, deodorants, and toothpaste. And to clothes worn while eating, or those saturated with roasting hot dog smoke. And to women during their period, in our case, one named Cat.

Diligently following the preaching of my Camping Bible, I stuff the attractive edibles into my backpack and hang it twelve to fifteen feet in the air between two trees, ten feet apart, a hundred feet from our campsite. Always attractive and edible, and though normally flexible and amiable, Cat refuses to spend the night safe and secure… inside my suspended pack.

As clouds roll in and the sky darkens, a game of cards distracts us from the anxiety of the unknown. I glance up

from my cribbage hand to see Cat's wide eyes, her jaw resting in her lap, her quivering finger pointing behind me. I whirl around to behold a massive hairy Sumo wrestler with poorly manicured fingernails and jumbo teeth. After a quick glance, he shinnies up the tree toward my backpack.

My heart officially stops, but my hands grab pots as I leap up while pounding them together. Being wimpy lightweight aluminum, the pots don't bang and crash, but only clatter meekly, as intimidating as a cheap wind chime.

Sumo pauses, calmly gazes down at me, and communicates telepathically: "You're next." Then climbs effortlessly up to the rope securing my backpack.

I continue tinkling my wind chimes and yelling stuff I don't remember, but being the seasoned warrior that I am not, they might've been random battle cries I'd learned in school. "Remember the Alamo! Give me liberty or give me death! Tenno heika banzai!"

Sumo pays no attention to us, as if we are dead Barbie and Ken dolls. Unable to reach out and grab our attractive edibles from the tree trunk, he chomps through the rope, and my pack drops to the forest floor. Agile as an ape, Sumo slides down the tree, jumps to the ground from about six feet, picks up my jam-packed backpack as if it were a helium balloon, and scampers into the brush at thirty-five mph.

I bravely follow him for two inches, shouting, "C'mon back, you coward, and face the wrath of my Plastic Fork and Spatula of Death!" Trying to quell my trembling, I turn back to Cat. "Ha! I scared him away!"

She voices another view. "You didn't scare him. He scared you. He completed his mission and left."

[Bear in mind this trek took place in the early '80s, before the advent of the internet, portable cell phones, or GPS trackers with SOS panic buttons that send emergency messages to your selected contact list like, "Up Shit Creek. Paddle up my ass. I want my mommy." That day SOS only meant "Stay or split."]

Soon it will be pitch black. We can't build a raging bonfire since the wood I'd scavenged is waterlogged. If we try to leave with Cat's mini-pack and minus mine, we'll have to sacrifice our gear, our flashlight batteries will quickly die as we get lost in a deluge, fall off a cliff, break our legs, and become a free buffet for reptiles and insects.

An adult bear's home range can be up to *eighty* square miles. Sumo had no problem tracking us after our short retreat from the BEWARE BEARS campsite. For a bear, that's like padding from the kitchen to the pantry. He's an evolved "panhandler" bear, one who's learned that tasty granola bars don't grow on trees, but might be *hanging* in trees. It's a walk in the fucking park for him to snatch an array of goodies from skinny, two-legged, pasty natives as they lapse into their entertaining ritual of singing, hopping, and banging aluminum bongo drums.

Though black bears normally don't attack sleeping humans, they're known to go after a pocketed candy bar and bite off more than they can chew. Praying that Sumo won't harass us since he'd already stolen all of our attractive edibles, we slink into our flimsy tent so cramped it barely holds our sleeping bags.

"Forget the Holiday Inn," Cat growls. "If we get out of here alive, you owe me a week at a Hilton, in the city of my choice, with the man of my choice, which undoubtedly will *not* be you."

I retaliate mentally. *Oh yeah? It's all my fault, is it? Well, I might be lying next to our one remaining attractive edible, Miss That Time Of The Month.*

We surrender to fate. I try to sleep as a ditty from my youth invades my brain and plays like a creepy theme from a horror flick sung by demented *Children of the Corn*:

If you go out in the woods today,
You're sure of a big surprise.
If you go out in the woods today,
You'd better go in disguise.
For every bear that ever there was
Will gather there for certain, because
Today's the day the teddy bears have their picnic.

Gee, thanks brain, for helping drive me insane. I eventually float off to Scottyland… until Cat's whispers and pokes yank me out of my dream into a real nightmare.

"Did you hear that?"

"Hear what?"

"That."

I listen, breathless, in total darkness, like being in an elevator during a power outage, a much safer place than where we are. I hear nothing…

No, wait… faint clattering. My wind chime pots hanging in the bush?

Then dead silence. Then something.

Maybe a heartbeat. Mine? No… Shit. Rustling… soft padding in the pine needles?

Nothing again…

What's that? A twig snapping? Damn it. Breathe. Listen. Wait. I hear breathing and it's not mine! And it's not Cat's.

It's inches from my face on my side of the tent. Oh my god, it's back! Or it's another one! The Teddy Bears are out in force, and we're their picnic lunch!

I sit up—the only thing there's room enough to do in the tent—with a Swiss Army knife in one hand and a penlight in the other. The thin beam of light reveals a hump of tent fabric pulsing from Sumo's curious snout pressing against it. Camping Bible says, "Keep a safe distance from bears."

Shit! Shit! Shit! This one's only the width of nylon away!

View of a black bear on the outside of tent
from the inside at midnight.

A plan hatches in my head, waddles one step, and dies. *If Sumo's paw slashes through one wall of the tent, I'll cut through the other side, and we can escape! Escape? Escape to where? We're fucked.*

Sumo creeps around the tent and rummages through our gear for ten eternal minutes. Then silence again… for a while that feels like forever.

I stick my penlight through a gap in the tent flap. The ebony night sucks the weak beam from my midget flashlight into oblivion. Beneath an overcast sky and canopy of tree branches, outside is as dark as the inside of a black hole.

Lying back down, I share more bear survival tips from my Camping Bible: "If you encounter a bear, stand up tall with your hands over your head to make you look bigger. Try not to panic and while slowly retreating. Do not run as this will excite its instinct to chase prey."

Cat's whispers slither into a pursed shriek. "Put my hands over my head so I'll be scary as a bunny with big ears? Retreat backward in the dark into one of your 'how the hell did I get in here if I can't even get back out of here' thickets? If this is the last day of my life, at least I'm gonna get a good night's rest." She turns over and feigns sleep.

I start to slip on my sneakers.

Cat snaps, "Now what are you doing?"

"If the bear slashes through the tent, we'll have to make a run for it."

"Now you're losing it. You can't outrun a bear."

"I don't have to outrun a bear. I only have to outrun you."

Cat rolls her eyes and drifts off into a catnap, leaving me alone with my inappropriate jokes, life-saving plans, Camping Bible scriptures, and "The Teddy Bears' Picnic" eating me up from the inside out.

If you go out in the woods today,
You'd better not go alone.
It's lovely out in the woods today,
But safer to stay at home.
For every bear that ever there was
Will gather there, etcetera, ad nauseam

I don't sleep for the rest of the night. Sumo or his teddy bear buddies come back at least five more times. Each visitation delivers more nerve-wracking, indistinguishable sounds, then stillness, muffled snorts, semi-muted footsteps, more snouts probing and pushing in the walls of the tent. *How can anything that big be that quiet?*

Moronic mental gymnastics keep my mind off our dilemma during the silent spells. *Hmm, the letters of Cat Borreesha can also be rearranged to spell 'Hot bear scare' or 'Bear actors, eh?'* Did she set this all up to spring the Hilton

Ultimatum on me? If I live to write about this, I'll call it "Chaos in the Campsite or The Terror Was in Tents." Let's see. If I remove my Swiss Army toothpick and tweezers, then unfold its scissors and file, maybe Sumo will trade our lives for a haircut, manicure, or teeth cleaning. I wonder if the sun will ever rise, but it finally dawns on me.

Day Three. A hundred yards from the campsite, I find the carcass of my pack. Despite being constructed of industrial strength Cordova nylon, Sumo has shredded it as easily as if it had been our skin. No matter what kind of containers I'd packed our grub in, every morsel is gone. *Tin cans of beans bitten open and licked clean. The heavy plastic egg protector crushed like an eggshell. Ziploc bags of power bars, Kool-Aid, hot cocoa and instant coffee devoured. With that much sugar and caffeine coursing through his veins, it's no surprise Sumo stayed up all night. He even ate half of my Mennon deodorant stick. An after-dinner mint?*

I scrape up a few grains of rice, dried beans, and crumbs from the grass. Over a meager breakfast of mush, wild chives, and our last wine spritzer, we weigh our two options:

Plan A) Stick with our planned trip, ambush feeble hikers along the way, and steal their food.

Plan B) Scratch Day Four and get the hell out of here.

We discuss these in depth for three or four seconds before selecting Plan B, revised with more succinct words: Holiday Inn, Home, or Bust!

I plot a five-mile, straight shot to the nearest road so we can hitch back to the van, then cram gear into my butchered backpack, crudely duct tape the gaping holes, and tie clothes around the whole mess to keep it together. As we hike, I imagine meeting other humans along the way who will point and laugh at the madman they see carrying a pile of garbage lashed to his back.

I'll fervently warn them about the Campsite from Hell and Sumo and offer to sell them my Plastic Fork and Spatula of

Death... then I'll ambush them and steal their food.

We make it to the van without being killed, or killing each other, and head for the park headquarters to tattle on Sumo. Park rangers appreciate it when hikers let them know they survived, and we want them know we almost didn't.

Upon hearing our story, Mr. Ranger says, "Way'll, y'all's ain't the first report. Might 'ave to relocate this'n or send it off to a zoo." [Translation: "Well, yours isn't the first report. We're gonna wait until a few more of you Yankee meddlers die before we take this soldier out of action."]

As I hope Sumo's head won't be relocated to a tavern wall via the taxidermy shop, Cat points at me and asks Mr. Ranger, "Can we use your relocation system for him, preferably a life sentence in a nearby zoo, naked in a monkey cage where I can throw bananas and peanuts at him?"

After our trip, I researched how to keep black bears away from campsites and learned they hate the smell of Bounce fabric softener sheets for the dryer. I secretly planned another adventure and posed my question to Cat. In a manly attempt to transfer the blame—for our night of mayhem, my destroyed backpack, and the natural behavior of bears—onto her personal reproductive cycle, I mooted my suggestion. "Hey, I have an idea. How about another holiday in the woods during a better time of the month?"

"Honey, I'd only consider it if you bring three things: a titanium tent with a secure basement, a flame-thrower to scare any creatures while you're drying out sticks to build a fire to scare any creatures, and... a helicopter."

I elected *not* to reply thusly: "But sweetheart, there's a cheaper option. We can order a new tent, sleeping bags, backpacks, hiking clothes, and panties—made entirely from fabric softener sheets!"

~ ~ ~

Seeing It Another Way

IT'S EASY TO HANG OUT WITH FOLKS WHO CAN'T SEE since they don't care how you look. You don't have to worry because it's a bad hair day, or fret about the shard of broccoli stuck between your teeth, or be self-conscious about the jumbo glowing pimple on your nose ready to explode, or all of the above, plus your t-shirt's inside out and strangers offer to give you a lift back to the funny farm.

Blind Tom always set us at ease with his ability to laugh at his disability. "Last night I got into a fight with another blind guy in the parking lot. Someone watching in the crowd yelled, 'I'll bet ten bucks on the guy with the knife!' We both ran away."

He called speed bumps in the road "traffic signs for the blind." Tom wanted a seeing-eye giraffe so people would know he's coming and a seeing-eye zebra for formal black tie events. "When I'm in a hurry, I'd like a seeing-eye wasp to clear the sidewalk in front

Speed bumps in the road:
"traffic signs for the blind"

of me. A seeing-eye elephant would be super for getting through crowds at a football stadium, but I couldn't see the game with it sitting at my feet. Oh, I forgot. I'm blind. Once I had a seeing-eye snake, but it kept slithering out of its leash."

During my formative years as a teenage musician, my personal hero was blind: George Shearing, the stellar British jazz pianist. I stumbled onto a book with transcriptions of his song arrangements and painstakingly learned his unique dissonant chord structures. I couldn't imagine how he came up with those strange combinations. Perhaps he kept putting his fingers on the wrong keys? The idea fit in with advice from another teacher:

"That's the beauty of jazz. If you make a mistake while you're playing a song, just make the same mistake when that section comes around again. No one will ever know."

Shearing's influence still shapes my style today. You don't jump from one chord to the next; you slink from one to another with passing notes in between, like feeling your way along a wall in a dark room—his everyday reality. Thirty-five years later I met and heard him perform live at a club, more of a master than ever. His blindness wasn't a disability; it enhanced his abilities. His tender touch gently caressed the tones out of the keys. I only *played* the piano; he *became* the piano.

A friend whose blind father had been George's piano tuner in New York related a story the artist like to tell. In the early days of commercial airlines before security checks and gates inside terminals, George sat in a mid-size prop plane on the Tarmac, hanging out with the pilots while waiting for passengers to board. One pilot asked if George wanted him to take his seeing-eye dog for a walk. He said, "Sure, thanks!" The pilot donned his official airline hat and sunglasses before the dog led him down the roll-up front stairway—as the passengers walked up the rear one.

Everyone was visibly upset at the concept of a blind pilot, praying he'd have a seeing-eye eagle while flying.

I drove a taxi for a few months and regularly picked up an elderly blind couple. The routine required that I back into their driveway and position my rear door by the sidewalk. Always ready and waiting when I arrived, they'd probably heard my taxi a mile away… or smelled its stale odor. They'd prance down the walk and slip into the back seat as if they had sixteen eyes between them, and then give me a running commentary on sites we passed.

"The Johnson's have painted their house pink!"

"The court house here is under major reconstruction."

"Honey, the traffic is terrible. I hope we won't be late."

I don't think they were really blind. They wanted the extra special treatment I gave them.

Maurice was the proud blind father of ten strapping sons and daughters who lived on a horse ranch in Wisconsin. A massive St. Bernard dog with a huge drooling mouth and dripping eye slits, Maurice lived a great life in the country with his loving, seeing-eye humans. When I rode in on my bicycle, he'd follow me by crashing invisibly but noisily through the woods next to the driveway. He didn't trust the parking lot where cars would be in random locations—trees grew slowly, and he knew where each one stood.

He liked me because he could feel I liked him and would follow me around by leaning his 250-pound body on my leg, almost knocking me over. One day a sinister someone came to the ranch, and to eliminate him, Maurice used his practiced technique of rising on his hind legs, putting his fat front paws on the man's shoulders, his drooling face a few inches from the intruder's wide eyes, and walking him backward down the driveway. One reverse march with Maurice was enough to keep a salesman away for life.

For a decade, my house sat across the street from Jeanette—blind and living alone in her home. Watching her work in the garden, you'd never know she was visually impaired, only that she loved to touch her flowers. She'd set up the sprinkler and walk around it in a circle, feeling the mist, making sure the water fed each one of her babies.

On a frigid winter night at two a.m. after a foot of snowfall, I went outside to help a guest dig out his car. He left, but since I'd bundled up, I started shoveling my sidewalk. The sound of another shovel caught my attention. Across the street, Jeanette was clearing the walkway to her house. She could hear the scrape on the pavement below the snow and *feel* when her shovel was full. No problem with the job or the time—it was always night in her world.

While mowing my lawn on a summer afternoon, I felt a presence and glanced across to see Jeanette waving frantically. I walked over to learn that her phone didn't work and she needed to make a call, so I handed her my mobile. She dialed a tad slower than the speed of light, unlike me, who needed to see the screen while stumbling through seven numbers with five thumbs. At the end of her call, she asked, "Thanks a lot. Who are you?"

"Scott, your neighbor across the street."

"I never see you!"

Hmm. How do you respond to that? Blind Tom never let me get away with any of my language faux pas.

I'd ask, "Are you seeing anyone?"

He'd say, "No, I've *never* seen anyone. Are you mentally handicapped?"

I'd say, "Look at it this way…"

Immediately he'd interrupt, "Sorry, but I can't even look at it my way."

I'd say, "Okay, see you later."

He'd grumble, "You lucky bastard."

Tom had the perfect job: an engineer at a radio station with a bevy of knobs to turn to tweak the tunes for his sensitive ears and our average ones. Born with a degenerative eye disease, he'd seen a bit of the world before losing his vision.

One summer weekend, I bring Tom and my friend Rob to my family's country cabin. I, being a rabid water-ski addict, am jonesin' to hit the boards. Rob can't swim and has never even been in a speedboat, but my tiny obsessed brain cells cranks out, "Rob can walk and ride a Vespa. He can learn to drive a boat right now!"

The law requires a second person in the back of the boat to keep an eye on the skier—the "spotter." In another moment of misplaced sanity, I choose my fate. "Okay, fine. Blind Tom can be the spotter placeholder!"

After a hasty driving lesson, I'm racing down the river on one ski, creating ten-foot sprays to impress my audience of cattails, more cattails, and one loon, a not-so-distant ancestor. Staring straight ahead, with a double death grip on the steering wheel and the throttle, Rob makes a beeline for his future, which holds a safe dry cabin not surrounded by a potential watery grave. Tom is immersed in the feel of the hot rays on his skin and the vibration of 250 horses pulsing through his elbows perched on the padded engine cover.

I lose it on a tight cut-back and become a gaggle of arms and legs skipping across the waves. As the boat disappears around the bend, Moron Buoy (me) treads water while replaying Rob's maritime driving lesson that did *not* include the vital chapter, "When a skier falls…"

Somewhere down the river, Petrified Pilot Rob shouts, "How's he doing?"

"He's fine," Clueless Tom shouts, "I think I hear him."

Sometime later, Rob realizes the water-ski handle is sans human and figures out how to turn around a speedboat n a narrow river. Tom sits calmly viewing the scenery inside his mind. I've become a purple prune man in the river, winner of the Worst Idea of the Weekend Award for putting my life on the towline of a non-swimming, non-driving skipper with a sightless spotter. Eventually they find my wrinkled body and pick me up without tangling my legs in the prop.

That night we decide to play croquet under the spotlight in the yard. Tom explains that he has severe tunnel-vision, and though legally blind, he can see a tiny speck of light in one eye, like looking down a long railway tunnel. It doesn't do him much good in daily life, but tonight in the dark, he can focus on the shiny croquet hoop at the end of his personal micro-telescope. With a mallet doubling as his white cane, he wins the game and never lets us forget it.

"So you guys can't even beat a blind guy at croquet? I've got a mute friend you should debate."

We offer to get him a rental car so he can drive home, or anywhere else—alone.

On the way back we stop at a gigantic petrol station, store, and restaurant complex—a vivid lesson for me to walk a mile in a blind man's shoes. I guide Tom across the busy parking lot, through heavy double doors, down aisles, around corners, locate the men's room, negotiate more doors, then sidle up to yellow-stained urinals and dirty sinks. I don't want to touch any surface in that filthy toilet. It's hard enough to do that with 20-20 vision, let alone with 0-0. Of course, while standing at our respective urinals, Tom has a story for the occasion:

"One time I flew to Dallas and said to the passenger next to me, 'Boy, these seats are big!'

"The guy grinned and replied, 'Everything's big in Texas.'

"At the hotel I ordered a mug of beer and told the bartender, 'Wow, this is a big glass!'

"Like the other guy, this one said, 'Yup, everything's big here in Texas.'

"I went to find the bathroom, walked through the wrong door, fell into the swimming pool, and screamed, 'Don't flush! Don't flush!'"

~ ~ ~

Veg;tablosophy 101

Confusing Menu Options for Vegetarians in Thailand

FRIED THING SOUP IN FIRD PAN

Vegetarian? Is your Thai good enough to ask what a "fried thing" is? Or "fird pan"?

DEEP FRIED WHITE GROUB IN BAMBOO

The jury is out on this one. Is "groub" an animal, mineral, or vegetable?

PORK STEAMED WITH LEMONADE

Can I just have the lemonade, please, hold the pork?

Spicy nork egg with mush room soup

Okay for veggies who don't eat anything with a face... if you can handle a "nork" egg.

Beef step on by me.

Maybe there's a militant vegan cook in the kitchen?

FRIED SALTED CASHEW NUT

Definitely vegetarian, but it's a very light meal – you only get one cashew nut.

I WAS BORN A VEGETARIAN, but I don't remember that part. My mother told me she had to disguise the meat in my food until I was six, and I do have a faint memory of eating a hotdog wearing a nose with glasses and a juicy red "gingerbread man" for dessert.

After succumbing mindlessly to meat until age 20, I gave it up several times, while wandering through the various vegetarian commitment levels. During a particularly zealous period, I only ate nuts and fruit, which compelled friends to call me a nut ("a foolish, silly, or eccentric person") or a fruit ("someone considered peculiar or insane"). I didn't care. I had thick skin, like an over-baked potato.

Experts say, if you are a vegetarian, you'll live longer, have more energy, save money, reduce pollution, avoid toxic chemicals, ward off disease, keep your weight down, and increase your sexual longevity, plus your car will run better, world peace will be achieved, and your bowel movements will be regular, which ties into my main reason to ditch meat—laziness. Digestion is a snap. Vegetables are easier to eat and excrete.

Your Four Basic Options: The categories of vegetarians depend on each person, on where you draw your personal lines, and perhaps on the pulse of Uranus.

1) The "Sure, I'm A Vegetarian" Vegetarians—Normally male, these sly chameleons eat meat daily, unless surrounded by real vegetarians, markedly so if an attractive female herbivore is nearby. You can identify them by their lame pickup lines: "If I said you had the body of an all-natural, organic-living, animal-loving, environment-nurturing, whale-saving sex machine, would you hold it against me? Please?"

2) The "I'm A Vegetarian, But I Eat Fish And Chicken" Vegetarians—This category has always puzzled me, since the mere mention of it exposes the ignorance of its adherent. Did I miss biology class about fish and chicken being vegetables? This is like someone claiming, "I'm an independent republican democrat." Or "I'm celibate except for my sister and the sheep."

3) The "I Never Eat Things With A Face" Vegetarians—I slip in and out of this category. Milk and eggs are okay. I still have a deep feeling for udders, though I am guilty of cradle robbing from hens.

While on a back-country Vietnam motorcycle tour in the northern jungle near China, I quickly fell into the "I'll Eat Almost Anything" category when confronted with a spread of homemade mystery dishes served with great care. Equipped with a meager vocabulary of Vietnamese numbers and everyday phrases, I had no desire to tackle the vegetarian topic and refuse their hospitality.

Encircled by our curious hosts, I ate energetically and matched their big smiles, while secretly sticking strips of meat jerky (complete with hair on one side) into my pocket, and discreetly pouring their clear rice whiskey (decanted from a large plastic Coke bottle filled with hundreds of huge hornets) under the table. Learning the phrase "Where's the toilet?" in every country you visit is indispensable.

I discreetly poured many shots of the hornet whisky under the table.

4) The "Meat Is Death, Go To Hell" Vegans—These people won't even touch an animal cracker. Eggs and dairy products are definitely out. It's taboo to wear fur, leather, or clothing made of excretions from silkworms' butts. Some have mock duck pets, and are directly descended from, or married to, a cow.

I respect these people and their dedication, and cannot find fault with one word from vegan bodybuilder Robert Cheeke's quote: "The standard diet of a meat-eater is blood, flesh, veins, muscles, tendons, cow secretions, hen periods, and bee vomit. Once a year during that November holiday, meat-eaters use the hollowed-out rectum of a dead bird as a pressure cooker for stuffing. And people think vegans are weird because we eat tofu?"

Lively and vigorous vegetarians? Bodybuilders? Are you surprised? The Vegetarian Society, founded in 1847, says that the word "vegetarian" comes from the Latin word *vegetus*—meaning lively or vigorous. Strange how that meaning has flipped around today: "I'm gonna veg out on the couch and brainwash myself with soap operas."

How many times have I worked circles around meatheads on construction sites? There's no lack of energy or endurance from a balanced diet of vegetables, though I had to endure snide comments at lunchtime from manly coworkers as they hauled out their geometrically shaped, luncheon meat sandwiches. "Hey, Veggie! Whacha got there'n yer box today? Sticks 'n' stems 'n' grass clippin's? Ah'll trade ya mah hot dog fer yer carrot 'n' five bucks!"

Self-righteous bigots will harass you. These people might say, "All vegetarians frown and eat alone, at least the one I saw did." Or "Vegetarian is an ancient word meaning poor hunter." After his daily routine of blood and guts, my surgeon stepfather ordered his steak raw. He'd tell the waitress, "Just put a saddle on it, and ride it in!"

Peering over at my wimpy veggie medley, he'd have to comment, "A couple bites of meat won't hurt you." I always wanted to say, "Right on, Dr. God! You're Catholic, you chant that 'thou shalt not commit adultery' commandment thing, and you love my mother, so a couple affairs won't hurt you," but then he wouldn't have paid for dinner.

You can be a self-righteous bigot and harass other people with your vast knowledge of cows. Memorize this rant and spew it forth whenever you feel it's time to lose a few friends. "We're eating too many cows, folks! Well, *you're* eating too many cows! Production of one pound of beef compared to wheat takes 18 times more fossil fuel, 15 times the land, and a whopping 200 times the water. If Americans alone ate 10% less meat, the savings in grain and soybeans could feed the world's 80 million people starving to death each year. The earth's 1.5 billion cattle intensify the greenhouse effect by passing about 75 million tons of methane gas each year—more than cars, trains, and airplanes combined, but a little less than men drinking beer, eating chili, and watching football on one Sunday afternoon."

[Now wrap up your presentation with a "punderful" rant in case there are any people who haven't fled the room.] "Cars run on methane. Why hasn't General Motors designed a vehicle that carries a heifer in the back? Stick a tube in the Bovine Methane Emission Center, connect the other end to the engine, and revolutionize the auto industry. A sports car called the Cowvette! A large, luxury model with several cows called the Cattle-act!"

You'll upset the lives of your family and friends. The vegetarian path becomes your normal painless routine, but when you decline an offer of meat, the plot thickens. Everyone else feels self-conscious, assumes they've offended you, imagines you think less of them, and asks lots of philosophical questions. You suddenly want to be invisible. The table is brimming with bread, veggies, salad, condiments, dessert, and one plate of flesh that you don't give a shit about. But they don't get it, because in the carnivore mind, if you don't eat the meat, the meal's a failure and you'll starve to death.

While visiting relatives on Easter, some of whom I'd never

even met, I decided to avoid any confrontation by eating whatever they placed in front of me. I hadn't eaten pig for a decade. Soon I stared down at a thick, pink slice of baked ham. It tasted delicious; the conversation was pleasant: the holiday was a success.

Later on that day my digestive tract began a churning, gurgling conversation with itself, and screamed, "What the hell is this?" I'm pretty sure that slice of ham reformed into its original shape—like those flat, round, rubber stoppers for the drain—and sealed my stomach shut. My bowels didn't move for days, and when they came alive, I was Liquid Lad, never venturing far from the White Porcelain Loveseat.

Your carnivorous friends will suffer. As Mr. Carnivore took a bite of the hot dog from a New York sidewalk vendor, Mr. Veggie said, "Do you have any idea what that is? An intestine filled with leftovers from the slaughterhouse floor! You are what you eat!"

Beating his chest, Mr. Carni shouted as he stepped into the street, "I am what I eat, a vicious animal!"

A speeding truck struck Mr. Carni, and an ambulance rushed him to the hospital. After a lengthy operation, the surgeon discussed the results with Mr. Veggie in the waiting room. "Your friend's going to make it, but he'll be a vegetable for the rest of his life."

The term vegetarian confuses people. Don't let it bother you. Stick with your convictions. Be regular. At an ashram near Chiang Mai, the English-speaking assistant, a devout vegan, told me about a miraculous healing at their facility. "After a bad motorcycle accident, paramedics delivered a young boy to the hospital. He had major head injuries, but somehow he survived, came here, and is now recovering wonderfully. The doctor thought he'd be in a coma for the rest of his life, like a vegetarian."

~ ~ ~

Quit It!

Today officially begins Clean Week #2—last week we quit smoking. My wife Joomi quit once. I quit three times: Tuesday till Friday night, Saturday morning till last night, and again today. We went to the allergy clinic when her skin rashes became unbearable, after her neck turned red and inflamed when I kissed it.

The doctor said, "You're either allergic to the polluted air in Chiang Mai, to cigarette smoking, or… to your husband."

Me, indignant: "Well, we'd like to get a second opinion."

Doctor, nonchalant: "I think your breath might be killing my office plant."

Joomi decided to keep me if we quite smoking by taking the doctor's advice and expensive medicine. We set a quit date in one week, started popping his pills while focusing on the ugly, wicked, bad, and nasty parts of this disgusting habit, and smoking till our

Got a light? I hid these cigs from the doctor but he took away my matches.

lungs burned and nose hairs turned to ash. Doctor Allergy said, "Avoid your friends that smoke," but we couldn't think of any. We are the people we're supposed to avoid.

We didn't understand exactly what the doctor's pills do, though they're touted to reduce the craving desire. The fine-print warning on the pamphlet lists a raft of "common adverse reactions: insomnia, hypersensitivity, rash, anorexia, agitation, anxiety, depression, headache, tremor, dizziness, taste disorders, concentration and visual disturbance, abdominal pain, constipation, lack of energy, sweating and fever," which are the same adverse reactions of smoking, minus lung cancer and death.

The insomnia is formidable, stealing from us those peaceful, unconscious, smokeless hours when we have no desire for, or capability of, lighting up. I lie sleepless in bed every night for hours, ruminating relentlessly:

Did I sleep yet? I don't know, did I? Wait! I think I just slept… but maybe not.

Did I dream I smoked, or did I get up and smoke?

Honey, will you please hand me the sledge hammer?

Would I rather smoke comfortably until I'm dead, or anxiously stay awake until I kill myself?

I quit taking the sleepless pills after a few days, before the black bags hanging under my eyes were threatening to rest on my chest.

Most of my life I didn't smoke and hated cigarettes. I started as a junior in college, but my mother said she'd quit if I'd quit, and if I didn't, she wouldn't send me any more brownies. Luckily her mouth-watering delicacies were way more addicting than stinky cancer sticks, so termination was simple. I tried rolling up her brownies and smoking them, but they wouldn't stay lit.

While traveling overseas, I started again for two reasons:
1) In 1972, everyone smoked;

2) When you're thumbing across Turkey and are picked up by gypsies in a horse-drawn wagon, who, though dirt-poor, offer you a gesture of friendship in the form of a grimy coffin nail, you either accept it or stab them in the heart.

I smoked for a few months, then quit for 28 years. I'm not sure how the Fag Demon crept back in when I was 50, possibly because of a personal mid-life crisis. I'd rather blame it on my neighbors, well, the one neighbor who smoked… and on Paul, a crazy Brit who lived with me for a month before leasing my house when I moved south. Fiercely intelligent and equally ridiculous, he'd party too hearty and daily smoke scads of, as he called them, "gaspers." One night I found him in the backyard, smoking and meticulously burning his "flaming car accident victim costume" for a Guy Fawkes Party.

Me, concerned: "How worried should I be that my future renter is using my pricey set of barbecue utensils to roast his clothing on my Weber grill?"

Paul, nonchalant: "Oh! They're not *my* clothes. They're your clothes." (Cheeky Limey stole them from my Salvation Army donation bag.)

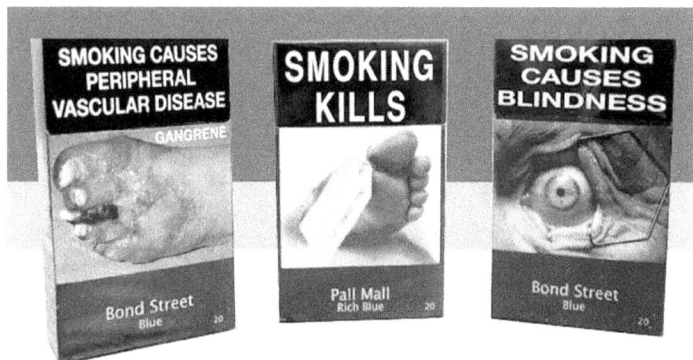

Hmm. So many grim options! Which disease shall I stoke today?

Why is it so hard to give up something you hate? The only semi-positive reason for smoking is the companionship with other druggies, like singing the blues with your buddies while everybody drinks themselves to death. It's the destructive, abusive relationship you can't leave.

Let's call her Anita Drag. You're sick of her; she beats you up; she's even illegal in public places, but you still want her all the time. You must take her everywhere even though she smells revolting, and your friends hate her. She tarnishes your image and your teeth, but you can't stop sucking her butt, you pathetic ash hole.

Dr. Allergy suggested we tell everyone that we've quit so they'll give us support. Following the doctor's order, I hereby inform local citizens of my decision to quit via *Chiang Mai Mail* newspaper, in hopes I'll get accolades and encouragement on the streets, but mainly so I *cannot* start again, since anyone who sees me smoking will know I am still a spineless addict, still stuck on Anita Drag, still kissing ash.

[FYI: I quit several hundred more times since writing that column twelve years ago, however, six months ago smoking went away. I didn't really even have to quit. I felt quite happy about it until I read this quote from Johnny Carson. "I know a man who gave up smoking, drinking, sex, and rich food. He was healthy right up to the day he killed himself."]

~ ~ ~

Skeletons of Songs

WARNING! Literary Verse Alert! Proceed with caution!
If you have an aversion to poetry, please take your allergy
pills immediately or skip ahead five pages.

Most poems I've written are skeletons of songs created during inspired times and the music is fleshed out later. They might appear during a 500-mile drive between gigs when the monotony of the road gave way to the rhyme and rhythm inside my mind, or better yet, on location with pen and notebook in hand.

This first poetic experience—"Dance of Desire"—at the Viking Saloon in Hampton, Iowa, was an empty night in between gigs.

The second—"Carnival Time in Larnaca Town"—happened during an overseas backpacking adventure while passing through the Republic of Cyprus, a Mediterranean island on the ferry route between mainland Europe and Israel. I remember nothing about Cyprus besides the carnival. This memory loss could've been caused by Ouzo, the anise-flavored, brain-melting liquor so popular in the Greek islands I'd left previous evening.

The third—"Keep a condom on 'em"—I penned for an AIDS awareness event with vulnerable Thai women in mind and addressed vital aspects of this issue and the day: 1) men don't use condoms, 2) men use the wrong size, or 3) men reuse them. These three poems don't really need the music. I think the words shine just fine on their own.

Dance of Desire

way down in the heartland of iowa
i strolled into the viking saloon
with walls like a cave
it felt like a grave
where men come to get marooned
vultures hunched over the bar
sucking on soggy cigars
two bulls in a booth reliving their youth
comparing old wounds and scars
way in the back an unruly pack, in to monkey around
the lady bartender
no one to defend her
just smiled and brought them a round

i put quarters into the jukebox
the song list was mighty grim
then a woman said, "hon, you can only press one
cuz i am about to begin"
her skirt was slit up the side
she had high heels and black ratted hair
she punched out her tunes, stepped out of the room
as the catcalls filled the air
then her dance of desire set the fellows on fire
they're drinkin' to douse the flames
only pacified, never satisfied
they felt better before they came

a man with a voice like a chainsaw
he let out a lecherous cheer
"you go-go right purty but get down, get durty"
and chain drank a case of beer
he'd forsaken his farm and his family
for the visions he'd seen on the screen
left the old nitty-gritty to sow seeds in the city
but he planted them all in his jeans
as her dance of desire set the fellows on fire
he's drinkin' to douse the flames
only pacified, never satisfied
he felt better before he came

it seemed like a dog food commercial
where the dogs had been starved for days
their tongues were waggin', their eyelids were saggin'
she's draggin' them in to a maze
a dead end for the hungry and unfulfilled
the drinker whose dreams are all wet
she's just food for thought, can't even be bought
what you see is what you get
her dance of desire set the fellows on fire
they're drinkin' to douse the flames
only pacified, never satisfied
they felt better before they came

Carnival Time in Larnaca Town

it's carnival time in Larnaca town
from every village the family comes down
wearing red ribbons and dressed with such care
a fair may be only a one-time affair
they gawk passed the midway, glide right by the café
it seems as though they simply came here to stare

hot roasted peanuts homemade with sea salt
hamburgers, hot dogs, a tall chocolate malt
pink cotton candy is stuck on a stick
just thinking of eating it makes you feel sick
you barter for everything, end up with nothing
you have to be quick cuz old ladies are slick

with bean bags and baseballs and blue feather darts
the gents flex their fetish for swooning sweethearts
a cigarette gambler, he rolls up his sleeve
and then rolls an eleven gets livid and leaves
each game he chooses he gives up and loses
this man is the moron mirages deceive

there are no neon lights in Larnaca town
just bare-naked light bulbs hung upside down
the crowd is elated and waits round the stage
for wrinkled musicians to turn the next page
soon the folk dancing sparks playful romancing
now everyone's prancing no matter what age

Cabbages & Condoms
Resort & Restaurant Thailand
Keep a condom on 'em

When you're getting it on, get a condom on 'em
And when they're getting off, don't ever take it off 'em
Wear it in and out and in and out and in and out
But never let it wear out: prevention is what it is all about

Keep a condom on 'em... 24/7
Keep a condom on 'em... 365
Keep a condom on 'em... 24/7
Keep a condom on 'em and keep alive

A woman should have a few sizes on hand
You can't trust a man with that kind of a plan
Never give the green light till it's just right,
Snug and tight on his stick of dynamite
If it fits like a tent, get the rubber cement

Hot and heavy lovin' is hell on any condom
Next time you'll be freakin', the old condom's leakin'
He might be sowing more than oats
Make sure he's got a brand new rubber raincoat
You reuse, you both lose. Choose... Brand... New.

He can show his affection with more that his erection
And pay some attention to protection and prevention
Keep a condom on 'em... 24/7
Keep a condom on 'em... 365
Keep a condom on 'em and keep alive

~ ~ ~

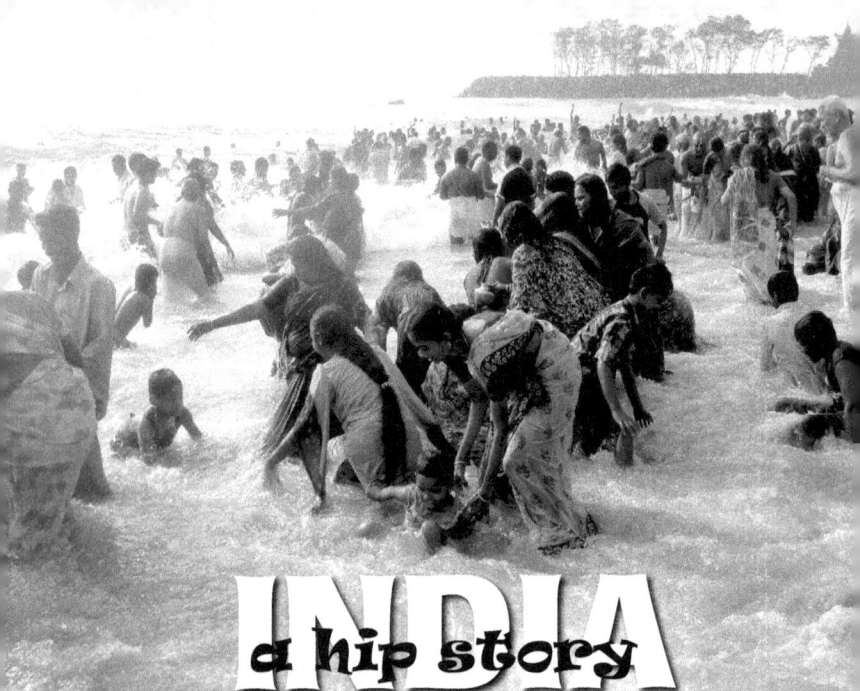

INDIA
a hip story

INDIA: a hip story

I HAVE ONLY THREE WORDS TO SAY ABOUT INDIA. *I love Thailand.* I used to be concerned that Thailand was too damn comfortable, charming, and enchanting which prevented me from getting off my cozy ass to explore other countries in my Southeast Asian neighborhood. After surviving twenty-four hours in the teeming city of Chennai, India, my love for Thailand tripled. I may never leave "The Land of Smiles" again.

Besides the other 15,000 words about India in this tale, three more complete the top six. *Trash and traffic.* Granted, upon arriving I was an invalid with a cane and a recovering patient with a cane when I left. I only visited four cities in southern India during my three-week "medical tourism" foray, but that won't stop me from making sweeping generalizations about the entire country and its diverse people. If India's minions spent some time sweeping, it would be considerably more attractive.

first impressions last

A sprawling, grimy conglomeration of over six million people which might reach seven million by the end of the day, Chennai has only three public trash cans. No one has bothered to empty them in 2,000 years. They now peek through expanding mounds of garbage crossbreeding in the sweltering heat and creating new biological species of living debris with eyeballs, tentacles, and genitals. Besides the bane of advanced civilization—plastic whatever—these piles are composed of decomposing produce, rocks and rubbish, sticks and stones, broken bones, slimy paper this, rusted metal that, and decaying everything else. Omnipresent piles of bricks—modern or primeval, smashed or intact—give the impression that the city is constantly being torn down and rebuilt into a dirtier copy of itself, and it's been going on for centuries.

Like stray dogs, sacred cows wander aimlessly in the streets and on the sidewalks, spreading their sacred shit to fertilize these germinating piles, or squish up the side of your ill-placed sandal onto the skin of your bare foot.

In stark contrast to the trash, the women float above the rubble like innumerable delicate butterflies, resplendent in their intricately woven, multi-colored saris. They wear these flowing shawl/skirt/pants combos as their daily uniform for

life whether going to the market, work, or school, shoveling sand from here to there, raking molten asphalt in the road, or carrying ten bricks on their heads—do not try this at home—in pairs, five high. (If I tried this, my neck would be an inch shorter within the hour.) Saried ladies fly by on scooters, scarves fluttering three feet behind in the breeze, ready to tangle in the side mirrors of passing buses and rip off their heads.

The frantic traffic makes Bangkok seem laid-back. New York is calm in comparison. Everyone is in a major hurry while barely moving. The idea of "lanes" is a foreign concept. Your personal space around your vehicle isn't measured in feet, nor inches; it's determined by the millimeters between the vehicles surrounding you and what the speed limits of your chosen mode of transportation might be—huge new truck, little old truck, first truck ever built on earth, automobile shrouded in black smoke, motorbike, sacred cow, elephant, horse, oxcart carrying a billboard the

size of an intersection, a 300-year-old emaciated man pedaling a 400-year-old bicycle, or two legs beneath two arms lugging a monkey, and a computer, and enough fruit to feed a family of fourteen for a week.

Auto rickshaws, three-wheeled motorcycles with a passenger seat similar to Thailand's tuk-tuks, are manhandled by Maniacs of Death, whose role in society is to reduce the excess population by their reckless driving.

Our personal Maniac lures us into the very-common-so-why-did-I-get-sucked-in-again shopping scam of "I Take You Sightseeing Cheap" (Then Drop You In Deserted Areas Populated Only By Fancy Museum Stores Selling Goods You Don't Want For A Hundred Times The Going Rate). After smoking an aromatic and powerful doobie while driving, our Maniac causes two accidents, one of which leaves a pile of motorbikes in our wake that will still be there in two centuries under a mutating glob of garbage.

Everyone honks their horns incessantly for these apparent reasons:

• **"Another vehicle, person, animal, or vegetable is within three kilometers of me."**

• **"I love my horn. It's my favorite sound in the world."**

• **"My car doesn't run unless I honk."**

• **Logic and excuse from a famous Indian philosopher, "I honk, therefore I am."**

Truck signs say "Sound Horn" to remind people that they're already doing it.

Enveloped by an incomprehensible number of honks equal to the number of air pollution molecules surrounding you, it's impossible to determine what they mean, or who will smash into you from where.

~

rewind time

In high school, I only knew that "India" was a kind of black ink and another country (or planet) where American Indians must have originated. I was a naïve lad from Fargo, North Dakota, where hardy Scandinavians were very skilled at shoveling snow, hibernating inside at 30 below zero for months, growing wheat during the three days of summer, and telling non-stop Norwegian or Swedish jokes.

Ole the Swede says: "Did you hear Sweden got a new zoo? They put a fence around Norway."

Ole the Norwegian says: "How can we tell when the Swedish Air Force flies over? They're the planes with hair under the wings."

While attending the University of Wisconsin in the

High school senior: I'm not sure if this is my hair or a skull cap. The tie might be from India.

late sixties, I became intrigued with India when an extraordinary guy appeared in this ordinary guy's life. He was in an entirely foreign subcategory of Homo sapiens than my two roommates and me. (FYI: to protect the innocent or guilty parties, I have rearranged the letters of their names.)

Roommate "Honk Minuet" was a white-bread Protestant from the dairy state of Wisconsin where folks excel at milking cows, drinking brandy by the barrel, and telling Polish jokes.

"Did you hear about the Polish guy who thought his wife was trying to kill him? He found a bottle of Polish Remover under the sink."

Roommate "Mr. Bagels Her ChiChi" was a button-down Jewish boy from Long Island, New York, where people are well-versed in mafia wars, gang murders, and corporate mergers. He'd come to study law with the gentle jerseys before tackling the bulls on Wall Street, and, unlike every other college student in Wisconsin who guzzled beer 24/7, only drank milk. Mr. Bagels was the neatest person I'd ever met besides my mother. Even his underwear was expertly pressed with visible creases. He saved the tiny plastic hangers that came with new socks and hung them in his closet. He arranged his toiletries geometrically on his dresser in columns and rows. We'd sneak into his room, mess them up, and kill a cockroach with his hairbrush.

While visiting Mr. Bagels' family home in New York, I felt an itching sensation in my nether regions and was dispatched to the family doctor. Diagnosis: NSU—nonspecific urethritis—a common, innocuous, but indeed, gasp, a venereal disease. After I left, his mother bought new toilet seats for every bathroom, forbade Mr. Bagels from associating with gentiles of either sex, and, with a Jewish Menorah candle, ceremonially burned out the state of North Dakota on any household map.

Enter "Om Grandness," who answered our newspaper

ad for an additional roommate in our rented house. With shoulder-length hair, exotic hemp shirt, moose-hide pants, and dark eyes sparkling mischievously, Om was an American maverick who grew up in Delhi. He later confided that he took the room because of an immediate attraction to my German Shepherd, not to the three of us.

In college I wore a headband to hold my hair down
so I wasn't mistaken for Bozo the Clown.

He threw a mattress on the floor, decorated the walls and ceiling with a kaleidoscope of imported fabrics, read fascinating books by candlelight, and wore a razor-sharp, leather-sheathed knife a bit shorter than his leg. Odors emanating from Om's lair were a medley of marijuana, incense, and India. From Mr. Bagels' room came the faint smell of dry cleaning, shoe polish, and legal briefs. As Mr. Bagels' days wound down at 10 p.m., Om's were revving up. Their rooms shared the same wall, and Mr. Bagels complained about things that go bump in the night, all night. A procession of sensuous women entered the Den of Om as sounds of love, harmony, and rhythmic writhing punctuated the air. From Mr. Bagels' room came sounds of rhythmic writing and judicial punctuation. The only women in the Efficiency

Apartment of Mr. Bagels Her ChiChi resided in magazines.

Om and I spent countless hours talking and hanging out as my hair lengthened, my pant legs widened into bell bottoms, and my major shifted from boring business to Political Science and Indian Studies. Though he'd eventually return, Om didn't stay at college for extended periods. His dad worked for the World Bank in Delhi, and every year sent Om a free plane ticket home, which he'd transform into a round-the-world trip to New York to Spain to Morocco to India to Indonesia to Hawaii to countries I'd never heard of, and occasionally back to Wisconsin. An accomplished carpenter, horse trainer, auto mechanic, pool and ping-pong player, wilderness guide, artist, and world traveler, Om had already experienced more than his professors would during their entire lives.

I learned to read and write Hindi, studied international politics and religion, smoked whatever we could roll up, and barely finished college. A hopeful hippie, I graduated with dreams of touring India, hiking the hills, meeting religious masters, and sampling the drugs. I never made it. Music, marriage, divorce, and everyday life got in the way. I forgot every Hindi word I knew except "Hindi."

Wisconsin-bred Honk Minuet disappeared into his world, though he's undoubtedly still milking, drinking, and wearing an enormous, cheese-shaped, foam cowboy hat in the Dairy State while chanting its official slogan, "Come Smell Our Dairy Air."

A successful corporate lawyer in Manhattan, Mr. Bagels has a mansion in New Jersey, a second home in Vermont, and a fiery Italian wife—a very ungentle gentile—who probably beats him with magazines in the bedroom. Since becoming the stepfather to his wife's daughter, siring two boys, adopting three orphaned sisters, plus an array of dogs, cats, and divorced neighbors, Mr. Bagels now drinks wine to subdue his unattainable goal of keeping even one of his many rooms tidy. On the side he teaches Advanced Punctuation and the Fundamentals of Sock Folding at a local community college.

Om and I have stayed close from afar as he evolved into Dr. Om Grandness, an internationally known environmental biologist, who occasionally lets me win at the pool table, sometimes one game in a row.

~

from hippie to hippy

Thirty-some years later, my hip degenerated due to age, heredity, mileage, and a motorcycle accident. My ability to walk decreased as the pain increased, and an X-ray showed bone-on-bone, which explained the grinding agony I felt with every step. The grim diagnosis? A hip replacement. The cost? $12,000 in Thailand or $60,000 in the USA.

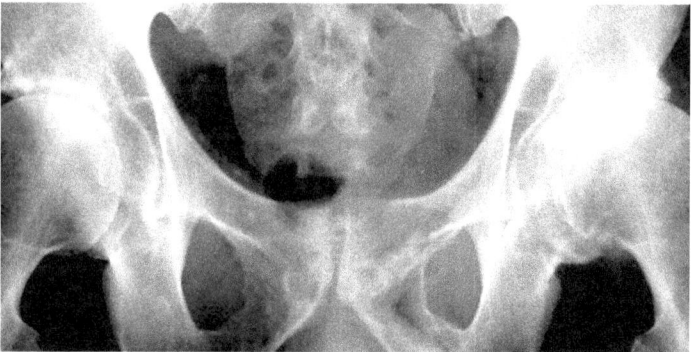

Left: good round femur with abundant cartilage in hip
Right: square peg in not-so-round hole, bone crunching on bone

After extensive research, including emailing my X-ray photo around the world and communicating with forward-thinking surgeons, I learned I didn't need the hip replacement described on the internet with unnerving, unmedical terms: doctors "saw" off your leg bone, "ream" out your femur, and "cement" plastic in your body.

I discovered a less-invasive, bone-conserving, hip "resurfacing" in India for $5,800, which employed chromium cobalt-steel from England plus posterior surgical entry techniques from Belgium. This sounded infinitely better than the frontal technique where the doctor's knife could slip and sever the precious soft tissue hanging in that general area. The super steel of the components had been created for the exterior of a space-shuttle to withstand intense heat during reentry into the earth's atmosphere, so I knew at least one part of me would survive my cremation.

Hmm, let's see, tough decision. No health insurance, airline tickets for two to India are $700 versus $900 for one to America, so I can save $55,000.

The official term? Medical Tourism. I was again, though spelled differently, a Hippy, dreaming of touring India, hiking the hospital hallways, meeting surgical masters, and sampling drugs—morphine, antibiotics, general anesthesia, plus typhoid, tetanus, and hepatitis vaccinations.

After emailing doctors in India, I settled on Dr. Balasubramanian in Coimbadore because he charged less, had plenty of experience, and had worked in England for ten years with the physician who'd developed the resurfacing technique. He responded promptly and booked our flights within India. Besides, I just liked his style.

"Can we schedule the surgery on February 29?" I ask during an international phone call.

"There is no February 29," Dr. Bala responds astutely. "How about March 1?"

"Good call," I say. "Can you please tell me what day of the week today is?"

Joomi and I bid farewell to friends, most of whom are shocked that we're off to a scary, over-populated, third-, fourth-, or fifth-world country for major surgery, and assume they'll never us again.

"Give me a ring when you get there," a friend who'd been to India requests. "You can hop down to phone stalls on any corner and call me."

"I'm going for hip surgery. I won't be 'hopping' anywhere unless you know of special crutches with pogo-stick ends."

With tickets in hands at the ends of arms throbbing with germ-cocktail vaccinations, we head to the Chiang Mai airport in plenty of time to board our flight only to be removed for two hours while they fix one of its engines. Passengers grumble in the terminal, but I'm always pleased they solve any engine issues *before* the plane leaves the ground.

In Bangkok, our Air India flight to Chennai is delayed because—yes, they really did announce this on the airport loudspeakers—"the pilots are tired and have to sleep." I'm also heartily in favor of wide awake pilots. We muse that India is a mellow place where time stands still during mandatory siesta periods, but after experiencing the frenetic pace of India for a few hours, we realize that every pilot must be terminally exhausted just from living there.

While purchasing our tickets two weeks earlier, we'd inquired about the time difference between Thailand and India. The answer had been "one-and-a-half hours." I'd scoffed at this, having traveled a bit in the world, and hadn't experienced time-zone changes measured in partial hours. Well, the time change is indeed one-and-a-half hours… backward, though in some respects it seemed like eons in the past. During the next few days, we begin to understand that India is in a mysterious time warp where the past seems to have folded over the present.

~

hello, goodbye, Chennai

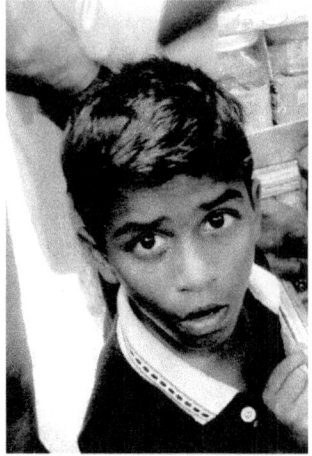

At the airport in Chennai, the staring begins. It appears there is only one multi-racial couple in India—a tall white male with a short, vaguely Indian-looking, darker female—and it's us. The sum total of three bare-shouldered women are currently in the entire country, and Joomi is one of them.

"Honey, we're not in Kansas anymore, and we're certainly not in Thailand."

The most experienced starers are professional beggars in all shapes, ages, and sizes. Mumbling and pleading, their eyes like black vacuum cleaners sucking on our hearts, the word "no" absent from their vocabularies, they float away with our ten rupees to their next victim. It must be a bitch to spend your life asking for money from strangers, who might give you something so you'll go away.

The dirty disheveled woman with an outstretched arm stands one foot away from us like a sad primeval statue and lets her pet monkey do the severe emotional work. The toothless old man peering out of a rat's nest of hair. The prematurely aging boy with an arrow through his tongue. The hag with gnarled wrinkles and crazy eyes straight out of a Steven King movie.

The heartless local advice we receive? "Don't give any-thing to anyone. It only encourages them." Whether we give to one and ignore another is immaterial; they are everywhere and leave their mark on our conscience. Each of these experiences carves another notch on the bedpost of our nightmares. This staring continues throughout the entire trip. It's not that people never smile, or they're un-friendly; it seems like those traits are buried under some unsaid burden or cultural cloud of gloom.

Several traffic snarls later, a taxi deposits us at our hotel. We enter the lobby to tight-lipped glares from the door-man and receptionist. No "Hello!" No "How are you?" No "Welcome! Can I help you?" Only stark stares that seem to scream, "What the hell are you doing here?"

Is it my breath? Or is my fly down? Do we look like the mass murderers whose photos are hanging on the post office wall?

We christen our lodging "The Frown Hotel," chuck our bags in our room, and head for the Maharaja Restaurant, heralded in *Lonely Planet* guidebook as "vegetarian… fan-tastic… popular with locals and travelers," in an area teem-ing with activity, like boiling water with trash floating in it.

As we sit down in the Maharaja, an adolescent boy in-stantly spreads two large banana leaves in front of us and sets bowls of miscellaneous condiment hoohah on the

table. No ordering necessary here. A barrage of waiters carrying metal pails slops rice and mystery vegetable stuff on the leaves. Errantly we wait for a fork or spoon while glancing around the room as locals grab glop with their fingers, pound it into the rice with their fists, and pop it down the hatch. Not sticky rice, the plain old, individual grain variety. It tastes okay, but we feel like inmates at the Frown Prison whose eating-utensil privileges have been revoked.

After lunch and politely refusing ten auto rickshaw Maniacs of Death, then haggling with one, we take a Cheap Tour Of Places We Don't Want To Go, see more mind-boggling amounts of trash, a plethora of traffic accidents, and "the world's longest beach," which is beastly hot with no palm trees or even a sliver of shade and stretches forever in both directions. No other people are on the beach because they're much smarter than us.

"Honey, I think that we're trapped in one of those desert scenes in a movie where lost souls slowly bake into pottery replicas of themselves, their ears burst into flames, and their lips fall off."

We resolve to leave Chennai as soon as possible or earlier. That night we eat a marginal meal at our Frown Hotel in a dark bar filled with dark men, a light one (me), and Joomi somewhere in between. The staring is almost painful.

~

the village idiot

Before we left Thailand, a friend had demonstrated the peculiar Indian head movement which means "yes." She shook her head side-to-side—not the "normal" side-to-side or back-and-forth shake which means "no"—side-to-side from the top, as if trying to remove water from her ears.

In America, this particular side-to-side technique would mean "I don't know" or "whatever." In India when you ask, "Do you have anything besides curry?" and the stone-faced waiter gently wobbles his head, he isn't a clueless novice wordlessly saying, "I have no idea." When you ask the taxi driver if he'll take you to the airport, he doesn't mean, "Whatever. Maybe. Who knows? What's an airport?" They're silently saying "yes."

This peculiar head wobble is universal in this subcontinent with, gasp, 780 different languages—not dialects, *languages.* (Another 250 died out during the last 50 years.) Besides "yes," I learn the wobble can also be a friendly greeting: "I am a peaceful man. I don't mean you any harm." Or the person might be using their head to "draw" the symbol for infinity in the air—a figure 8 or ∞.

You'll see a bus full of strangers mutely wobbling at each other, like a bunch of those plastic, bobble-headed, toy dogs staring out through the back window of a car, not yours I hope. Until you get it, this wobble might confuse you, but once you do, it's very cute and addictive. You'll unconsciously start wobbling, and when you return home, this peculiar movement will convince friends that you're mentally deranged, and they'll alert the authorities.

The next day we load our bags into a taxi van to find a bus, train, or oxcart to take us to Mamalapurim, a whistle-stop seventy kilometers south on the Bay of Bengal, undoubtedly still on "the world's longest beach." Our driver Basha's head wobbles perpetually, while genuinely smiling, and we negotiate a fair rate for the trip. The smog lifts after thirty kilometers so we can see the trash on the ground better. Sing along now, "On a clear day, you can see the litter."

Upon unloading our bags at a Mamalapurim guest house, I realize my computer bag is missing. The computer is one thing, but the two external hard drives are everything—essential things have all my information and files, the back-ups, my virtual life. Before I can wail and drop to my knees in prayer to every deity in the vicinity, the shopkeepers, guest house owners, and random people on the street already seem to know the Village Idiot has arrived.

Basha rings The Frown Hotel in Chennai to check if

they have my bag. Counter help says, "Call back in fifteen minutes," the longest fifteen minutes of my life. The good news? I'd been the *City Idiot* in Chennai. In our haste to get the hell out of town, I hadn't bothered to check out, and my computer is still inhabiting the room. *Hey, I'd paid on the internet and who wants to see your frowns again?* The bad news? I must return to Chennai and pay for an extra day of lodging while they hold my computer hostage. More good news? Basha and I have a grand time chatting in the taxi.

Basha grins and asks, "Do you like Indian women?"

"Yes, they dress like goddesses and are wonderful to watch."

"They are the most beautiful in the world."

"I disagree. Thai women are the most beautiful. And they don't wear as many clothes."

While trying not to shriek in terror, I instruct Basha on driving as he's passing a bus on a curve in the two-lane highway, careening into the path of a truck, a horse, and a 600-year-old limping man who couldn't afford a hip replacement. "If you drive like this in America, the police will take away your license."

"Why?" asks Basha.

"Because you're trying to kill me."

"We all drive like this."

"They would lock you all up in a big prison in America."

"Ha, ha, ha."

"And if you honk this much, they'll put you away forever in a rubber room at a mental institution."

After two hours of seeing the same trash from the other direction, I'm groveling at The Frown Hotel in Chennai and bartering for my computer. Three more hours of inching through rush-hour traffic and experiencing the same trash for the third time, I arrive back in Mamalapurim. Five minutes after Basha drops me off, I realize I'd left my paperback in his taxi. I mentally vow to tell no one else, ever. *This secret is between me, myself, and I. If it gets out, I might have to change my name legally to The Earth Idiot.*

Fifteen minutes later, as Joomi and I relax over a cup of coffee, Basha strolls into the restaurant, head wobbling intensely with a sly smirk on his face, and hands me my paperback, setting in stone my role as Universal Idiot in the mind of my mate.

Beside an expansive beach, Mamalapurim's primary attraction is one touristy street not lined with trash. All the mustachioed shopkeepers grin, wobble, and have tremendous discounts for us, complete strangers who have become their best friends in three seconds.

"How much is this?" I ask, pointing at a Persian rug.

"Oh," the shopkeeper wobbles, "money is not everything, my good friend,"

"Okay, fine. But what does it cost?"

"I give it to you for less than I paid."

The Silent Patient Idiot imagines what Mr. Shopkeeper wants to hear. *Gee whiz! You're the nicest man I've ever met! Here, take all my money and credit cards.*

Once he had seduced us into his shop and locked the door, his helper brings a serving of tea and sets it on the floor. Distracted by amazing textiles, jewelry, and religious gizmos, I promptly kick over both cups of tea and the teapot, luckily not onto the handwoven rug that he would've compelled me to purchase, possibly at knife-point. Mr. Shopkeeper's mouth drops open, but his mind delivers no words, since his brain is firmly ruled by the dollar signs in his eyes, which linger momentarily on my cane as they dream of his hands snatching it and beating me into a pulp.

Later that day in a young rock carver's cramped shop, I hold in my palm one of his incredible sculptures—an eggshell of flowering vines, with a mother elephant standing inside, with a baby elephant standing inside the mother elephant, like a ship inside a ship inside a bottle, but carved from a single block of marble.

While peering inside it and attempting the head wobble, I exclaim, "This is amazing!"

"It took three months to make," he announces proudly.

"I don't know how you have the skill or patience to do this without going insane!"

Without warning, the Village Idiot once again takes over, pushes his thumb through the delicate vines, destroying the sculpture in front of the boy's horrified eyes. No part of him wobbles or signals, "I mean you no harm."

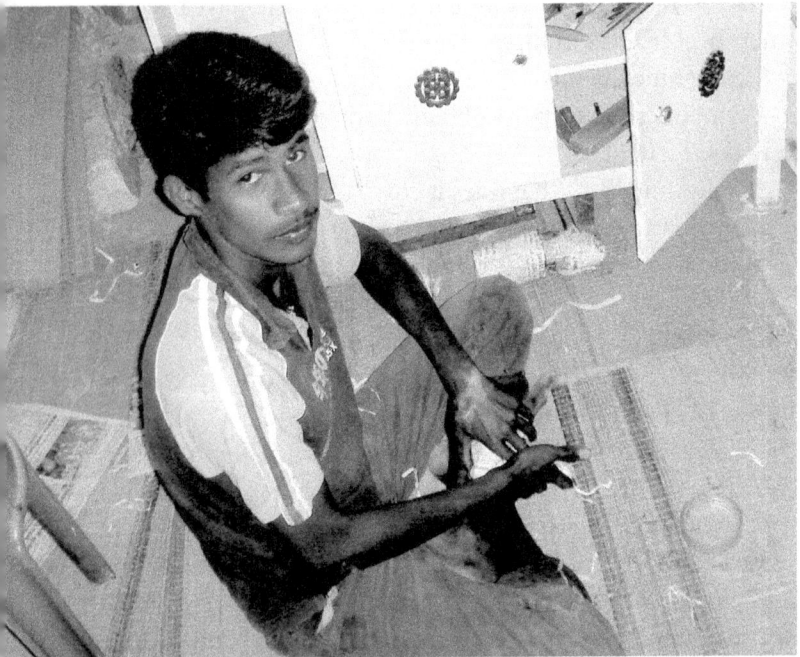

Wary carver with watchful eyes hoping the Village Idiot won't touch anything else.

I try to distance myself from the Village Idiot, but regrettably, he's me. Joomi pretends she is not associated with me in any form whatsoever while wishing she were invisible. I buy the hundred pieces from one rock that used to be an egg with elephants, plus more sculptures to assuage the revenge of my karma. We slink back to our guest house and wait for the knock on the door when the Tourist Police come to escort us out of the country.

Near dismemberment by the Hindu Generator of Light and Death

The full moon rises, and a Hindu festival consumes the village. We struggle through a mass of humanity to view stalls selling anything and everything, plus the illegitimate children of Anything and Everything. We marvel at a fireworks display comprising seven bottle rockets and cower at the sound of rapid explosions from somewhere on the ground, possibly from a machine gun. While locating the exact opposite direction of the reports for our escape, the Caned Crippled Idiot is nearly crushed by a large generator on wooden wagon wheels which powers a tiny parade of one religious float and its three light bulbs.

We try to elbow our way out of the dense crowds but are sucked along by multitudes making their way to an immense filthy pond surrounded by cement steps, possibly honoring the Hindu God of Garbage. As usual, the women are brilliant in their rainbow saris, the same ones they'll wear the next morning to swim in the sea.

As the sun climbs above the horizon on a high Hindu holiday and thousands of families flow down the world's longest beach to frolic in the waves, I am an extra in the movie *Gandhi* and understand why the Brits gave up trying to rule the hordes, throngs, and mobs of India. (Photo of this phenomenon on the first page of this chapter.)

~

hand grenades and meat cleavers

It's time to head inland to the hospital in Coimbadore, a non-touristic city that tourists tolerate on the way to somewhere they actually want to visit. *Lonely Planet* says the only thing to see is a yoga ashram thirty miles out of town. I'm beginning to grasp why religious meditation is so popular—locals and travelers alike need some method of escaping everyday mayhem in India.

We arrive at the airport in plenty of time to marvel at the security warnings on the overhead LCD screens. In most airports, photos of restricted items on panels moan about the danger of scissors, box cutters, and aerosol cans, "common" stuff that fits into carry-on baggage and meets the airlines' dimension requirements.

In the Chennai airport, the list includes items I've never considered taking on a plane anywhere. "Portable power saws and drills, pistols, automatic weapons,

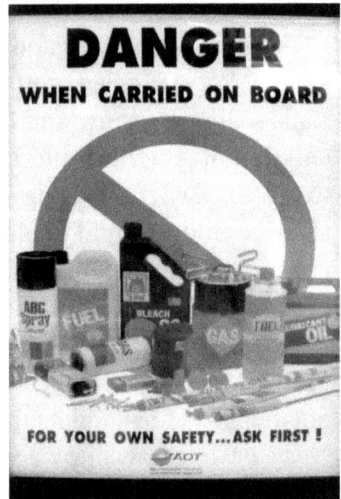

DANGER
WHEN CARRIED ON BOARD

FOR YOUR OWN SAFETY...ASK FIRST !

Airport security warnings in most of the known world.

blasting caps, baseball bats"—and on other signs in the lobby—"hand grenades, sabres, swords, crowbars, darts, spear guns, shotguns, ice picks, and hatchets."

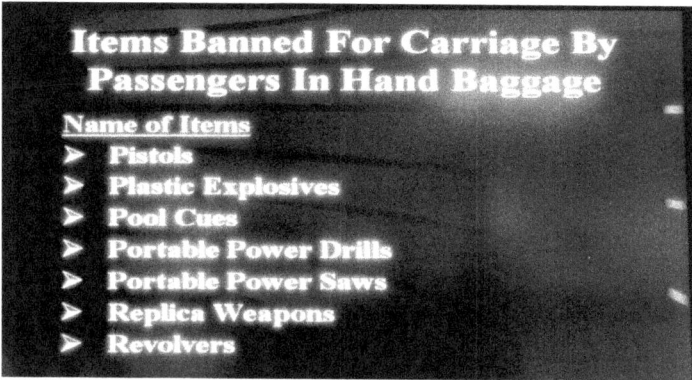

Items Banned For Carriage By Passengers In Hand Baggage

Name of Items
- ➤ Pistols
- ➤ Plastic Explosives
- ➤ Pool Cues
- ➤ Portable Power Drills
- ➤ Portable Power Saws
- ➤ Replica Weapons
- ➤ Revolvers

Damn, I can't even bring my meat cleaver or hand grenades! "Dynamite" is listed right before "chili powder, spices and pickles," which gives us an idea how hot the food might be. I'm suspicious that terrorists in the security line might be concealing a power saw in their pants or wearing a heavily sprayed hair-do constructed from plastic explosives. *Are they expecting the extended Osama Bin Laden family to travel through town?*

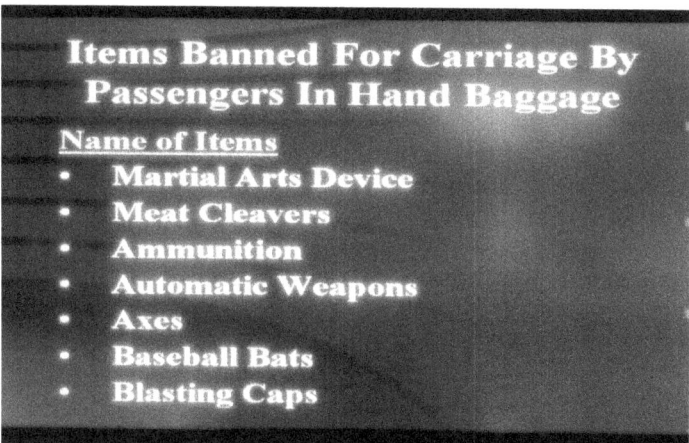

Items Banned For Carriage By Passengers In Hand Baggage

Name of Items
- • Martial Arts Device
- • Meat Cleavers
- • Ammunition
- • Automatic Weapons
- • Axes
- • Baseball Bats
- • Blasting Caps

"But Officer, you must understand! We couldn't put the meat cleavers and automatic weapons into our checked luggage, because we must destroy infidels immediately upon leaving the ground!"

"It's okay, honey. Give the nice man the hand grenades in your purse."

"Oops! Sorry, Officer. One of the pins came out…"

Once scanned, patted down, and released into the waiting area, we have no clue what to do. Our boarding passes list no gate number, and no airline agents are in sight, only security guards and streams of travelers. Flight announcements broadcast in Tamil and English (pigeon English or maybe bird-flu English) that squawk out of speakers are reminiscent of drive-thru windows at McDonald's.

"Flight two-crackle scratch-saven-tane will something-buzz-whenever from gate unintelligible-squelch-hiss. Would you like fries with that?"

After watching monitors in Tamil and English *not* tell us where to go as our departure time has slipped into the past, I show our boarding passes to a guard herding a crush of people through a gate. The man's eyes widen and arms flail as he whisks us onto a huge bus that carries only us.

"Where are the other passengers?" Joomi asks.

"Waiting on the plane, I hope? Start praying fervently."

The bus careens across runways toward parked planes, nearly collides with a baggage truck, approaches one jet, hesitates, and then lurches off to another that's fired up and ready to launch with its entry door closed. The ground crew rolls the walkway back up to the airplane. We race up the stairs, slink down the aisle like hunchbacks, and slump into our seats as a tempest of non-wobbling stares fling unconfiscated daggers at the time-thieves who just robbed 160 innocent victims of a few precious moments.

~

we're off to see the wizard

In the Coimbadore airport, a friendly taxi driver greets us and takes us to meet the doctor at an elegant hotel. We experience our first smiling doorman, who resembles Dr. Bala, though every photo on the doctor's website is serious and sour-faced while posing with the semi-genial original creators of the new hip resurfacing technique.

Routinely unsuccessful in the facial hair department, I covet the doorman's eleven-pound mustache that could conceal hand grenades or meat cleavers. After several months of concerted whisker growing in college, the eleven wispy hairs on my chin made me look like an elderly Chinese man. When my father saw me, he asked, "Is that a beard, or are you cultivating dental floss?"

Smiling and casual in his polo shirt, khaki pants, and sandals, Dr. Balasubramanian greets us and leads us to a fancy restaurant. His warm welcome makes us feel at ease, though I had discovered that you can rearrange the letters of his name to spell a wealth of warnings:

"A mad brain runs a lab."
"And barbarians maul!"
"I am a drab, nasal burn."
"Rabid banana murals."
"Anal urban barmaids."

An energetic man with extensive experience in hip re-surfacing, Dr. Bala appears to spend thirty-six hours a day greeting patients, disassembling and reassembling their bodies, or talking to prospective surgical candidates in every global time zone. Half the dinner we are alone while he's on the phone. We doubt if he's seen his family in months.

"So Dr. Bala, how soon before I can ride my motor-cycle again, learn to bungee jump, or take sumo wrestling lessons?"

"Most people have hip replacements in their 40s to 60s and surgery is not advisable in their 90s. One of my patients, a 95-year-old woman, didn't want to go on living with the constant suffering that kept her awake day and night. She told me, 'Either I survive and have no pain, or put me to sleep.' We did the replacement, and now she's pain-free and happy."

I want to ask this, but don't, since we just met, and soon he'll have a scalpel in his hands. *Gee, thanks for the evasive answer, Doc! How long before the happy, pain-free, 95-year-old lady got back on her motorcycle?*

Dr. Bala mentions he'll soon be off to Thailand for the first time, to give a hip presentation in Bangkok, and then head down to Pattaya. *Hmm. Anal urban barmaids?*

"Pattaya isn't Thailand," I advise, "it's only Pattaya. It's full of sex, drugs and rock 'n' karaoke—no place for a family man to vacation. If you go there, I'll send your wife digitally enhanced photos of you with naked women."

"I did not know. Many India people vacation there."

Perhaps they're learning advanced Kama Sutra positions in Pattaya?

After dinner, he takes us "home" to the hospital, not in a Mercedes, in his Hyundai. So far the India Doctor Experience is at odds with America, where doctors are wealthy god-like creatures who bless you with their presence for a few seconds while looking at and talking to your medical records on the clipboard. American doctors' answers to your questions are terse with the underlying message, "I know what I'm doing. You don't, and I don't want you to know. Shut up and pay the bill."

Dr. Bala personally escorts us to our suite, which is not sweet. It's semi-sterile, square yardage with attached sitting room, kitchen, and bath. The open windows in the hallways reveal courtyards being torn down, rebuilt, or somewhere in between, like the rest of India.

Mmm, Doc! You went all out with the stark and cold theme! Bare white walls, bare light bulbs, kitchen utensils heaped on the table, and two orange plastic flowers. So generous! One for each of us! An electric hot water kettle with a rusted element to poison our tea, window bars like a prison, no screens, and several hungry mosquitoes already in the room. Which diseases do they carry here in India?

Dr. Bala informs us that tomorrow, Sunday, will be a day of tests, and he has scheduled surgery for Monday morning. I ask if we're free to roam until then. "Of course!" he says.

When Joomi and I stroll past the main desk toward the front door, the nurses become visibly upset, mumble something in broken English like "cannot do, contamination, go back to your room," and call someone to tell them the Bad Children are escaping. We smile and walk out the door.

There's not much in the neighborhood, and judging by the stares, foreigners are scarce. The river next to the hospital is a stinking ditch full of filth. We hang out with the local homeless cows, score some juice, snacks, and a couple cans of flat Indian beer that tastes like it might have come from a sacred cow's urinary tract.

If they threw leftovers from the morgue into The Ditch of Death next to the hospital, no one would ever notice.

Back in Sterile Suite, we do not have a pillow fight, since one whack with these hard bags of straw might require a trip to the emergency room. I seem to remember "hospital pillows" on the list of restricted items at the airport.

~

tests, more tests, and terrified testes

The next morning, they X-ray my hip with a machine that might be a prop from an old war movie. And without the customary lead apron to protect my chest and nearby sperm, any children I procreate might glow or turn into X-Men as they leave the womb. After an adolescent attendant clumsily positions my body and escapes into his safe room, I wait alone for a long time while he scans the instruction manual to locate the ON button.

"Holding your breathing!" he says, as I try to lengthen the sacred sac so my family jewels drop below the dreaded mutation ray. Instead of the standard, one-second-exposure hum, this machine buzzes for several seconds.

It must be powered by two rats running on a treadmill hidden inside the closet. Or because he had to wait for a bolt of lightning to hit a rod on the roof?

The blood test begins with Nurse Sans Rubber Gloves, who ignores my bulging, cavernous veins with enough plasma to launch a small ship, and attempts to make medical history by plunging her massive needle into invisible, heretofore undiscovered blood canals. During three unsuccessful probes into nonexistent veins, she tries to suck solid muscle tissue into her syringe, using both hands to pull back the plunger. Headlines read: "Nurse Discovers New Arteries During Routine Blood Test As Patient Fights Back And Plunges Ballpoint Pen Into Her Jugular Vein."

After hours of tests and exams and not filling out extensive pages of informational forms like in America, Joomi and I ask Dr. Bala if we can go explore the city.

Amiable as usual, he says, "Fine, but be back by 6 p.m. to meet with the anesthesiologist. And don't eat or drink anything after 10 p.m."

We attempt to slink past the nurses' station and again are confronted with "danger, alarm, pollution, cannot do, stop where you are" as they phone Dr. Bala. The Bad Children smile and wait, acutely aware of a communication problem in the system, and imagine the ordeals ahead with these sergeants-at-arms. The doctor releases us without bail.

Nyah, nyah, na, nyah, nyah.

Coimbadore, known for its textile production, is known as "the Manchester of India." The markets overflow with incredible fabrics, saris, shirts, gowns—anything created from cotton woven with metal threads, bobbles and bangles, shells, beads, and trash from the streets.

"If you sit and watch India for five minutes," a friend had told us, "you'll see more than you've seen in your lifetime." He didn't mention that India constantly stares back at you. No other foreigners are in the central market, and we feel even more foreign than in the area near the hospital.

The anesthesiologist is professional and cordial, and for our benefit, called Dr. GBS, since his full name has several hundred syllables. His role in the operation is vital.

Whatever Dr. Bala decides to do to me, for however long, I don't want to experience any of it, nor wake up in the vicinity of sawing and sanding in my personal hip zip code.

"Are you a religious man?" Dr. GBS asks.

You ask me so the appropriate monk, rabbi, or priest can be on call for last rites? Well, Doctor, I'm spiritual, a devout Buddhist by now, after living in Thailand for years."

With disappointment and condescension in his voice, he states, "Well... *I*... am a Christian."

No shortage of deities in the hospital lobby to summon for help.

Oh my God—or your God—India has them all! I definitely do not want to get on your bad side. "Oh yes, Christ was

a great holy man. I'm a baptized Episcopalian, graduated from Lutheran Sunday School, and plan on going to
heaven, but hopefully not tomorrow."

After each doctor and their assistants have interviewed
me, I try to quell a rising fear of the operation because of
three misgivings.

One: The final question any staff member asks is, "Do
you have any doubts?" That's a pretty negative way of saying, "Do you have any questions?" I chalk it up to seman-
tics, but their questions alone give me doubts.

Two: No one seems to take notes, and I never see an
expanding file or medical report on Scott Jones. I decide to
mark my entire body with arrows in permanent ink pointing toward my left hip with a bright red X-marks-the-spot
on the correct operation site.

Three: When my mother was about my age, she had a
hip replacement—and then another—marking her drift
into a terminal depression from inactivity and unfortunate
impediments.

The biggest danger of surgery for older patients is post-
op complications, and Mom had more than her share.
After the second hip replacement, her leg transformed
into a pink, bloated, water balloon, and her ankle was as
thick as her thigh. More hospitals, more treatments, deeper
depression.

During my mother's hysterectomy, a doctor accidentally
sliced an innocent organ next door to the uterus, obliging
him to carve back in at a later date. Because of his mistake,
Mom had to wear a colostomy bag and carry her crap at
her side, not the fashion statement a snappy dresser like my
mother cared to make. The first day she ventured downtown, barely navigating with her Sack o' Shit—and I'm not
making this up—a wind-borne, inflatable child's swimming
pool knocked her down onto the sidewalk.

After a lung operation, her bowels refused to cooperate,

etcetera, creating the irreversible complication of... death.

These grim memories cause me to question my own miserly decision to opt for a cheap way out with Operation India. *Stupid Scotty, have you turned Scottish? Can you afford a bigger casket now with the money you're saving?*

The moment the medical worker ants complete their tests, we Bad Children race out of the hospital in search of my Last Supper, one more layer of curried whatever in my stomach. The Military Nurse Police purse their lips and eyes in an anticipatory glare. Soon they'll have the upper hand in the War of the Nurses—when I'm scrubbed naked, taped with intravenous tubes, drugged heavily, and stapled to the operating table.

Our last visitor for the night is a nurse with papers to sign to certify that I consent to the operation, that I'm personally responsible for the removal of any scalpels or sponges that Dr. Bala may forget inside my body, and that I won't reach up and strangle Dr. GBS when I wake up screaming during the operation. Joomi signs as a witness.

I sign another written paper in Hindi, Tamil, or Sanskrit that might say what the nurse said it did, or maybe not. Joomi signs as a witness.

Finally, during a sudden loss of common sense and intellectual sanity, I sign a blank sheet of paper the nurse says she has to fill in later. Joomi is again the witness. We are indeed the witless.

I expect all my worldly assets will be transferred electronically into Dr. Bala's Swiss bank account and my Harley motorcycle shipped to the nurse's husband while I'm required to obey every command from every nurse or face additional suffering in the Blood Test Torture Chamber as they extract sperm from a distant testicle through a secret vein in my neck.

As sleep takes me, I pray Dr. Bala has agile hands protected by sterilized rubber gloves, that Dr. GBS has a barrel of morphine near the operating table, and that any hungry mosquitoes conk out from a proboscis full of the drugs in my veins before they can inject their malaria parasites.

~

the war of the nurses

Before dawn I arise to scrub my body with the prescribed dark brown liquid that is so abrasive it must contain sulfuric acid, shards of steel wool, ground glass, and antibiotic curry powder. Soon bags of murky fluids drip into my arm as nurses roll me in to meet Dr. GBS, who administers his magic epidural concoction.

"How do you feel?" asks Dr. Bala cheerfully.

"Somewhere between drunk and stoned. Maybe droned, maybe stunk."

"Don't worry," he says, his head bobbing from side to side. "I'll be taking good care of you."

"Remember, it's the left hip," I mumble, "but feel free to repair anything else… that might need resurfacing while you're exploring and excavating…"

As I fade away, I faintly hear Dr. Bala chuckling and Dr. GBS praying to Jesus. *I wish you'd summon the help… of a god that's a… little closer… to… India…*

While I'm flying high in the Scottosphere, Joomi lives in the Realm of Gloom and Doom for hours, alone in Sterile Suite with a clock that doesn't seem to move. The Indian images of trash, mosquitos, filth, and frowns meld with the movie scenes where the surgeon slinks up and says, "Sorry, ma'am, but he didn't make it." Until you've bitten your fingernails to the nub while waiting for a loved one to return from major surgery—or not return—you'll never really know the anxiety and fear of those moments that seem to last longer than forever.

Finally… a nurse enters and issues her commands to Joomi. "He is out. Come. Bring a straw to help him drink."

Joomi snatches a straw from the kitchen and follows on the heels of the nurse, who won't walk fast enough. Luckily Joomi glances inside the straw and sees it's filled with spider webs, bugs, and spider poop. She saves it to stick into Dr. Bala's beverage when he stops by our room.

Joomi, one inch behind the nurse, wends her way to another wing—not to a recovery room—to an empty hallway with one bed on one side, like an abandoned car on a deserted road, the discarded patient's own personal ICU, the Insensitive Care Unit. Naked except for a tiny blanket that's one cotton molecule thick, I'm still zoned out and plugged into several bags and machines. Two strange devices attached to my hip look like those electric shockers that restart your heart in an ambulance, though they're strange drainage containers filled with Liquid Me.

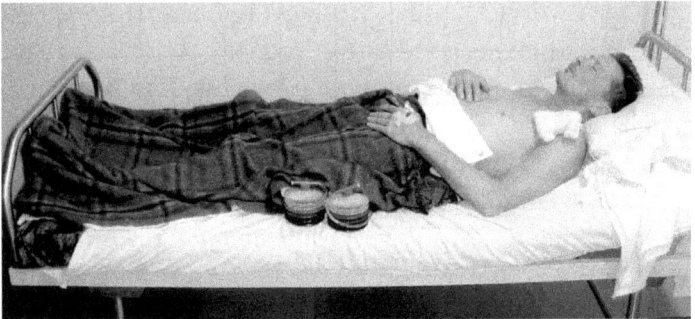

Comatose patient with taped manhole cover on wrist and dark containers filled with Liquid Me

"Scotty? Scotty, wake up!" Joomi pleads, leaning close to my face. Thank God, Bala, and GBS' holy anesthesia, I open my eyes and gaze vacantly at Joomi. She's comforted momentarily, but I don't remember the moment. I'm still trying to catch a train, plane, or coherent brain back to Earth.

According to Joomi, once in a while I crawl out of my mental haze, then drop back into Nonsenseville throughout the day. I whine about not knowing where I am, ramble on about Joomi saying things to me that I might have only dreamed, and apologize for forgetting whether I asked her for water, whether she brought it to me, or whether I ever drank it. Later, when I tell another patient about this stupor, she says tenderly, "Love, you're like that every day."

On Post-Op Day One, the War of the Nurses is in full-swing. I'm barely able to retaliate with cotton and tubes taped here, there, and on everything I want to move. I lay like a soldier at attention, so I don't knock the two jars of Liquid Me off the hospital bed.

Neither Joomi nor I care for fluorescent lights, especially four, glaring, yard-long tubes on the ceiling, so we use the one lonely light bulb on the wall. Joomi burns incense to thwart the chemical hospital odors wrestling with the air in our room. She keeps the door locked. The Stormtroopers have to knock before entering, and they don't like it.

"Wait!" Joomi shouts, then pauses for a few seconds to heighten their exasperation before opening the door. Charging into the room, the Stormtroopers turn on every light, the way *it's supposed to be* in their room, in their territory. Sniffing the air like narc dogs, they assume the Bad Children have established an opium den right under their noses.

"Take BP," one nurse demands.

I learn damn soon that BP means "blood pressure," and they take it 79 times per day.

"Give shots," the other snorts.

Perhaps they're shy about their remedial English, but the first words I learn in any language are, "Hello, how are you?" Every Stormtrooper in our Nurse Platoon is kind and warm in their own way, but their own way is puzzling to me. (My way is undoubtedly puzzling to them, because it's even puzzling to my own family.) They're like the hotel personnel who missed—or flunked—their classes in Remedial Smiling and Friendly Greetings 101.

Through a tiny manhole cover bordered by tape on

my wrist, Nurse Maniac pumps medicine into me with a needle-less syringe the size of an industrial caulk gun. Whenever any of the Stormtroopers do this, they seem to be rushing, like the traffic outside, in a hurry to barely move. They stick the gun barrel into the hole and press the plunger as fast as they can. Then they do their same trick with the next three shots.

Scotty's tortured artery and bulging wrist can only take so much pharmaceutical caulk at one time. My skin swells visibly around the manhole, and Nurse Nasty gets impatient, tapping and pressing the lumps with her bare fingers. I smile and say politely, "Slowly, please, slowly. Big syringe, little vein."

I know I'm just one of your patients, but you could have a little patience! And you're not the little Dutch boy sealing a dangerous hole in the dyke with your caulk gun!

Non-smiling Stormtroopers pose reluctantly with the Bad Children

~

a pain in the ass

Post-Op Day Two begins early with incessant hammering, pounding, and scraping right outside our suite. Doctors, doctors' assistants, and doctors' assistants' assistants visit to inquire about my pain, naively presuming it's gone.

Dr. Bala: "Any hip pain?"

Recovering Patient: "Yes. Remember? I had an operation two days ago."

Dr. Ba La-la Land: "But not like the pain before?"

Patient: "Yes, that pain, plus pain from the skin you slit and the muscles you muscled out of the way to get to the bones you filed and resurfaced."

Dr. GBS: "No pain, eh?"

Impatient: "Yes, here, there, and over yonder."

Dr. BS: "But the pain from before is gone."

Sick and Tired of BS: "No, it throbs at night like before, but now other pains distract me from the previous pain."

And now you're a royal pain in the ass!

Dr. BS, formerly known as GBS, only likes to listen to what *he* has to say, scoffs at my answer, then mumbles something as he leaves the room.

Does he think I should leap out of bed, bless him, and present him with prepared testimonials of his divine medical skills?

It has become crystal clear that the communication problem is crippling the system. I'm continually asked questions I've already answered. When a doctor or their bevy of assistants tells *me* something, the Nurse Platoon doesn't hear it through the grapevine.

Private Nurse: "Give pain shots."

Bad Child: "Dr. Bala said I don't need them."

Nurse, disgruntled: "Don't roll over like that."

Smiling Child: "Doctor said I could." *Neener, neener.*

Nurse, rattled: "Eat breakfast."

Grinning Child: "Thanks, but I'm not hungry."

Nurse, wide-eyed: "Must eat."

Child, wild-eyed and demented: "No."

Private Nurse gives up and runs out to recruit reinforcements. Doctor's assistants come to remove my catheter and Liquid Me drainage system. Ah, freedom. I can roll over without worrying about spilling Me.

A physical therapist arrives with a semi-rusty steel walker that weighs as much as scaffolding for a two-story construction site and looks very good for building upper body strength. "Time to walk!" he says enthusiastically. It seems early, but I'm all for it. Mom couldn't put any weight on her leg for six weeks after her operation. It's been two days since mine. I'm stiff and sore and in pain, but I walk with my buddy "Walker." *He's very sturdy. I'm not. Cool.*

Later I inch out the door to check on the incessant racket and see if airplanes are landing in the hallway. Under the stairs across the hall, a worker smooths the massive marble tiles with sand and water, using an ancient machine rustier than my walker.

Great. I'm recovering from hip resurfacing to the sounds of floor resurfacing which are drowning out the Sound of Silence I really want. Could this be the same machine they used on me during the operation? The same guy, too? I wonder if he washed his hands?

It feels grand to walk again, even though I have to carry the six, count 'em, *six* fucking keys to our suite of rooms—skeleton keys that look like they'd been used in a dungeon during the Iron Age and are almost heavy enough to drag the green hospital pants off my ass and onto the floor during therapeutic creeps along the corridor.

"Hi, there!" I call merrily and wave as I shuffle past the Nurse Platoon Guard Station, "I'm going for lunch in Bombay!"

It's not funny to the Stormtroopers, because they think I'm not only a Very Bad Child, but clinically insane, and I just might try the two-hundred-mile schlep.

Meals are confusing. In America hospitals serve routine, bland meals, three times a day, whether you want them or not, with no discussion of any choice—geometrically-shaped meat, mystery vegetables microwaved for eleven hours, and unidentifiable objects suspended in green Jello.

Dr. Bala had said to us, "Order whatever you want," whatever that meant. It doesn't include the mouth-watering Thai meals we dream about daily. "Whatever you want" in this hospital means pizza, or selections from the takeout menus of nearby Indian restaurants that offer Curry, Mother of Curry, Second Cousin of Curry, Bastard Child of Curry, plus pages of obscure menu items with no pictures. Once ordered via the Nurse Platoon, these meals arrive within a half-hour to two-and-a-half-hours to never.

A pair of nurses knocks on the door. Safety in numbers.

"Patience, please!" Joomi yells and smirks mischievously while I hide the opium pipes, send the other addicts out the back window, and flush the heroin down the toilet. Immediately upon hearing the lock click open, Nurse Pester and her sidekick barge in, flick on all the lights, and begin their interrogation and torture.

"Eat lunch?"

"We ordered it two hours ago. It hasn't come. Did you eat

it for us?"

"No. Stop doing that."

"Physical therapist said I could. Remember I'm walking."

"Take BP."

"Take yours instead. You seem stressed."

"Take temperature."

"Okay, where do you want it this time?

The temp thing is a little too random for me. I think all members of the Nurse Platoon use the single thermometer stored in our bathroom. At first they put it under my tongue, but lately they stick it into my armpit.

When I was still lost in Scottyville after surgery, I wonder where the thermometer went? No, I don't want to know.

Post Surgery Nurse: "Take BP."

Incoherent Patient: "Want BM."

"I get pan."

"I'll hold it."

"Take temperature."

"Who are you?"

"Spread 'em."

"Whatever."

~

molten curry

I loved Indian food before coming to India. Although Joomi and I eat some splendid meals while on the coast in Mamalapurim, most of the dishes look alike: orange-brown mush covering vegetables grown in soil fertilized with curry or chicken force-fed with curry-infused grain. And they look about the same on the way out as on the way in.

My bulging bowels haven't moved since before the operation, four days ago. All my pre-op curried meals have merged into an immobile mass expanding somewhere between my stomach and lungs, because I am trapped in bed and would be forced to poop in the pan. I refuse to eat until something comes out the other end.

Constant pain in my abdomen masks the sporadic aches in my hip. Joomi calls the Nurse Platoon to request an enema bag or suppository. Two Nurse Soldiers enter gleefully, ready for excavation, wearing miner's caps with spotlights, carrying pickaxes, safety ropes, two suppositories and surprise, surprise—a pair of rubber gloves. I imagine one will spread 'em while the other deposits the suppositories an arm's length up my ass, somewhere near my collarbone.

Soldier One: "Have suppositories."

Bad Child: "Thank you very much."

Soldier Two: "We put in."

Very Bad Child: "No, thanks. I'll do it."

Soldiers One and Two, speechless: "…"

Very Strange Bad Child, smiling: "…"

Soldier Two, eyes narrowing: "We put in."

Very Strange Deranged Bad Child: "I put in. Thanks for the gloves. I didn't know you had any."

Both Soldiers, heads bobbing frantically: "…"

Very Strange Deranged and Dangerous Bad Child: "Thank you very much. See you later."

The soldiers race out of the room to tell their mothers, the doctor, the Head Nurse, or to apply for a position in Intensive Care, where the patients are unconscious, or better yet, at a morgue. It's comforting to know they might wear rubber gloves to insert suppositories in the patient next door before they arrive to give shots or—don't even think it, Scotty—put the thermometer in my mouth.

The suppositories do their job (one would probably have sufficed) and the runs begin. Unfortunately, I'm incapable of running to the toilet. Though I can slowly do the Walker Walk, getting out of bed takes about eleven minutes of intense concentration on correct leg position to avoid piercing muscle cramps which feel like they're tearing out internal stitches.

Sitting up is hard enough, but sitting down is painful and precarious while balancing with one hand on the toilet reservoir and one on the sink—no handrails next to my porcelain throne. A hard plastic extender rises a foot above the toilet seat, which makes it convenient for a nine-foot, 300-pound person. When my vast reservoir of molten curry presses down upon the soft, round door without a lock, it wants out: not in fifteen minutes... now. During my hundred expeditions to the Discomfort Station, I somehow manage to hit the bulls-eye without spraying curry puree on the walls. Indian food will never be the same.

~

Superman Marshall and his Nursettes

Marshall Cooper, a dramatic operatic tenor, voice instructor, and fellow Hippy with wild curly hair trying to escape from his head, arrives from New York and takes the room next to us. It's great to hear his surgery story and have a second foreign opinion on the Indian medical adventure. He'd hoped for hip resurfacing, but once Dr. Bala saw the caverns in the not-so-round end of his femur during surgery, Marshall got a complete hip replacement, plus a free, non-related tendon repair the doctor thought he'd appreciate. Very proactive, Dr. Bala!

"Marshall, my man!" Dr. Bala says to his patient struggling out of anesthesia. "While touring your pelvic area, I fixed other things I thought you'd like. You now have a new tendon, an auxiliary bladder, and an eleven-inch penis."

The man can sing and does so regularly. I do love a good ol' barn-burning Italian aria, and Marshall's resounding voice fills the wing, almost drowning out the rumble of floor resurfacing in the hallway. I've never been a fan of interminable, incomprehensible operas that aren't over until the fat lady sings. I always wish she'd sing first so I can leave.

Like musicals, dialog that is too stupid to be said is sung. I picture Marshall stabbed on stage nightly, but instead of dying, he gets up and sings about it.

Having traded my buddy "Walker" for a cane, I often hobble over to visit Marshall and covet the fresh bouquets given to him by his groupies, the Fawning Nursettes, who even bring by their friends to hear him sing. I'd heard of singing for your supper, but I didn't realize I'd have to sing for flowers in India. Joomi and I are still lower-caste Bad Children with our two complimentary dingy plastic flowers, the same ones that have been gathering dust and airborne germs from the hundreds of previous patients who've passed through our suite.

I also admire the "cane" presented by Marshall's wife in America—an exotically carved, six-foot staff used by Gandalf to slay dragons in *Lord of the Rings*.

How'd he get it on an Indian airplane that doesn't allow pool cues, sabers, or swords in carry-on baggage? In zealous Bollywood style, I picture him singing through security as guards and adoring flight agents fling fresh roses in his path. My cane is a light, metal, adjustable variety with the brand name "Singha" prescribed in Thailand for incapacitated people damaged by too many Singha beers.

I am most jealous of the way Marshall sits upright in a flash and whips his legs over the side of the bed, causing me to grimace in pain at the very thought of doing this myself. And my operation was two days before his.

Marshall is only a man, not a superman, and I am a complete wimp! But wait! I've never seen his incision! Marshall must be an actor employed by the doctors to harass, depress, and convince me that I'll never recover and will need a personal nurse to lift my invalid body onto my Harley motorcycle equipped with chrome training wheels. Hmm. Any nurse would fit the classic role in Bikedom: the bitch on the back.

~

bordering on insanity

The War of the Nurses reaches a pivotal battle around Post-Op Day Four. One Nurse Commando flanked by two bodyguards penetrates the security precautions of Joomi and advances menacingly with four or five large syringes. The taped medical manhole on my wrist now sits high on a hill of pus created by the fermenting reservoir of every shot from the past few days. You can't see veins or bones in my hand because the skin is thin and stretched like a water balloon ready to burst. It hurts.

Commando Nurse: "Give shots."

Bad Child: "No, thanks. Too much pain. Look."

Commando: "Must give shots."

Impudent Child: "Not here. How about somewhere else, like in *your* arm?"

Commando, advancing with bodyguards: "Give shots!"

Devil Child, hiding blimp hand under the bed covers: "No way. Get Dr. Bala!"

I consider trying to strangle her, but can't do it with only one hand. It's an Indian stand-off, but they finally back off, and later switch my manhole to the other wrist.

How can these medical professionals look at my hand, ignore my pleas, and imagine they'd add four more syringes of liquid? Of course! They want to see it explode.

Red bumps that itch, break open, and ooze have overrun my back, like measles or chicken pox.

It must be curry pox!

A skin doctor checks me out and says it's a reaction from too many antibiotics and painkillers. *Plus chili powder or floor scraps "accidentally" added by the nurses.* He suggests pills instead of injections.

Yes! Justified! The nurse probably missed my artery altogether, but kept tapping and pressing and squishing the medicine around to my back and out my pores.

A scarlet welt or bite or something infectious on Joomi's thigh itches and swells and expands—from one inch… to three inches… to six inches in a half hour. A member of the Nurse Patrol escorts Joomi to the Emergency Room, and I expect never to see her again. An hour later after a tetanus shot, the swelling has subsided, and she returns feeling much better.

Unlike in America where we're taught tetanus comes from stepping on rusty nails, Dr. Bala explains matter-of-factly, "Insects carry Tetanus in India."

They've undoubtedly been feeding on the rust from my walker, the electric kettle in our room, and the X-ray machine!

For several days Joomi takes over the chore of giving me a sponge bath in bed after watching miscellaneous medical hands on my naked body. But one morning—*or is it the middle of the night?*—a persistent knock on the door rouses us. At 4:45 a.m. Joomi staggers to the door, opens it a crack, and glares Indian-style at the intruder. Nurse Nuts announces she's here to give me my bath. Coursing with rage and adrenaline, Joomi picks up our refrigerator and chases her down the hallway.

At 6:15 a.m., Nurse Clueless raps on the door and wants the wash cloth from our kitchen. We've traveled thousands of miles and are paying thousands of dollars, and this wacko worker ant wants our wash cloth at dawn. Their terrorist tactics have escalated to psychological warfare. Joomi turns into Exorcist Girl as her ears steam, her head spins around, and green projectile vomit splatters onto the nurse's chest. We plan escape routes while we're still semi-sane.

It's great to have a personal caretaker during this saga, but this being Joomi's first trip to a "developing" country, the days start to take their toll. Sometimes the caretaker roles are reversed, and all I can do then is listen and sympathize. She doesn't feel safe walking alone in the neighborhood for a Tour of the Trash. She's sick of the food, the sterile room, and watching me wince with pain. She's hopelessly outnumbered in the War of the Nurses and tired of being mosquito bait. If we're in a room with fifty mosquitoes, all fifty will ignore me and choose a blood cocktail from her tender, sweet skin. Luckily she meets a friendly Indian woman and they go out for a relaxed afternoon of shopping before Joomi sneaks out to catch a plane back to Thailand.

~

premature escape

On Post-Op Day Five, the doctor gives the go-ahead for our hospital release to journey somewhere for a week of recovery before bandage removal. My mom had been in bed or on crutches for six weeks, and I'm out of the hospital in six days! She'd be proud... or jealous.

Perusing our *Lonely Planet India* Travel Bible, we're attracted to the town of Ooty in the Nilgiri Hills and the narrow-gauge train that runs there via the steepest track in the world—360 curves, 16 tunnels, and 250 bridges in 40 kilometers. The train takes five hours to crawl up and nineteen minutes to careen down. Dr. Bala suggests we take a taxi up and the train down.

On the internet, every hotel in Ooty features rooms decorated in shades of orange-brown curry, but we find two charming resorts with photos captioned "a private garden with each room and stunning views." We want a place that's quiet,

Non-smiling Dr. Bala agrees to discharge patient under threat of strangulation with Singha cane

beggar-less, trash-less, and traffic-less so I can practice walking sans Nurse Commandos.

I stroll slowly but handily with my cane to the modern sport-utility taxi-van, gingerly lift my frail self into the back, and sit sideways with both legs on the seat. Sitting is still a chore, and I can't really bend the gimp hip more than sixty degrees. Despite our explicit direction of "please take it slowly," our driver cannot shake his hereditary speed of breakneck, which today could be break-hip.

Though the scenery through miles of marvelous mountains carpeted with terraced tea bushes that appear to produce enough caffeine for the known universe, I am soon focused solely on levitating above the seat so the incision in my leg doesn't wear down to the bone or metal joint. Our driver saved at least three seconds of travel time by honking continuously and passing buses on blind curves while forcing motorcycles off cliffs. Shoulders on this road are composed of sand, trash, sharp rocks, or only thin air. I'm not sure how we survived the oncoming truck while passing this bus with no room for us on either side of the road.

My hip throbbing, my arms weakening, and my hands raw from hours of advanced levitation techniques, we arrive in Ooty, a hillstation from colonial days, originally built so the British could escape grass-roots India during the hot season for a measure of peace, cool climate, and splendid scenery.

Our driver has no clue regarding the location of our hotel. He asks directions from street people who've never been beyond their three-block neighborhood. They gesture vaguely up, down, or over yonder. Mystified, the driver takes off again on marginal pot-holed roads surrounded by piles of cement, rock, and sand (delivered sometime during the last decade) which might be repaired (sometime during the next decade).

An hour later we stumble upon Lodging Choice Number One which, unlike the cheery photo on the web, looks like a haunted resort. It's late afternoon, Ooty is cool, the rooms are dark and cold, and staff is colder. Of course, the Uniformed Frowns don't have my internet reservation, nor do they care to help, though there's not another guest in sight. The private gardens with each room are hard, curry-colored dirt with dead bushes. I struggle back into the taxi to search for Lodging Choice Number Two. We never find it, and once again see all of Ooty while bumping over its rutted roads and stopping to ask directions from more locals who've never ventured out of their neighborhoods. We pass Internet Lodging Options Three Through Ten that must have used grand opening photos shot before the mold had enshrouded the buildings.

My patience is worn thin, about one irritation atom thick. After a quick perusal through *Lonely Planet*, we decide to go upscale at the Savoy Hotel built by the British in 1829. I politely demand that the driver call the hotel, reserve a room, and ask directions from local taxi drivers instead of beggars in the street.

By the time we arrive, the temperature is downright cold. I want a derrick to hoist me from the car and deposit me in a bed. As usual, it's run by the Frown Corps, and counter help informs me they have no double rooms for their quoted internet price of $75, only suites for $130, the cost of one of my favorite guest houses in Thailand for a month. At least the grounds are Britishly clean and tidy, present a trash-less place to walk, and our suite of four rooms is almost elegant. We're most attracted to the LCD wide-screen TV so we can bury ourselves under blankets, watch a movie, and fall asleep to dream we're someplace else.

A tropical lass at heart, the frigid temperature has turned Joomi into a coughing thing, and I'm not well enough to be a doctor to my nurse. While waiting for delivery of our room-service order, we discover the rental DVDs advertised in the hotel literature do not exist, and there are no movie channels.

The room service fare is a speck of good news surrounded by bad. The tea is nectar from the gods, but the tomato soup is Dishwater brand, not Campbell's. The fries taste as if sliced from potatoes harvested in 1829 by the Brits. The club sandwich is unquestionably the worst I've ever eaten since I visited England, where I learned the only decent food besides fish 'n' chips is found in countries other than England. I think we order supper, too, but I've successfully blotted the tasteless glop out of my mind.

I venture into the bathroom and gaze vacantly at the toilet located just above the slick tile floor, about twenty feet below eye level, and try to figure out how the hell I'll get down there and back up again. Sure, I've mastered getting in and out of beds or cars, but so far I've only used the tall hospital toilet with its plastic extension. I honestly don't know how I'll manage without my leg cramping, causing me to lurch in pain, lose my balance, and fall backward onto the seat which dislocates the hip and tears open the incision allowing the steel-capped femur to rip out of the skin, and clank onto the blood-stained floor. I may have to ask two of the Frown Corps to form a circle with their arms and suspend me above the porcelain hole.

As the space heater warms the room, removes every moisture molecule from the air, and flavors it with the odor of baked metal, Joomi's cough approaches pneumonia levels. I wonder if we can survive the trip back to the hospital the next day. I'm confused why Dr. Bala allowed us to risk destroying his recent surgical masterpiece on the road to too cool Ooty and tackle very inhospitable accommodations where even a trip to the bathroom is a dangerous endeavor. *Ah, ha! I get it now! The nurses convinced the doctor to dispose of me!* Superman Marshall probably would've driven here himself or trekked alone with his magnificent staff, the wooden one, with nurses swooning behind him.

That evening and the next morning, I see only two other guests, which tells me the receptionist must've had a double room, and she scammed the caned cripple ready to pass out when he checked in.

We enter the empty dining room for breakfast and are

greeted by three silent waiters, waiting for something they seem to have forgotten.

I address their blank stares. "Breakfast?"

This reminds them why they, and we, might be in the dining room at 10 a.m. We choke down the cold scrambled eggs, lukewarm beans, and dishwater tomato juice while sitting as far away from the curry buffet as possible and listening to orchestral hits from the colonial era crackling out of one eleven-rupee plastic speaker.

Unable to brave the escape from Ooty, the next day we book a room at King's Cliff—"an intimate retreat high on Strawberry Hill in a colonial mansion with superb views." We're thrilled to check out of the Savoy until counter help gives us the bill: 8,000 some rupees = $200.

~

escape from the escape

As we exit our taxi at King's Cliff, our last chance lodging choice, two members of the local Frown Corps lead the limping invalid to a distant room with a private porch. Smiling despite their blank stares, I say, "Perfect! Jolly good! We'll take it!"

They gesture across the expansive courtyard we'd just traversed, perhaps toward the office, perhaps toward England, and motion for me to follow.

Mr. Limp totters back to the exact spot he'd recently been (several meters behind the Frown Corps who had been scurrying in an attempt to lose the cripple) to learn that the room he previewed isn't available. As luck would have it, or maybe it's the foam dripping out of my mouth, or I momentarily lose consciousness and scream, "Honey, get the police, an American Consulate General, or a meat cleaver!"—the manager appears and asks graciously if there is a problem.

"Why, yes," I say calmly and consistently without allowing him to speak until I've finished my humble rant, "but not a big one. I'd like someone to smile and say, 'Welcome to King's Cliff! How are you? Can I help you?' I'd say, 'Hello! I'm Scott Jones. This is Joomi. What's your name? It's nice to meet you.' Then I'd like to view a room we can rent without stumbling throughout your entire hotel grounds, give you cash, eat your food, have a drink, relax, and lie down before my leg falls off, and I bleed on your nicely manicured lawn. This may be the last day of my life."

Thank Whichever Hindu God with several arms, heads, trunks, and vicious teeth, the man is helpful, even smiles once, and offers us the room we first viewed. It has a lovely fireplace. Their tea is perfect. The view from our porch is delightful because we feel like we're not really in Ooty, only looking over it.

Joomi's cough is progressing downward in her lungs, and we need medicine, sweaters, and phone cards. We trudge back to the lobby to summon a taxi which "will come in ten minutes." Not relishing the round-trip back to the room, we wait ten minutes which changes to "will come in twenty minutes," which becomes forty-five minutes, while we alternately sit in the sun that's too hot, then in the shade that's too cold, in textured metal chairs that leave imprints in my tender buns. *Has anything ever gone smoothly in India for anyone in the last 5,000 years?*

While waiting we gain bewildering insight into the non-smiling phenomenon while watching a group of twenty people posing for a photograph at what appears to be a family reunion or post-wedding party. The women wear the typical, pouty model frowns, and the men scowl like death row inmates marched into the shot at gunpoint. If the photographer is saying "smile," no one in the party is having any part of it.

"Okay, fine, you can take my picture, but I want everyone to know that I don't want to be here, and I can't stand any of these people around me."

If the photographer is muttering "say cheese," these people hate cheese. Perhaps it's a post-divorce party.

Ooty department store with only one department with everything.

Our two hours of errands throughout Ooty via taxi are taxing. I get a glimpse of markets I'd like to walk through but can't, more trash I don't want to see, and a plethora of beggars I'd rather not meet. We return to the King's Cliff with pills and sweaters for Joomi, books and Tiger Balm for me, but no phone recharge cards.

India is a world telecommunication powerhouse. When you call the info line of a major company in Bulgaria, it's answered in India. We'd purchased our new India SIMM phone cards near Chennai, a few hundred miles away. Though we could use our phones in Ooty *and* Coimbadore to call anywhere in India and the world, we could not buy recharge cards here, only back near Chennai.

Go figure. No, why bother? Let's just jump off King's Cliff and be done with it.

We choose not to purchase the school shoes and belly.

Joomi puts on all the clothes she brought from Thailand, plus the two sweaters she'd purchased in Ooty. She looks like a round sweet potato with a small Asian head, but she's warm. I light a fire in our room and order a beer, and that's not easy either. They don't serve beer at the hotel. They summon our taxi driver again, who returns a couple of hours later with a couple of warm beers for a couple of hundred rupees. However, the hotel's room service food is fit for a king, which is what we feel like in this mansion above the masses constructed by the now deposed colonials. Psychologically comforting? No. Physically? Yes, very, but we want out.

I call Dr. Bala. "Would you send our taxi driver to take us back to Coimbadore? And please ask him to drive gently and carefully… like an elderly American… or I'll stick my cane into the orifice of his choice… sideways!"

"Why?" he asks, surprised.

"Because it's cold here, and I'm cold here, and my nurse has pneumonia. Please see if you can put us in that snazzy Residency Hotel where you took us to dinner when we arrived."

"Okay," he agrees. "I'll call you back."

The friendly hotel manager authorizes the delivery of

a stack of wood sticks that snap, crackle, and pop in the screen-less fireplace. We drift off to sleep imagining cinders from the blaze, one meter away, will shoot onto the bed, setting fire to our hair and crispy clean sheets. At least we'll die warm.

Dr. Bala never called back, but at 9:00 a.m. the next morning, our original taxi driver arrives with another man who we pray has elderly American driving skills. They are ready to roll, and the driver gestures impatiently towards the taxi.

Wait a minute! I've paid till noon! It's warm, and I'm going to get my money's worth.

"We're not leaving until after brunch, and I'll buy both of you breakfast. Relax until noon." I ask how much he'll charge me for the delay while bending over and handing him a tube of KY Jelly. INDIA has become an acronym that now stands for "I'm Not Doing India Again."

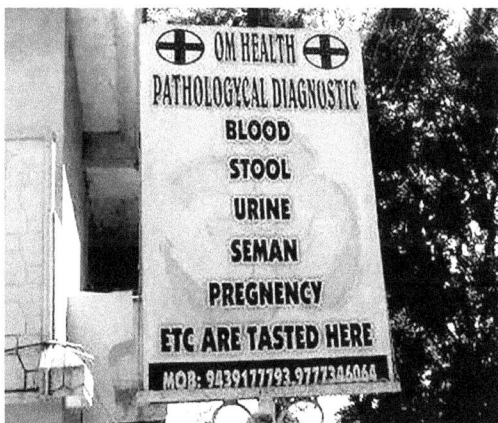

We're pleased to return to Dr. Bala's medical facility instead of this one.

~

the bad children return

Our return trip to Coimbadore is pleasant, and we savor the views of infinite tea fields we couldn't fully appreciate on the Death Ride up. However, toilets on the trip back are difficult to reach and look like no one has cleaned them since the birth of Buddha. Though I have to touch sinister areas of this one, at least there's a Brillo pad on the sink for cleaning my hands. I consider ending it quickly and electrically by attempting to turn on the fan.

Complication

Disinfection

Electrocution

As usual, the driver does not take us where we want, and instead deposits us at the Jenny Club which has a dramatic, brightly illuminated, photo-billboard of itself at the entrance that doesn't resemble the hotel in real life. The lobby looks like a hospital waiting area with white walls, and the rooms are as characterless as a furniture store for the dead, although the brochure contains an impressive list of amenities, which is spelled "amnesties." The swimming pool, the Ayurvedic Health Spa, and a beautiful lawn catch our eye.

We check in, but during our tour of the grounds, we find the swimming pool is empty while they're removing some black muck with a rotting odor that almost triggers

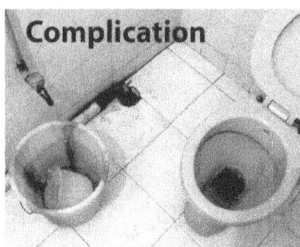

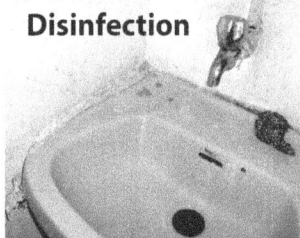

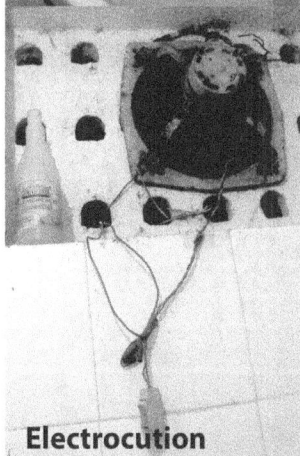

the vomit reflex. This noxious smell wafts over to the pool beside the Ayurvedic Spa building, which looks like an abandoned insane asylum. Strange grass-covered lumps and bumps, perhaps made by gigantic malignant moles, cover the lawn. This alien area becomes the venue for an international cricket match that evening, set with tables, chairs, stacks of speakers, and drunks bellowing at a mammoth projection screen below our hotel room window.

Try walking on this lawn without a cane.

Good news? I can maneuver down to the toilet, room service delivers beer, and an internet connection allows me to plan our remaining days in India in the most peaceful place we have experienced so far—back in Mamalapurim on the Bay of Bengal.

The next morning the Bad Children return to the hospital for a bandage change, mini-copies of my X-rays, plus a letter from the doctor certifying that I have metal body parts which could be mistaken for a hand grenade surgically implanted in my hip, guaranteed to set off airport security alarms.

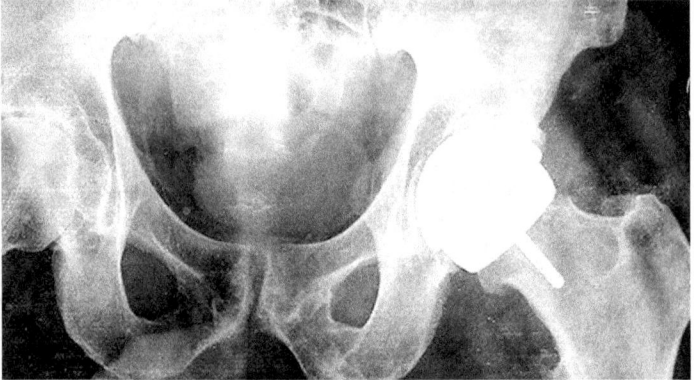

New hip x-ray with chromium cobalt joint or is it a hand grenade that will precipitate our arrest in the airport security line?

We have a departure dinner back at the Residency Hotel with Dr. Bala, who asks me for a testimonial. I agree to send him one in three months—when I'm back on the bike, and when he promises to prescribe lessons for every one of his nurses in hospitality, in hospitable hospital procedures, and in the English language. As we bid the good doctor adieu, he says, "Call me anytime if you ever have a problem." I plan to call him whenever I have computer, motorcycle, or relationship problems, when I have mental math lapses like forgetting how to divide, and definitely from the next toilet where I can't manage to sit down.

~

the final trial

The next day goes reasonably well except for the delayed flight, which is airline business as usual in India. During our taxi ride from the airport, Joomi survives the worst pollution we've yet encountered on the way out of Chennai by wrapping up in a silk face mask like a Muslim woman, but as we enter Mamalapurim, the smog clears. The shopkeepers and beggars are glad to see us return with our wallets. We check into the Shiva Guest House and select a room with an ocean view on the breezy third floor since I'm mobile enough to negotiate stairs. Life is good and relaxed, though we dream of Thai food, smiles, clean streets, and Thai beaches with palm trees instead of trash.

Dr. Bala calls to see how I'm doing, but has a not-too-hidden agenda. "How are you, Mr. Scott?"

"Great. It's hot and relatively honk and trash free. The hip is healing. I walked here from Chennai."

"Right. Where are you staying?"

"In Mamalapurim at the Shiva Guest House."

The motive for his call becomes clear. "My nurse accidentally gave you all the Visa receipts for your hospital bill."

"Cool. That means I got the operation for free. In that case, I'm staying at the Seaview Lodge, and I'm changing my mobile phone number."

"I know someone in the area who could pick them up."

"Policeman, secret service, or Nurse Swat Team?"

"No, no, just a friend."

"Tell you what, you needn't bother a friend. There's a post office here surrounded by holy cows and their sacred pies. You should get your receipts in a few months delivered by an oxcart pulled by their cousins."

"Yes, yes, thank you. Please send them."

"I'll make you a deal."

"Okay, whatever."

"I'll send the receipts tomorrow if you promise not to visit Pattaya when you come to Thailand next month."

"I promise."

I imagine he crossed his fingers during the promise.

After five relatively splendid days dining on fresh seafood, visiting our shopkeeper friends way too often, and carefully climbing the three flights of stairs made for folks with feet much shorter than mine, we're off to Chennai in a taxi, hoping our rupees will last the trip.

Refreshment stop, tolls, and taxi fare take all my rupee bills, plus a five-dollar American greenback, leaving us with 75 rupee coins for the two-hour wait at the airport, that becomes, sigh, four-hours, trapped without an ATM. They won't let us back out through security, because... um... because... because it's India!

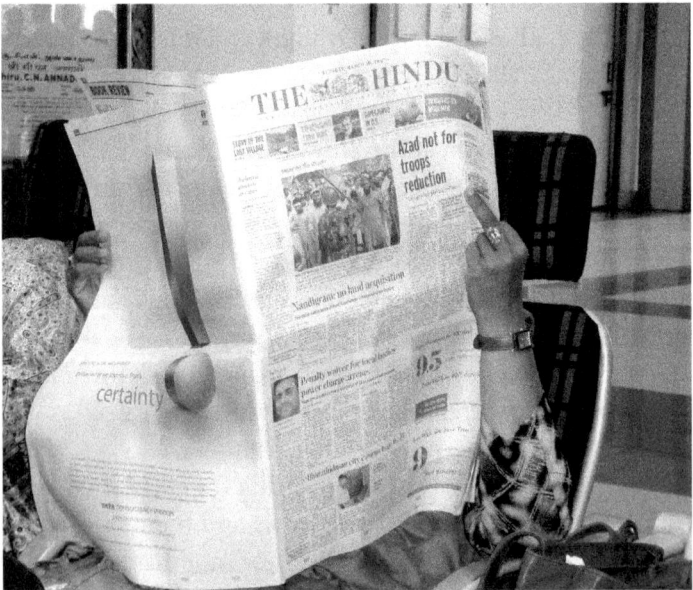

**No staring from this woman in the airport...
only the traditional finger gesture**

We choose a miniature meal from the only glass food case in the only shop. *Nope, can't afford the Snicker's Bar for 85 rupees = two dollars.* "We'll have those two aloo-who-ha-bindimabobs and a small bottle of water, please." Barely warmed in the microwave, they are curried potato gunk inside fried shells made from clay a some time during the last three years. We mask their lack of flavor with the contents of an entire ketchup bottle.

After our Last Indian Supper we're forced to move as the coughing and hacking Tubercular family overtakes our aisle and surrounds us. We flee a few rows over, but are then confronted by the Wheezing Sisters across from us, spewing their pestilence into our air. *Where's the transporter button to beam us outta here?*

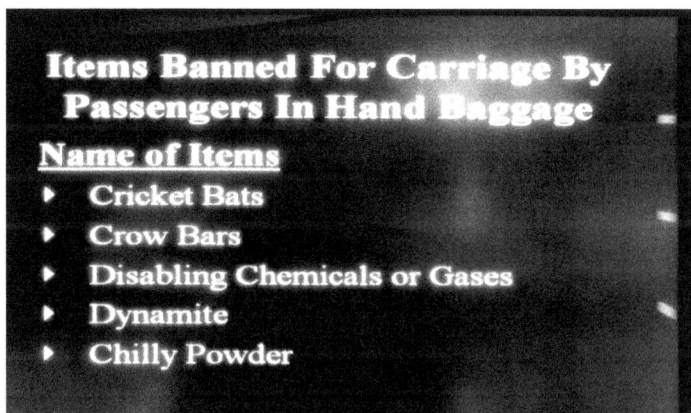

Items Banned For Carriage By Passengers In Hand Baggage

Name of Items
- Cricket Bats
- Crow Bars
- Disabling Chemicals or Gases
- Dynamite
- Chilly Powder

Damn! Had to chuck the Chilly Powder.
Too hot. Right next to dynamite.

On the plane we're fed our final curried fodder that tastes like Styrofoam packaging material it came in. The flight to Bangkok is roughly comforting because the intense turbulence keeps the pilots awake. They execute a marvelous landing on one tire and one wing. Whatever. They didn't execute us. We're home.

We step off the plane onto another planet—modern, casual, and smiling. Delightful non-curried food is everywhere, and I have a wallet full of Thai baht. Outside the terminal, taxis are orderly and quiet—not one honk—and the air is clean even though it's Bangkok. I've never cared for this metropolis, but today I'm madly in love with it.

Hometown Chiang Mai is heaven on earth, nirvana, utopia. We count three tiny pieces of trash on the ten-kilometer ride down flower-lined streets to our bungalow. Sweet success. I'm alive, upright and walking with a cane. I saved $55,000. And Joomi is the only nurse in sight.

~

the last word

People often ask, "So how was India?" I'd prefer to hand them this story, but a short answer suffices: "Let's just say I have no plans to go back."

Contrary to what you've read here, I think India is a wildly fascinating country. We had great times in between the gritty times. I'd like to return when I'm fit and healthy and can go where I want to go instead of where I have to go. I went in pain, endured more pain, and finished with healing pain, so I could eventually have no pain.

This account is not a cheery journal about a delightful jaunt for some slick travel magazine. That's another piece. Nor is it a tale of Medical Tourism written about a hospitable experience in tidy Thailand, Singapore, or Europe. It's a saga of Medical Adventurism in India, where you get advanced procedures right alongside age-old poverty.

Do I regret going? No, not at all. The price was right. And OMG! So much to write home about!

I have trouble with nurses anywhere who treat me like a pincushion or dart board. Except for the Soccer Ball Hand Incident that still hurts three weeks after surgery, my Indian caretakers were very sweet, competent ladies doing their job to the best of their abilities. Well, there was the knock on the door at 4:45 a.m. for the unscheduled sponge bath, but maybe that nurse fell in love with me and wanted to sneak in for a rendezvous before Joomi woke up.

Would I go back to Dr. Bala? If he upgrades the hospital, I'd consider it. Twelve years after the operation, the joint makes strange squeaking sound but both feet still touch the ground. I heard great testimonials about new facilities for foreigners at the Apollo Hospital in Chennai, but chose Dr. Bala because he charged $1,300 less. Maybe the Apollo has real flowers, fewer mosquitoes, and no spider webs.

Would I suggest you do it? That depends on you, your stamina, and your tolerance for life as it careens into the unknown. If you're a frail, elderly person, I'd say, "Hire a helicopter to the hospital, and stay there until the helicopter takes you home. If you try the taxi ride to Ooty six days after your operation, you'll go home in a wooden box."

Would I suggest you go alone or with your mate? It depends on your mate and their adventure level. You can always pay someone to carry your stuff, but it's great to have help during private moments. Often I wanted to be alone in a cave to sleep, do my physical therapy, read and move at my snail's pace without having to wonder about the welfare, boredom level, or sanity of my mate. The War of the Nurses would have been less intense without my personal gatekeeper. I might have kept the doors unlocked so the Nurse Troops could enter, do their business with my body, and leave before I woke up.

Your mate's mental anguish will equal your physical anguish. My wife Joomi wanted to help but mainly could only watch and worry. When she found a few ways to help, they would quickly disappear. I had to learn to do the chores myself. That's an essential part of the healing process. Joomi was like a parent to a dependent kid, who must become independent, but with an infinitely shorter time line.

Patient, one day: "Honey, will you please help me put on my socks?"

Impatient, next day: "Mom, leave me alone! I can do it myself!"

Near the end of our trip, Joomi tried to help a little too much. In Mamalapurim, Joomi picked up our bundles and trotted down the street. As I searched for my cane, I was momentarily bewildered until realizing she'd grabbed it with the bags and was carrying it away.

"Honey! Thanks for all your help, but I have to carry the cane. Honey? Joomi!!! Please come back! I'm trapped! I don't want to spend the rest of my life in India!"

Luckily she came back and took the beggar home.

Post-op postcard to Dr. Bala: "Thanks a lot, Doc.
When I got home, my leg fell off."

~ ~ ~

Thailand Is Not Fargo, Part II

S OME DAYS I FEEL as though I am living on the pages
of *National Geographic.* Kids ride bicycles while carrying their pet chickens; anyone seems to be comfortable walking around in their pajamas at any time; last year
an elephant sauntered through town. We consider village
traffic "busy" if we meet another car on our road, or follow
the huge open-bed truck from the local Slaughter House
and Crocodile Farm filled with disassembled pigs, their silent heads gazing down, ears flopping in the breeze. Like
a time machine, an hour's ride on the Harley takes us 500
years into the past to visit hill tribe folks living in the mountains as they've done for generations.

Gardening with a vengeance! My grandmother had a grand garden in Fargo and planted a seed in my brain that took decades to sprout. Gardening as a teenager meant weeding and lawn mowing, conscripted labor to get my allowance, and summer never lasted very long. (The saying goes, "If summer falls on a Sunday, we'll have a picnic.")

During my twenties in Virginia, my green thumb grew into an oversized appendage, then evolved

In the USA, I raked leaves. Some days in Thailand it's impossible to rake leaf.

into an entire green body inflicted with horticultural psychoneurosis after relocating to Minnesota.

When Joomi and I moved into our own place with neglected lawn, trees, shrubs, plants struggling in puny containers, and space begging to be filled, the garden monster was unleashed. I saved the orphan plants and put in 1,000 herbs, bushes, water plants, and flowers from one inch to ten feet tall. (None would survive Fargo's climate unless reproduced in cement.)

Plants are amazingly cheap in Thailand! One cut stem of a bird of paradise in America might cost $20 = 600 baht. Here, eight-foot living plants cost three bucks—healthy ones will that double in height, spread out till you hack 'em back with a machete, and produce 12-inch flowers that bloom year round.

A bunch of fifty stems of orchids or roses costs 50 baht = $1.75. In the USA, you might get *one stem* for that amount.

I remember stumbling upon the Rose Deal of a Lifetime in downtown Minneapolis, where I delivered an exquisite, off-the-cuff quip immediately, as opposed to most times when I think of punch lines a half-hour too late. An aging hippie tended a stall sporting a sign that screamed, "FOR SALE RIGHT NOW! TWO DOZEN ROSES FOR FIVE BUCKS!"

I opened my wallet to find *one* five-dollar bill. "I'm using my last five dollars to buy my girlfriend two dozen roses."

Mr. Hippie grinned and spit out these words. "If it was my last five bucks, I'd buy liquor!"

Tuned into the cosmic comedy universe, I replied, "When I give these to my girlfriend, she'll make me lick 'er."

Thai seasons are shuffled up and delivered in a funky new order. The majority of mainland America claims four seasons: spring, summer, fall, and winter. Thailand only has three: the rainy season (May-ish to October or beyond), winter (November to January, but more like Fargo in late summer) and the hot, dry season (February into May). Any Fargoans visiting would refer to these seasons as Hot, Hotter 'n' Hell, and "Uff da, I'm melting."

North Dakota officially has two seasons: Winter and Road Construction. Marigolds die from the cold in the fall. In Thailand, they die from the heat in March. I planted "fragile" impatiens in pots, which in Fargo would last about three months because they're absolute sissies in the cold. If an impatiens plant even overhears a frost warning broadcast on the radio, it'll commit suicide by morning, a flattened road kill hugging the dirt. Impatiens planted here, two years in November, are still going and growing strong.

My chili peppers in America never made it beyond "plant" status into "bush" territory, but here I recently pruned one that was almost six-feet tall with hardy branches and official bark, hell bent for "tree" status. Ditto for the eggplant and basil.

A major horticultural challenge is my abundance of spontaneity coupled with a lack of knowledge of how large plants grow. I buy a "little" water plant and "big" impressive pot, but soon have a seven-foot plant and a pot brimming with roots but no room for water. My papyrus plant split its two-foot-tall ceramic pot in half like Superman busting out of a cement stockade.

Selfie with teak tree leaf

A tiny garden inside. My wife Joomi likes to purchase mini-plants in miniscule containers about an inch tall. They're cute, but the container cannot hold sufficient water so the plant dies requiring that she purchase ten more.

While Joomi visited the USA for two months, I was determined to keep one miniature fern alive, and set it next to the sink so I'd remember to water it daily. After a month, the plant remained verdant green and healthy. Picking up the fern for its routine dousing, I examined the leaves closely, which revealed the secret of my success. The plant was made of plastic. The container was indeed pottery, but contained fake dirt. I'm considering plastic grass for the yard.

My lawn standards are much lower here than they were in America. I inherited a mental disorder from my mother: the demented compulsion to seek the impossible dream of a weed-free lawn. In Thailand, if it's green and stays flat for a while, it's lawn material.

Mowing the lawn during the rainy season reminds me of both Fargo and San Francisco. Sign in a Fargo garden store: "Plant our grass seed and jump back!" Soil in the Red River

Valley is abnormally fertile and grass is highly motivated to grow after a six-month hibernation. Why San Francisco? I heard a team of workmen constantly paints the Golden Gate Bridge. When they "finish" and reach the other end, they turn around and start over. When I'm at the halfway point of mowing my lawn in Thailand, I look back at where I began and wonder, "Didn't I already mow over there?"

Varieties of bamboo grow everywhere, serving a myriad of purposes from the soft shoots in our Thai stir-fry to sturdy scaffolding several stories up the side of a building. My only recollection of bamboo in Fargo involved tales of the Chinese bamboo torture where bad guys strap the good guys to the ground over a stand of bamboo, which grows up through their bodies. I noticed an inch-thick teak board on the deck bent up a couple inches at one end. A baby bamboo spear had grown underneath and was patiently but persistently raising one end by prying out the nails. After witnessing bamboo grow six inches a day into two-inch wide, seven-foot spears in two weeks, I definitely don't want to get on the bad side of any bad Chinese guys.

You can take the American out of America, but you can't take America out of the American. Our favorite Thai trees, Lilawadee aka Frangipani, produce stunning blooms that are fragrant beyond belief. Their sweet odor fills your senses, as if a delegation of elderly ladies wearing thick cologne are attending a convention in our backyard. I've fertilized and watered and snatched the trees back from the Grim Garden Reaper. Busy with other tasks, I didn't notice their sick leaves, which had begun to yellow and fall.

One day, upon closer inspection, I see orange, scale-like, insects covering the leaves. Panicking, I race to the flower market to point, gesture madly, draw pictures, and seek a solution to the orange scourge on my babies. Mr. Flower Market Guy Who Can Barely Understand English But Knows I Have Money convinces me to buy chemicals and a manual pump sprayer. I'm mainly an organic kind of guy, but I succumb to altered ideals required for this life-saving emergency. I don boots, rubber gloves, glasses, hats, shirts, pants, socks, face mask, and a prophylactic for extra safety, then nearly collapse in the heat during my pathetic attempts to pump noxious potions into the tree and not on me. I pile up hundreds of infected leaves and trimmed branches while planning to fling them into a field and dispose of them with napalm in a valiant American attempt to eliminate the orange terrorists once and for all.

Curious what the hyperactive idiot is doing now, Khun Pa saunters over. My 79-year-old father-in-law's English is better than my Thai, but he's reluctant to use it and appear to be mentally challenged like me. Haggard and distressed, I point dramatically to the orange menace on the leaves and tree. Khun Pa doesn't know what it is nor care what it is. He wants the cut branches from my pile so he can plant them in his yard and along our shared fence. Stick a Lilawadee branch into a hole in the clay, and it'll become a tree.

My aggressive scheme to exterminate the orange species in a huge firestorm is foiled by a relative inviting my hostages into his home. Hmmm. Like the TV show back in Fargo: *Father Knows Best.*

Miss Fargo? No, I'm not, nor do I. Fargo is a fine place to be from, far from, but I've exceeded my Cold Quota. The inside of my refrigerator is seventy degrees warmer than Fargo in the winter. Except for family, friends, and the Grand Canyon, I only miss three things in the US of A.

Number One: high-speed internet. My connection speed varies from weak to power out in the whole neighborhood. Thai wiring is seldom done by licensed electricians, just Random Guys With Tools, who create intricate wire patterns that look like my tangled fishing line when I first learned how to cast near Fargo. I tried to download a hefty music program. The Estimated Time Required meter vacillated between 52 and 104 days, which would take decades considering how often the electricity fails. I'm currently trying to locate a wood-burning router.

We lose electricity less often than the water, which is routinely repaired by More Random Guys With Ancient Tools Whose Names Make Great Scrabble Words Like Adze. Judging by the amount of times they've fixed the water main in the half-mile to our house, I suspect the pipe is composed of 350 individual sections, lashed together underground with bamboo, duct tape, and sticky stuff.

Number Two: good tape, the Scotch packing type. It's a scientific marvel how Thai manufacturers can make a layer of adhesive that is *one molecule thick* stick to a *one molecule thick* piece of tape. If you can ever find the end, it peels off in a thin strip until it's gone again. You start more strips and end up with a higher bunch of layers on one side, which completely prevents you from finding your original strip or the key to the strip maze. During this process, severe exasperation sets in as you rip off tiny shards that stick to your fingers, but you can't flick 'em off because you're taping something, and your other hand is holding whatever you're taping, so you use your mouth, and then tape gets stuck between your teeth. If you extract a respectable piece of tape and mount a poster on the wall, it falls down the moment you turn your back. Packages sealed with Thai tape spontaneously pop open moments after you leave the post office.

Number Three: Pepto-Bismol. Nothing works as well as the pink stuff, and you can't find it in Thailand. No matter what travel guidebooks say, I'll never give up food from street vendors. It's the best, particularly when the ladies know exactly what I want and proudly tell me, in Thai, so I don't have to pronounce it incorrectly and have them laugh at me. Many dishes include unordered bacteria that can peel the lining off your stomach. Somehow the pink stuff does the trick, unlike traditional Thai potions and pills filled with Chinese herbs, scorpion tails, and ant testicles.

Okay, fine. Thailand Is Fargo. After writing this comparative narrative, I realize Thailand is Fargo, from another point of view. I'm just a naïve kid again, barraged by foreign experiences, new subjects to study, and vast horizons to explore. Instead of escaping on my Schwinn, one-speed bike enhanced by playing cards fastened to the spokes with wooden clothespins, now I ride a Harley with 1200 throbbing cc's. Summer vacation lasts all year long, though I still need to find a summer job. I can make ridiculous mistakes here which are promptly excused. "Hey, he's just a foreigner." = "Hey, he's just a kid."

During this COVID Era, leaving the house any day in Thailand takes as much time as in frozen Fargo during the winter. Gotta put on the mask, surgical instead of ski. Hand-sanitizer bottle in hand instead of hand-warmers inside gloves. Ventilators, defibrillators, and a hospital cot in the car trunk instead of jumper cables, snow shovels, and a few Duraflame, 6-pound, 4-hour Firelogs.

Fargo was a great place to evolve while listening to the rest of the country make fun of it. That taught me to make fun of me and enjoy it! Now on the flip side of life, twilight in Thailand is divine. I've achieved two life dreams—one clear, one more of a misty musing. For years, this dream was imperative: *I want to live where I'd vacation.* Thailand made that dream a reality. One down. Next!

When I thought about the end of my life, I imagined peace, and had this vague idea of being 1) a gardener, 2) for some rich landlord, 3) who's never home. However, I never pictured myself as 1) the landlord with lovely, loving, landlady Joomi; 2) I've learned that rich is directly related to where I am and who is standing, walking, or lying next to me; and 3) I am home. Two dreams down. Next!

~ ~ ~

Shepherd vs. Siberian

And in the German Shepherd vs. Siberian Husky category, the winner is...

I'VE HAD THE DISTINCT PLEASURE OF LIVING with two extraordinarily different yet look-alike dogs, both intelligent and independent in their own eccentric ways.

Marcus was a 100-pound German Shepherd marked like a Malamute.

I'm reasonably sure, at 88 pounds, Chance is a Siberian Husky/Malamute mix, maybe a Malausky, as in malaprop or malarkey. Over the years, his name is often lengthened to Chancellor because he rules our entire universe.

When I told Marcus to do something, he'd say, "Sure, cool. I'm on it."

Chancellor says, "Yeah, whatever. I'm very busy resting. Do it yourself."

Marcus loved sticks (or logs) and would bring one home after every walk, fetch them, play tug o' war with them, or tear them apart until they were twigs.

If I try to interest Chancellor in a stick, he says, "No thanks. It's a fucking stick. Call me when you have a cookie."

Marcus retrieved tennis balls flung far into a lake until my arm was ready to fall off, and I'd give up.

After three half-hearted retrievals on land, Chance stands motionless and watches my fourth throw. "Game over, man. Been there, done that."

Marcus chose to sleep alone on the floor, never in the bed with me.

Chancellor owns the bed and sometimes leaves enough room for me.

Marcus ate Gravy Train dog food once or twice per day.

Chance will eat anything at anytime. When he hears the crinkle of a plastic bag or snack wrapper within a three-mile radius, he will immediately be there pleading with his baby browns. If I want to enjoy all three of my (and his) favorite Ovaltine Malt Cookies in the package, I have to hide like a closet alcoholic pounding down three shots behind the barn.

I assumed that Marcus considered me his master.

I know that I am Chancellor's slave.

Marcus didn't need a leash, hiked miles of circles around me in the wilderness, and always knew where I was.

Chance is ALWAYS on a leash so when H.A.D.D. (Husky Attention Deficit Disorder) kicks in when he spies a cat, he won't chase it five thousand miles to Siberia with me lagging three countries behind wearing out my flip-flops.

Marcus barked once in a while and growled menacingly at any person wearing a uniform.

Chance talks back routinely or begins a conversation that involves us getting him food. During his vocal episodes, he will howl like an operatic baritone, tenor, alto, or soprano, depending on who starts it: a malamute on the web (baritone), a wolf on the web (tenor), a puny dog next door (alto), a baby crying (soprano), or his slaves (us) while we drive away and leave him home alone (all of the above).

Marcus loved and protected me, but also liked to play with people or startle them by sticking his nose in the crotch of their legs… from behind. If they didn't quickly produce a tennis ball or a stick, he'd could be rather aloof.

Chance is Love Incarnate and adores everyone. When people arrive (friends or strangers or thieves casing the neighborhood with an empty truck), he yells with unbridled joy as if God is at the gate.

"Look at these beautiful beings who have arrived! Oh, I love them sooooo much, and I haven't even met them yet! Can they pleeeaaase live with us? Do you think they have any cookies?"

Chance wants to put his paws on their shoulders, look right into their eyes, and lick them eternally… pretty intense for someone who might not care for dogs, specifically a big, super-friendly, invade-your-space kind of canine.

I loved Marcus till death did us part, but after having the chance to hang with Chance for eight years and 6,000-plus walks, I'd never choose a breed other than a Husky.

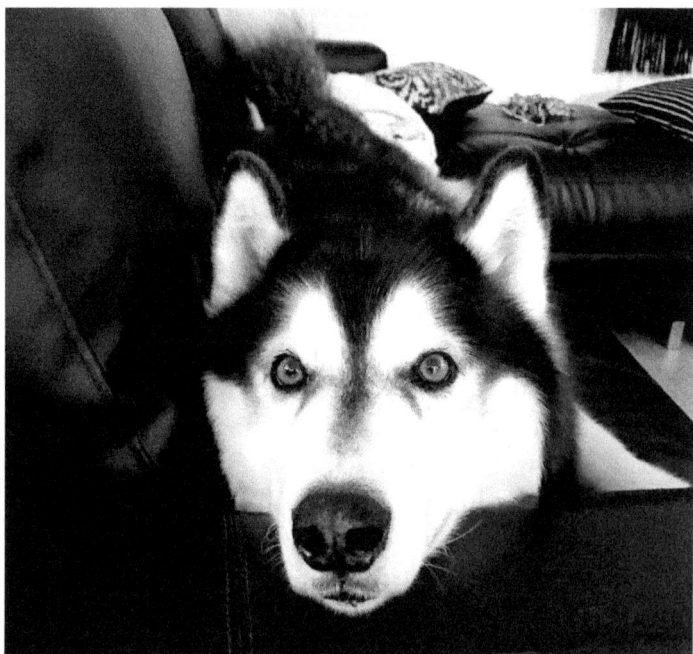

~ ~ ~

Way to Go

D YING? I'M NOT REALLY AFRAID OF IT. I am afraid of pain, but not death, that fast-acting, over-the-counter painkiller. Death is merely page two of the two-page life deal, neither a secret, nor illegible fine print on the contract. Ben Franklin said, "Nothing in life is certain except death and taxes." (It's too bad they don't come in that order.) Sometimes you don't have a choice. It's just the way it is. My tent is staked in the Mark Twain camp: "I do not fear death. I had been dead for billions and billions of years before I was born, and had not suffered the slightest inconvenience from it."

I'm curious about the other side. I don't recall stories from folks who've come back and said it sucks. I want to see that brilliant light at the end of the tunnel. No, I want to *be* that light.

Perhaps this is home. It looks nice.

The word "death" has such a grave, grim reaper reputation, notably in the West. No matter how splendid you are, or what your first name is, if you're saddled with the grim surname of Hitler, people get spooked. Gandhi Hitler? Mother Theresa Hitler? Pooh and Piglet Hitler? They still mean death. How about some laid-back, inviting names for death? Mister D. The Big Sleep. Another Chapter in the Long and Winding Road. Going Home.

Mister D and I have had several close encounters of the scary kind. While climbing up a steep rock wall, I stopped to catch my breath thirty meters above a canyon floor. My foot slipped on loose stones, and I fell backward off the thin ledge. Somehow the fingers of one hand found a branch that held me at a 45° angle from the wall, leaning on a breeze, praying that my little bush angel had titanium roots firmly planted in bedrock.

Years later I had fallen asleep and was dreaming peacefully. However, I was also driving my van on the turnpike. At the last millimeter and nanosecond, I jerked awake, lurched left, and barely missed the truck trailer guillotine that would have severed my head. I was okay, but my heart almost beat me to death from the inside out.

Each of my three big-sister cousins have mentioned saving me several times from drowning, when I was two or three, and they were five to ten. I doubt if I was suicidal at two, or they had early Alzheimer's, so I suspect their conversations on the dock went something like this:

Cousin 1: "I'm gonna to throw him in the lake."

Cousin 2: "No! Me! You got to do it yesterday!"

Cousin 3: "Do we have to save him again?"

I nearly died of boredom when my stepmother sentenced me to a week of Bible school, right after fifth grade. As my teacher, Helen Brimstone, told far-fetched parables of eternal burning in the furnace below or eternal monotony in the clouds above, I thought, *Hell is right now, sitting inside, with you blathering on and on. Heaven is also right now, right outside this prison, playing in the summer sun.*

The Major Brand Name Religions never captured me. Dad was an Episcopalian, and Mom a Methodist, then he married a Lutheran, and she married a Catholic. My best friends were Presbyterian and Jewish. I was a Devil's Advocate for the Mixed Bagatarians. The Indian sage Krishnamurti said it all in three words: "Belief divides people." I watched and listened and questioned.

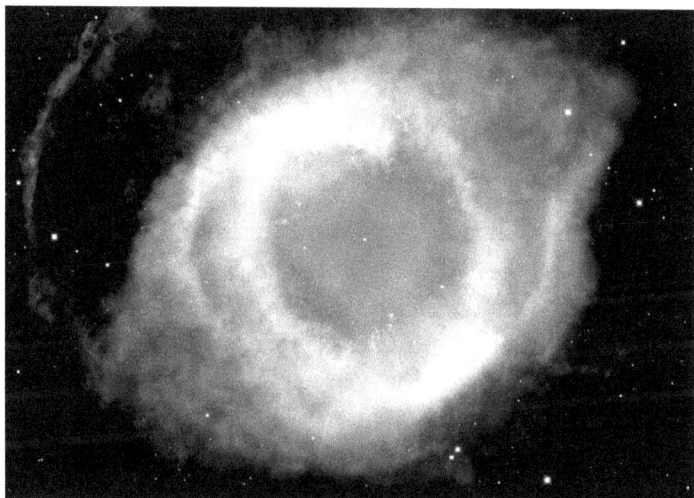

And maybe the universe watched and listened to me, too.

One day a female tag team of Jehovah's Witnesses rang the bell—a small talkative one and a large silent one. Miss Small told me that only 144,000 people, selected by God, would get into heaven, and eventually come back to live forever on earth. *Now that's a frightening thought. I'd have to clean the fridge and pay taxes forever?*

I asked her, "Why are you talking to me? Your saved soul quota must be filled. What if God changes his mind and selects me instead of you?" Neither my question, nor the answer, were in her script.

She launched into a personal testimony about how this

"heaven on earth" dream influenced her life—and I am not making this up. "I've always wanted to play the saxophone, but never find the time to learn. It feels good to know that I'll have eternity to learn when I come back to earth."

OMG! I mean, OHG—Oh, her God! The Lord of Procrastination! I don't have to clean the fridge! I don't have to exercise today, tomorrow, or this decade! I can stop shooting heroin sometime during the next century!

With tight lips suppressing the urge to burst out laughing, I politely escorted them to the door. I didn't want to say anything that might compel Miss Large to sit on my chest, while Miss Small rammed religious tracts down my throat.

Visions of life beyond this one didn't come to me in the square rooms where folks dress up for each other on Sunday. One came at the Grand Canyon with the help of LSD—Let's See Differently—when the infinite jigsaw puzzle put itself together. I no longer felt apart from the universe, just a part of it all. Experiences during holotropic breath work and meditation drove the revelations deeper than a pill could ever reach. Marvellous books by extraordinary people confirmed the mysteries I felt.

Even simple scientific facts provided spiritual support. Each one of us, and everything in the entire universe, is 99.9999999999% space, spirit, energy, The Force. Its name depends on who's talking, but it's not matter, and it doesn't matter what each of us call it. Humans are hung up on hard things in the third dimension. When we touch something solid, we don't touch matter; we touch the forces that hold it together or keep it apart. There's not much to "die" with so much life teeming within us. Why are we so afraid of being what we already are?

Of course, if you don't experience this energy yourself, you probably won't believe it—but you might have second thoughts. Woody Allen said, "I don't believe in the afterlife, although I am bringing a change of underwear."

Why are we so afraid of being what we already are?

My No Fear of Death Policy went on trial when Mister D and I walked hand in hand for a few elongated days. As I cruised on my motorcycle at 50 mph, a car swerved into my lane and hit me head on—a 100-mph impact. I immediately took a nap and didn't get to enjoy my 30-foot flight over the car. Neck broken in two places, fractured pelvis, internal bleeding, bruised ribs, sprained whatever, destroyed foot.

The bad news? An artery that fed my brain was severed, so they couldn't start remodeling the rest of me. I felt ready to slip away. With the help of Mr. Morphine, the notion of Going Home seemed better than being Paralyzed Vegetable Boy. I was in between, but I didn't know where. My sci-fi hero Isaac Asminov nailed the feelings: "Life is pleasant. Death is peaceful. It's the transition that's troublesome."

As I lay there in limbo, I thought about driving with my dad past Meteor Crater in Arizona—a 170-meter hole, 1,200 meters in diameter.

"Now that's how I'd like to go," I said, "vaporized by a giant meteorite. Poof!"

"Sounds good to me," he agreed. "Just take me when I'm happy."

Dad got his wish a few years later, but his meteorite was a 90-mph car that shot out of the darkness on a 45-mph road. He went home in a flash, unlike his mate, Maryanne, who the doctors reassembled with 34 screws. She lasted five years with her new constant companion, Mr. Pain, but somehow kept her humor intact. To pass through airport metal detectors, she'd carry a miniature x-ray, hand it to the guards, and smile. "The doctor put me to sleep and screwed me 34 times."

As I suffered through the sorrow, my dad's dad appeared in my mind, a gentle man who inspired me how to live— and how to die. When his time came, he went to sleep. The song I wrote about him floated through my heart…

one summer evening his lady passed away,
a wife who was half of his life.
but still he strolled through the park everyday,
and smiled through all of the strife.
then in the fall, his decision was made.
he went to his room and he pulled down the shade—
time to end the charade.

he went to sleep in his easy chair
and became a dream and a prayer.
his body is gone, but his soul's in us all.
his writing is still on the wall.
I remember him reading
always trying to understand.
cherry smoke in the air, and the pipe in his hand.
oh, you know he was grand.

Way to go, Grampy. You showed me the way to go.

Eighteen years later, I'm still here, but if I hadn't worn a helmet and sissy protective gear, I wouldn't be writing this sentence. The broken neck is still a pain in the ass. The old pelvis has a new hip. A quarter of my head is still numb, verifying my mother's foresight when she used to say, "You little numbskull!" The Big Sleep is a little closer, and I'm even more curious about the Big Dream.

These past few years have been one copious chapter after another as friends and family along the long and winding road pass on. A 95-year-old great uncle led the way over, followed by his son the next week, his wife a month later. A cousin gave up. My uncle's warranty expired. A drunk driver exterminated a dear friend. Her brother hung around with Mister C, Mister D, and Mister E—cancer, death, and mystery—until he drifted into The Big Sleep.

My wife has a genetic blood disorder that could take her at any time. One day, her heart will say, "I've had enough." When her temperature rises, her heart pounds, and her breath can't catch enough oxygen, she calls her kids on the other side of the world, so the last thing she does is love.

I dug out a poem from decades ago, hoping it might bring a moment of comfort to the folks left behind when their loved ones leave. I don't remember why I wrote it—whether it was for me, or someone else. Maybe my grandfather sent it special delivery from the other side. Maybe I wrote it for you, and you finally got it today.

the darkness of dying
a dream in disguise
to look at the lightning
and see without eyes
the thundering heartbeat
a hurricane's breath
for now is for ever
and life is for death

forever sits quietly
beyond the core
inside the moment
that opens the door
to a world within
and a world without
from one to the other
the soul will sprout

for spring is the promise
of every fall
as summer gives in
and winter takes all
the actors are lost
in reliving their roles
as silent seeds patiently
sleep in their holes

when shadows are long
and the nights never end
the unknown comes knocking
to call on a friend
it's just as a child
alone with his mother
she takes him from one breast
and gives him another

www.ingramcontent.com/pod-product-compliance
Lightning Source LLC
La Vergne TN
LVHW051541080426
835510LV00020B/2800